The Soul of an Entrepreneur

The Soul
of an
Entrepreneur

*Work and Life Beyond
the Startup Myth*

DAVID SAX

PUBLICAFFAIRS
New York

PublicAffairs
Hachette Book Group
1290 Avenue of the Americas, New York, NY 10104
www.publicaffairsbooks.com
@Public_Affairs

Printed in the United States of America

First Edition: April 2020

Published by PublicAffairs, an imprint of Perseus Books, LLC, a subsidiary of Hachette Book Group, Inc. The PublicAffairs name and logo is a trademark of the Hachette Book Group.

The Hachette Speakers Bureau provides a wide range of authors for speaking events. To find out more, go to www.hachettespeakersbureau.com or call (866) 376-6591.

The publisher is not responsible for websites (or their content) that are not owned by the publisher.

Print book interior design by Amy Quinn.

Library of Congress Cataloging-in-Publication Data
Names: Sax, David, author.
Title: The soul of an entrepreneur: work and life beyond the startup myth / David Sax.
Description: First edition. | New York: PublicAffairs, 2020. | Includes bibliographical references and index.
Identifiers: LCCN 2019041753 | ISBN 9781541736009 (hardcover) | ISBN 9781541730366 (ebook)
Subjects: LCSH: New business enterprises—Case studies. | Entrepreneurship—Case studies. | Businesspeople—Case studies.
Classification: LCC HD62.5 .S296 2020 | DDC 658.1/1—dc23
LC record available at https://lccn.loc.gov/2019041753

ISBNs: 978-1-5417-3600-9 (hardcover), 978-1-5417-3036-6 (e-book)

LSC-C

10 9 8 7 6 5 4 3 2 1

To Mom and Dad, Fran, Daniel, and Lauren . . .
my entrepreneurs with soul.

Contents

Give a man a fish, and you feed him for a day. Teach a man to fish, and you feed him for a lifetime.

—Unknown

If you lose your job and need to start a business, reading Elon Musk's biography isn't going to teach you shit.

—Michael Sax

Introduction

A FEW YEARS ago I saw two things that changed how I look at my life. The first revelation appeared to me from the magazine rack of a Hudson News store in Montreal's airport. Amid the sports, news, and cooking publications, the cover of *Maxim* stopped me in my tracks. The magazine was dominated by a black-and-white photograph of Heidi Klum, the forty-five-year-old German supermodel, who appeared completely nude from the waist up. Klum's eyes gazed down seductively, and her streaked blond hair fell just enough over her perfect breasts to obscure her nipples. But it wasn't Klum's flesh that held my gaze and had me pull out my phone to snap a picture (regardless of how creepy I looked). It was the words that appeared atop it. There, splashed across her bosom in bright red script, read the headline:

Heidi Klum
Inimitable
Entrepreneur

A few days later, back home in Toronto, I drove to a cemetery with my wife, Lauren, to visit her father Howard's grave on the eighth anniversary of his death. After a few minutes of standing there, I spotted the gravestone of a man named Freeman, who was buried in the row behind Howard's. The engraving on his stone listed the usual details; the dates of Mr. Freeman's birth and death, and the fact that he was a devoted husband, father, and grandpa, who made the world a better place. But below that, permanently etched in black granite, was the sentence that had me reaching for my phone again:

Brilliant salesman and entrepreneur until the end.

I have spent half of my life so far working for myself. Writing stories and books. Giving talks to whoever will pay me. Working from home, in shorts or sweatpants. Shaving once a week, unless I have to meet someone. I have no idea where the next payment is coming from, or how much money I will make this year, or what I am going to do the day after I finish writing this book. I haven't seen a regular paycheck or had a boss since I held a brief, miserable office job as a copy boy during the summer of 1999, and the only other jobs on my résumé are stints as a ski instructor and camp counselor (qualifying me for roles in an '80s comedy, but nothing else). I am certain that I will never work for anyone but myself for the rest of my life.

This is my reality. I am my own boss. A freelancer. Self-employed.

I am an entrepreneur.

A few years ago I doubt I would have used that term to describe myself. I employ no one, have never invented anything, or really innovated in any way. But something changed the week I saw that same word splashed across Ms. Klum's bosom and Mr. Freeman's grave.

I began to realize that something crucial was happening with entrepreneurs at this moment in time, which these two wildly contrasting visions of entrepreneurship represented. On the one hand, you had the sexy public image of entrepreneurship in the form of a celebrity who had parlayed runway, advertising, and television success into several clothing brands, ranging from baby wear to lingerie, turning her from a multi-millionaire into a multi-multi-millionaire. On the other you had the grave of an octogenarian businessman, whose legacy was forgotten except to his family and those who knew him, one of countless entrepreneurs in my city and in this world who identified with that title so much, that it followed him to the grave. Here was the tomb of the unknown entrepreneur.

I have always been fascinated by entrepreneurs. The articles I've written over the years almost exclusively focus on people who work for themselves, from a cohort of young bankers who went out on their own during the financial crisis (starting yoga studios, robotic toy companies, and solar finance firms), to the tribe of freelancers who plug their laptops into a Brooklyn café every morning. My books all focus on entrepreneurs. *Save the Deli*, which chronicles the rise and fall of the Jewish delicatessen, isn't as much about pastrami sandwiches as it is about the men and women who built the businesses that served them. *The Tastemakers*, which is about food trends, is told through the eyes of the dreamers who passionately believed that their cupcake shop, food truck, or new breed of apple was going to change the way people ate. *The Revenge of Analog* is riddled with analog entrepreneurs, from the plucky bookstore owners who faced down Amazon, to a pair of half-crazy Italians revitalizing a mothballed film factory.

I rarely wrote about big corporations and organizations, and when I did, I regretted it. They were cold and impersonal, and the people who worked there were always worried about saying the wrong thing. I was drawn back to entrepreneurs again and again; their stew of personal passion and hustle, a work life inseparable from their self, and a sense of purpose to everything they did.

Was it surprising? Not when I thought about it. After all, I was the product of entrepreneurs, from the immigrant ancestors who found their way into some corner of Montreal's garment trade a century ago, to my grandfathers, who both owned their own businesses. My paternal grandfather, Poppa Sam Sax, had a series of never quite successful companies in the schmatte business, while my mother's father, Stanley Davis, built a hardware company with his brother that continues to supply screwdrivers, pliers, and other tools across Canada. My father has spent his entire career since law school working for himself as a lawyer and investor, and even my mother ran a side business with her best friend Paula, selling wholesale women's clothing twice a year out of our basement for nearly two decades.

My wife Lauren's family was no different. On her father's side were Polish immigrants who founded a truck parts distribution business, while her mother's parents were Holocaust survivors who'd arrived with nothing and dabbled in everything, from stationery stores to feather collecting. My beloved mother-in-law, Fran, may hold one of the first MBAs in the country awarded to a woman, but she has spent her professional life at folding card tables in hospitals and at flea markets, selling all sorts of things: macramé planters, rattan furniture, and whatever inexpensive women's accessories China's sweatshops can churn out that season.

Each month I had friends leaving careers and steady jobs to build branding agencies, law firms, software startups, rug stores, cafés, bike shops, yoga studios . . . even a chopped liver company. My brother Daniel recently quit his job at a mortgage brokerage to launch his own real estate investment company in Canada's booming cannabis industry, while Lauren began her own career coaching business, after working as a corporate headhunter for a decade.

Outside my own world, something bigger was happening with entrepreneurs that drove my curiosity. There was already an inescapable buzz in the air about entrepreneurs: the crowded coffee shops packed with laptop wielding dreamers working on their ideas, the blossoming of coworking spaces to house all sorts of freelancers and new companies, the decline of the steady job and the eagerness of younger generations, like the Millennials, to go out on their own. And of course, the inescapable startup fever, which had spread far beyond Silicon Valley to inspire millions around the world to launch businesses like never before.

There was a noticeable change in the entrepreneur's value to society, which altered the way we spoke about them as a group. Entrepreneurs were cool. Entrepreneurs were brilliant. Entrepreneurs were in demand. Entrepreneurship had entered the core of the zeitgeist, not just in the contained world of business and economics, but out in the wilds of popular culture.

Newspapers and magazines regularly featured entrepreneurs on their covers, spinning exciting tales about their transformational businesses and thrilling lifestyles. They published endless lists of the top entrepreneurs to watch: the fastest-growing ones, the most inspiring, those who would change the world, the twenty under twenty, thirty under thirty, and so on. Headlines proclaimed entrepreneurs as the new rock stars, a group who were downright sexy, even if they weren't actually posing topless.

The bestseller lists became dominated by heroic books about the most famous entrepreneurs: biographies of Elon Musk, Richard Branson, Steve Jobs, Peter Thiel, Jeff Bezos, Nike's Phil Knight, and others, while airport bookstores featured a rotating selection of how-to books on entrepreneurship, ranging from online wine pitchman turned motivational guru Gary Vaynerchuk (*Crush It!* and *Crushing It!*), to less recognizable names like Miki Agrawal, a media fixture of New York's startup scene who had started a pizzeria, an underwear company, a bidet toilet seat company, a series of early morning raves, and whose book, *Do Cool Sh*t: Quit Your Day Job, Start Your Own Business, and Live Happily Ever After*, boldly sold the dream of entrepreneurship for all.

Who wouldn't want to do cool shit, especially when social media entrepreneur influencers like Agrawal were cheering you on, posting inspirational quotes and streams of advice on Instagram, lists of instructions on LinkedIn (Five Secrets to Hack Growth You Need NOW!), Snapchat videos filmed in cars, and a growing series of hashtags, from #startuplife and #founder to #entrepreneur and more specific ones, like #solopreneur, #serialentrepreneur, #mompreneur, or those meant to encourage entrepreneurs through the slog ahead: #wontstop, #beyourownboss, and the endlessly deployed #hustle (or its less committal sibling #sidehustle).

Podcasts? How about *Startup, The Foundation, The Introvert Entrepreneur, Eventual Millionaire, All In, Ambitious Entrepreneur Show*, and *Entrepreneur on Fire*, to name a few of the thousands out there. Turn on your TV and you could spend all night watching shows about cake-making entrepreneurs and matchmaking entrepreneurs, storage locker hustlers and bounty hunters out to grow their businesses. Willie Robertson, the star of *Duck Dynasty*, even authored a book called *American Entrepreneur*, a history of American entrepreneurship, told from the perspective, mostly, of Duck Commander's journey, while Kylie Jenner, of

Keeping up with the Kardashians fame, was declared the youngest "self-made" female billionaire by *Forbes* at age twenty-one, following the success of her makeup company.

Then there is *Shark Tank*, the American version of the global franchise *Dragons' Den* (airing in more than thirty countries), where a panel of aggressive investors are pitched business ideas by a series of budding entrepreneurs, in the hopes of securing coveted funding. *Shark Tank* is over the top, as you'd expect of a show where Jeff Foxworthy is being pitched a Mafia-inspired money clip called the Broccoli Wad, but it has become so successful that Sharks like Barbara Corcoran and Chris Sacca have become household celebrities, on par with Hollywood actors like George Clooney and Jessica Alba, who now sell their own tequila and diapers, and Drake, who not only hawks clothing through his OVO brand, but joined forces with Canada's largest bank to host his own entrepreneurship conference (one of thousands put on every year around the world).

In the public mind, entrepreneurs had become a force for unquestionable, unalloyed good in the world. They brought the necessary innovation and disruption that made economies competitive, spurring growth, creating jobs, and giving birth to whole "ecosystems" of startups around them. Entrepreneurs were hailed as creative and agile, able to think outside the box and tackle any problem with more efficiency and determination than even the most well-funded and experienced incumbent. "We don't know what the problem is, but the solution is entrepreneurship," joked Howard Stevenson, an entrepreneurship professor at Harvard, when I asked him to characterize this cultural shift, which he had witnessed in recent years. In a way he was right. The entrepreneur had come to symbolize the loftiest angel of our human nature.

Social and Economic Inequality, Labor Relations, Hunger, Homelessness, Public Transit, Incurable Disease, Climate Change, Failing Schools, Gun Violence . . . suddenly these intractable issues that had dogged our brightest political leaders and institutions were best tackled by young, eager entrepreneurs, who were rightly celebrated for their efforts. I never fully realized the extent of this shift until I was walking in the hallway of a conference center a few years ago, which featured framed portraits of inspiring leaders and their quotes. Alongside the faces of Albert Einstein, Winston Churchill, Mother Teresa, and Martin Luther King Jr. were those of Mark Zuckerberg, Jeff Bezos, Elon Musk, and Peter Thiel. The more entrepreneurs we encouraged, embraced, and set forth, the better we would all be . . . economically, but also socially, politically, and most important, personally.

Entrepreneurship studies were already transforming education, as universities rushed to set up and expand entrepreneurship departments, producing a growing trove of research on every aspect of the topic, while simultaneously encouraging students to start companies, with investment funding available from their in-house network of venture capitalists, and freshly built incubators, accelerators, and innovation zones to house those companies. To prepare your child for this future, there were now courses on entrepreneurship being offered in high schools and elementary schools, and if those were insufficiently motivating, you could send them to Young Entrepreneur learning labs, which taught children how to start businesses far more disruptive than a lemonade stand, then pack them off to Camp Inc. for the summer, where they could roast marshmallows *and* write business plans!

From nonprofits and arts organizations to government agencies, word went out across the land that acting, thinking, and working like an entrepreneur was the only thing standing between success and failure. Reid Hoffman, the CEO and founder of LinkedIn, suggested that every career should be treated as its own startup. Corporations, previously seen as the antithesis of entrepreneurs and all they stood for, eagerly embraced the importance of entrepreneurship with a vigor not seen since they discovered the open office. Suddenly blue chip firms like General Motors and Deloitte created official entrepreneur jobs (Entrepreneur in Residence, Disruptor in Chief), with offices, staffs, and executive salaries to match.

I got why this cultural shift made sense. Thanks to innovations ranging from cloud computing and smartphones, to coworking spaces, crowdfunding, overseas manufacturing, and social media, it was now easier to start your own business than anytime in history. Technology had put the tools of scale at everyone's fingertips, and drastically reduced the time and cost of market entry for any firm. At the other end of things, the allure of the nine-to-five salaried job was rapidly dissolving, especially in the decade following the Great Recession. Job security was a relic. The jobs that existed were being stripped down to the bare minimum in terms of upward mobility, benefits, and engagement. Was it any wonder that the Millennials were widely predicted to become the most entrepreneurial generation of all time?

"There are more entrepreneurs operating today than at any time in history," wrote Eric Ries, in his bestselling book *The Lean Startup*. "The side hustle is the new job security," wrote Chris Guillebeau, in *Side Hustle*. "You're lucky because you live in an age of unmatched opportunity for anyone with enough hustle, patience, and big dreams," wrote Gary Vaynerchuk in *Crush It!*, extolling readers, in his next book, *Crushing It!*, to "eat shit as long as you have to" in order to grasp the "brass ring of adulthood" (entrepreneurship) because there has never been a better time to . . . (wait for it) . . . Crush . . . It! The Freelancers Union, a newly formed group that provided benefits to self-employed workers, predicted that the majority of American workers would be freelance in some capacity by 2027. We were living in the midst of a golden age for entrepreneurs and I wanted to chronicle what that looked like.

But when I began looking at the data on entrepreneurship and speaking with the academics who studied it, what I found stood in complete contrast to everything I had assumed to be true. There are fewer people going into business for themselves today than there were twenty or thirty years ago. When Ronald Reagan was in office, two out of ten Americans worked for themselves in some capacity. Today that number is one in ten. This counted for individuals going out to work as unincorporated and self-employed (like me), as well as those starting up formally incorporated businesses.

But what about the Millennials? Turns out that the group that gave us Mark Zuckerberg is the demographic least likely to start a business and work for themselves in nearly a hundred years, a phenomenon that a

US Small Business Administration report dubbed "The Missing Millennials." One study found that college graduates with advanced degrees were half as likely to start a business that employed at least ten people in 2017 as they were in 1992. In fact, the density of startups around the country (the number of new businesses created in a given time period, for every thousand businesses that already exist) was down by more than half of what it was in 1977, when those statistics were first compiled. The data were riddled with all sorts of incomplete information, and these studies contradicted each other regularly, but even the best-case scenario had entrepreneurship flatlining in America and in much of the developed world. Entrepreneurship was not ascendant. In fact, it was declining and had been doing so for years.

Expecting to chronicle the golden age of entrepreneurs, I now found myself reckoning with something far more complicated. How could entrepreneurship be more revered, romanticized, and valued on a broad economic, political, and cultural level, yet when measured by the numbers that mattered (people going into business for themselves), it was stagnant, and in many areas, appeared to be dying? How had we come to revere entrepreneurship so highly, yet gotten it so wrong?

I started asking questions, beginning with academic experts on entrepreneurship. But within a few interviews, I noticed something at the start of these conversations that deepened my curiosity. "What do you mean by an *entrepreneur*?" they would ask me. I was surprised to learn that there was no single universally accepted definition of the word. An entrepreneur can be described as broadly as anyone who works for themselves. Or it can be as specific a definition as the founder of a business based around a particular kind of innovative technology that they personally invented, with a minimum number of employees, specific rates of growth, and particular financial structures. Some believed that being an entrepreneur had nothing to do with self-employment and described a series of behaviors that could take place anywhere, even in a salaried job. Others cast the word as a mold for a hero of modern-day capitalism, an *Übermensch* whose goals were nothing short of saving the world through business.

I quickly realized that this one question—What is an Entrepreneur?—was the key to understanding the seeming divide between our rosy perception of entrepreneurs and the more complicated reality of their decline.

And what I saw from the answers was an echo of the inequality of wealth and opportunity present in the rest of the economy. At the top, you had the popular image of entrepreneurship that had inspired all that "entrepreneur porn," a wonderful term from a 2014 *Harvard Business Review* article used to describe the way the media pushed an idealized lifestyle about entrepreneurs well past its reality. This was the startup myth forged in Silicon Valley, a well-oiled machine of entrepreneurship with defined roles and rules, sources of investment, and paths to success. This myth drove the headlines, captivated the public consciousness, and made household names out of its icons.

The startup myth dominated discussions of entrepreneurs in the media, institutions, government, and academia, and increasingly defined what an entrepreneur was supposed to look like, how they behaved, and what they did. It established that entrepreneurs were brilliant and young, mostly male and white, highly educated lone geniuses who frequently dropped out of college because they were so singularly focused on a brilliant innovation that would transform industry, and maybe even the world, through economic disruption driven by blitzkrieg growth and fueled by venture capital. These entrepreneurs were deemed the most valuable, because they held the promise of quickly creating the greatest economic benefits . . . jobs, investment returns, and new lines of business.

But like that airbrushed cover of Heidi Klum, Silicon Valley's entrepreneurship was far from reality for most of the entrepreneurs I knew. My entrepreneur was someone starting a business that ranged vastly in size, spanned every conceivable industry, and was inherently personal. It was the entrepreneurship of my father, grandparents, friends, and neighbors. It was more often self-financed and grew at a variety of speeds. It was entrepreneurship over the long term, sometimes spanning generations, and it wasn't captured in slogans or hashtags.

None of this fit into Silicon Valley's narrow definition of an entrepreneur. Not businesses run by women or minorities or immigrants or seniors. Not people in poor neighborhoods or rural areas, making things with their hands, or selling services that served a local market. Not someone who wanted to stay small so they could pick up their kids from school every afternoon, provide for a family, realize their values, or to scratch a need to do their own thing, in their own way. That was a problem, because out in the real world this broader group of entrepreneurs still made up the overwhelming majority of people going into business for themselves. They fixed holes in my roof and baked my bread, designed my website, changed my tires, and cut my hair. For men and women like Mr. Freeman and the hundreds of millions like him around the world, who toiled in relative obscurity running all sorts of businesses, and yet rightly saw themselves as entrepreneurs until the end, there was a deeper, more meaningful truth to being an entrepreneur that the popular mythology missed.

I came to realize that the way you define an entrepreneur has meaning. It establishes the story we tell ourselves about the inherent promise of economic opportunity and sets us up with the metrics by which we measure success. If that definition is becoming increasingly narrow and rarefied, and casts out the majority of the people in this world who are their own bosses, then what you get is an inequality of entrepreneurship that makes being an entrepreneur less accessible, realistic, or desirable. The system becomes rigged and exclusionary. The benefits and glory accrue to those at the top, and dangerous resentment builds below. The illusion of economic opportunity gives way to the reality of hopelessness. The so-called golden age becomes a veneer.

Over the months that I began having these conversations, my own thoughts about being an entrepreneur were rising to the surface. My wife, Lauren, had finally launched her career coaching business and, for the first time, was completely on her own. I was now witness to an individual's transformation from a salaried employee comfortably earning six figures, to an entrepreneur starting from scratch, who had to be taught during her first week of working from home that she no longer had to eat a can of sardines by her computer (Self-Employment 101: lunch is sacred). At the same time my brother Daniel worked to launch his own business, with much higher financial risks, in an industry on the cutting edge of uncertainty, and I watched the two of them weather the initial thrills of starting up together.

And then there was me. Nearly two decades into being my own boss, and still figuring it out. Still unsure about where that next check was coming from. Still nauseated by the fear of not enough work, or the stress of having too much. Always chasing that nagging question "What the hell am I doing with my life?" day in and day out. And now . . . "Am I really an entrepreneur? And if not, then who am I?"

This book is my search for the soul of an entrepreneur, and what that soul looks like today. If you are an entrepreneur, a family member of an entrepreneur, or just someone interested in entrepreneurship, I hope you get a sense of what that soul looks like, the different forms it can take, and why nurturing it across a wide spectrum of entrepreneurship is crucially important now. Because no matter what kind of entrepreneur you are, from the modest side hustler to the most ambitious captain of industry, entrepreneurship is a constant process of soul searching.

Unlike most books on entrepreneurship, I'm not at all concerned with the *How* (how to become an entrepreneur, start a company, or get rich), but *Why*.

Why do entrepreneurs do it? Why do they keep at it, even in the face of tremendous odds, and the daily personal sacrifices, and the imminent threat of financial failure? Why does the entrepreneur matter, why do different types of entrepreneurs matter, and what's at stake if we lose sight of their value?

My search for the soul of the entrepreneur led me to read stacks of books, articles, and research papers on seemingly every aspect of entrepreneurship, in addition to interviewing countless academic experts around the world. But at its heart were the conversations I had with more than two hundred different entrepreneurs over the past two years, on the phone and in their businesses and homes, when times were good and times were bad. I chose these entrepreneurs because their lives and experiences covered a wide diversity of backgrounds, industries, and economic circumstances. This book is a result of those conversations, and the journey that drove them.

Of course, every entrepreneur has her own story, and I found that each person's idea of entrepreneurship was closely tied to her identity. My own definition of the word evolved over the course of researching this book, and I've tried to replicate that experience in its pages. The first group of entrepreneurs described here were those just starting out: an immigrant story about beginning a new life; a woman who built her business around the life she wanted, rather than the other way around; and someone who found success, then turned it to the benefit of the community she came from. The second group was wrestling with their growth: a business owner who discovered what was important to him long after he started his venture; a family dealing with a legacy across generations; and an individual struggling with the personal cost of entrepreneurship for himself and those around him. Finally, I sought out someone reflecting on a life defined by bringing his entrepreneurial ideas into the world, and what that ultimately meant for entrepreneurs everywhere.

Yet I also found it nearly impossible to make sense of these stories without dealing with the singular narrative that still dominates our collective obsession with entrepreneurship: Silicon Valley's startup myth. This myth had so skewed our understanding of who an entrepreneur was, and what they did, that we had lost sight of its very essence. Before I could move beyond Silicon Valley to search for the entrepreneur's deeper soul, I needed to face the startup myth head-on. I wanted to understand what it looked like and why it had grown so prominent, what the startup myth's complications were, and why the imbalance between the myth and the greater truth of entrepreneurship mattered. So I began my journey in the valley, town, and campus where entrepreneurship has a particular name and meaning, defined by its own models and heroes, where the transformational act of becoming an entrepreneur is simply called starting up.

PART I

THE MYTH

CHAPTER 1

Starting Up

"O H MAN, WE'D better hurry," Nikhil Aggarwal said to his best friend Andrew Chizewer, as they walked up to Stanford University's NVIDIA Auditorium, and saw hundreds of bikes jammed together near the entrance. "I hope we can get a seat." They were too late. The 342 spots in the lecture hall had already filled up, so the three of us quickly grabbed a table in the lobby that faced a large television, which would broadcast the talk. Within five minutes, another hundred students surrounded us, sitting on the floor, and even standing against the wall.

Aggarwal and Chizewer were business partners in the startup Scheme, a new software platform that matched students with internships at different companies, mostly Silicon Valley tech startups. They tried to attend the Entrepreneurial Thought Leaders (ETL) lecture every week, which had brought the top entrepreneurs in Silicon Valley to speak at Stanford for twenty years. "Mindset matters," said Tom Byers, an entrepreneurship professor in the engineering school, introducing the lecture. "There's so much entrepreneurship and innovation going on in this world, and it's time to talk about it positively!"

Today's featured entrepreneur was Maureen Fan, a Stanford alumni in her early forties who cofounded the virtual reality animation company Baobab Studios. Dressed in a black leather jacket, Fan took the stage and recounted her professional life story with an easy command of the audience. "I'm going to tell you about my path to becoming an entrepreneur," Fan said. "I never expected to become an entrepreneur."

Fan quickly humblebragged through her journey from reluctant computer science major to discovering a love of animation, which she studied at night in community college, despite the protestations of her Chinese "tiger parents" that she would "be poor and destitute if I followed my dreams." They convinced her to get a job at eBay, even though she wanted to go to Hollywood, and then get an MBA from Harvard Business School, which led to a job at Pixar, where she refused an accounting position to work on *Toy Story 3*.

"The point is to always ask for what you want because people in general want to make you happy and want to help you," Fan said. Aggarwal and Chizewer rolled their eyes at this suggestion and returned to their laptops. They were half-listening to the lecture, while toggling between Excel spreadsheets (economics homework) and Google docs (formatting an email blast to send to possible companies who might want to be early adopters of Scheme).

Fan worked at Zynga after Harvard, where she managed the successful game *FarmVille*, became a vice president, and slept four hours a night. "It was traumatic but I learned so much about what it meant to be an entrepreneur and what it took to start a company," she said. "Because in business school they teach you to be a certain type of leader, which is very different from what it takes to be a startup leader."

Fan and some Pixar friends made a short film on weekends that won an Oscar, but kept wondering if she could turn her love of animation, and of virtual reality, into a viable business. She got the cofounder of Dreamworks animation to be her mentor by befriending his wife, then convinced the cofounder of Pixar to be her advisor by showing him the power of virtual reality in a crepe shop. "So it's about persistence and constantly asking," she said, moving on to investors and how she raised funding in four weeks, which felt like an eternity, until one connection led to a $6 million series A round, and then another few connections (via Stanford, Harvard, her old boss at Zynga, and the Taiwanese tech diaspora in the Bay Area), landed her in the arms of Peter Thiel, the famous venture capitalist.

"You should be honored that I'm even talking to you," she told the audience, pantomiming the overconfident tone she took with potential investors to convince them to back her. "You should be honored to give me money!"

Chizewer laughed out loud. "Oh man," he told me, "they'd laugh Nikhil and I out of their offices if we took that attitude."

Fan joked that her company was "poor," because it had raised a measly $31 million.

"No, we're poor," Aggarwal said to Chizewer, not looking up from his laptop, as Fan went on about persistence and connections and leveraging Stanford, stopping to apologize for using the word "asshole," then saying it was okay to curse, because one study showed that successful entrepreneurs cursed more.

"The mission of our company ultimately is to bring you back to that five-year-old self that you have inside you, to bring out your sense of wonder and inspire you to dream again," Fan said, playing videos of her company's virtual reality animations, which we couldn't actually see on the TV outside the auditorium, even though we heard the crowd *ooh*ing and *ahh*ing inside. "Because then you would all go for your dreams, you would realize how much potential you have, actually go for it rather than being scared that you can't achieve your dream and what an awesome place the world would be if everyone actually pursued their dreams. . . . Thank you."

Cue rapturous applause.

"Same old same old," Aggarwal told me, as he and Chizewer zipped up their backpacks. "It's inspiring to hear the success stories, but it would be more fulfilling to know how they figured out how to jump through the hoops that other entrepreneurs faced." The two had a lot of hoops to jump through before Scheme was off the ground, and they headed off to Starbucks to work for the next few hours on their company . . . just one startup among many being born in Silicon Valley that day.

Most of us tend to think about Silicon Valley when we talk about entrepreneurs. Silicon Valley is a catchword for an industry, built on a foundation of computers, which now touches nearly every facet of our economic and personal lives. And Silicon Valley is shorthand for the way that industry works. A mindset. The way it creates and values companies and the technologies at their core, but also the entire system of organizing, financing, and operating those companies, which is a model now deployed around the world, across industries. Silicon Valley is also a place in Northern California, stretching from San Francisco to San Jose; a string of towns, cities, and exurbs, punctuated by freeways, office parks, and dots of natural beauty. At Silicon Valley's geographic, financial, and spiritual center is the city of Palo Alto, built at the feet of Stanford University's expansive campus.

Silicon Valley is Stanford, and Stanford is Silicon Valley. This campus, and the world that grew up around it, largely defines what we think of when we talk about entrepreneurs today. The particular model of entrepreneurship cultivated at Stanford is rich with its own history and heroes, ideas and rules, benefits and drawbacks. All of this forms the heart of the Silicon Valley startup myth, a narrative around a particular kind of entrepreneurship that has come to dominate our conception of the word far beyond this place. To understand that myth's origins and evolution, its inherent business model, and the problems that presents for entrepreneurs and the wider world, I began my search for the soul of the entrepreneur at Stanford, by witnessing the process of starting up in its most fertile ground.

Chizewer and Aggarwal first conceived of Scheme in late 2017, when they were living together in a fraternity house during their sophomore year. Neither fit the typical computer science student startup archetype (Chizewer majored in political science, Aggarwal in economics), and neither was particularly interested in entrepreneurship when they got into Stanford. Both did well at school (but not exceptionally so), had social lives, extracurricular interests (Chizewer ran the debate team), and career prospects in the business world. Neither wanted to be cast as the "evil tech bros" in my book, in Chizewer's words, which was a simple task, because they are both very thoughtful, considerate young men, with a strong sense of skepticism about the world they are living in. The pair are reluctant entrepreneurs, in a place where that word is ripe with meaning.

"I didn't want to become the guy who starts a company at Stanford. I still don't!" said Chizewer, who grew up in a Jewish family in Chicago and has a fair complexion dotted with freckles.

"Even in high school, the stereotype about Stanford is that everyone here is trying to start a company," said Aggarwal, who is from an Indian family in Fort Wayne, Indiana, and is slightly taller than Chizewer. "I didn't just want to start a company just because everyone did."

Like most startups, Scheme began as a problem its founders personally experienced: the competition for summer internships. "What do you have lined up for next summer?" their friends asked them during the first week back from summer vacation of their sophomore year. Next summer? It was September. Chizewer had just completed an internship at a hedge fund, and Aggarwal one at a software development firm in Palo Alto. But many Stanford students had already secured the top internship spots for the following summer . . . internships that Chizewer and Aggarwal had no idea existed, let alone how to apply for.

The students who were ahead of this game seemed to be the same ones whose families had deep connections at Stanford or in the very corporations offering these coveted positions. "It's hypercompetitive," Aggarwal said. "Everyone here who is connected already has stuff." That seemed unfair, but also a tremendous missed opportunity. Students needed valuable work experience, while companies (especially smaller startups), needed young talent to help them grow. Many companies already offered internships, or wanted to create them, but lacked the resources to attract Stanford students. If Aggarwal and Chizewer could connect those willing students with the companies that wanted to put them to work, wouldn't everyone be better off?

"It was an opportunity to solve this problem," Aggarwal said. They began talking late into the night about ideas, surveying students and companies, sketching out a business plan, and coming up with a name ("scheme" is apparently slang for hooking up with someone, which they adapted to hooking up a job). Quickly, Andrew Chizewer and Nikhil Aggarwal went from students to founders, the particular term Silicon Valley applies to startup entrepreneurs.

BEFORE WE GET TOO FAR into the startup myth, it is important to know how we got there. Entrepreneurs are not a new phenomenon. There were merchants, traders, property speculators, and private businessmen in ancient Babylonia, Sumeria, and other market societies that set the stage for modern civilization. The word "entrepreneur" originated in France, and was based on a thirteenth-century verb meaning "to do something." It was used widely for all sorts of people doing all sorts of things, from an undertaker (a quite literal translation), a battlefield commander, or the director of a musical performance. The French/Irish economic scholar Richard Cantillon is credited as the first to describe the entrepreneur as something specific in the 1730s. Cantillon's entrepreneur occupied a wide range of businesses, from manufacturers and merchants, to small farmers and bakers. The central thing that linked all of Cantillon's entrepreneurs was the fact that they bore a personal financial risk, regardless of their profession, not knowing when or how much they would be paid, or whether they would make a profit or a loss. "The entrepreneurs are on unfixed wages while the others are on fixed wages as long as there is work," Cantillon wrote in chapter 13 of his posthumously published book *An Essay on Economic Theory* (*Essai sur la Nature du Commerce en Général*).

In the United States, the entrepreneur entered the foundational mythology of a society. The defining characteristic of America was commercial, rather than aristocratic. Each settler, from comfortable Londoners to poor Dutch fishermen, set off across the Atlantic with the same acceptance of risk and hope of the reward that Cantillon wrote about at the time. America's founding fathers (many of who, such as Ben Franklin and John Hancock, were themselves entrepreneurs) enshrined the importance of starting a business into America's laws.

America's entrepreneurial myth grew with the country, typified by the industrious merchants of New England and the hopeful pioneers seeking riches out west. By the later half of the nineteenth century, the American entrepreneur had become a fixture of popular culture. He ranged from self-promoting businessmen like ringleader P. T. Barnum (author of *The Art of Money-Getting*), to Ragged Dick, the namesake protagonist of Horatio Alger's largely forgotten 1867 novel about a loveable New York bootblack who persevered by working hard, finally befriending a wealthy young man who gave him a chance to make a decent living.

"There've been a great many boys begin as low down as you, Dick, that have grown up respectable and honored," Dick's patron says, after bringing Dick off the streets and buying him a new outfit. "But they had to work pretty hard for it."

"I'm willin' to work hard," said Dick, who quickly rose from poverty to the respectable middle class by sheer pluck. Hurray for Dick!

Alger's bootstrap pulling, get-rich-quick American fantasy was a myth, of course. A miserable street urchin like Dick was likely going to die a street urchin during that "gilded age" of inequality, but the fact that many of the robber barons such as Andrew Carnegie, Cornelius Vanderbilt, and John D. Rockefeller came from humble origins cemented the core American fairy tale of endless possibility for the entrepreneur.

"There was no higher goal for a young American male to pursue during this period than to become a 'self-made man,'" wrote Yale historian Naomi Lamoreaux. The examples of people rising up in society by starting businesses were so strong, she wrote, it was almost seen as wasteful not to become an entrepreneur. Hard work and the success it brought were a sure sign of a man's moral worth. "Indeed, in the late 19th century, to be an employee (even a genteel, white-collar employee) was to forsake a life of striving for a condition of 'dependency,'" wrote

Lamoreaux, "itself a moral failing." Entrepreneurship became the core of the American Dream.

That dream was challenged as the twentieth century dawned. Financial crises led to labor unrest, rising inequality, and poverty. The shared sacrifice of World War I, the crushing poverty of the Great Depression, and finally the mass mobilization required for World War II put America's entrepreneurial myth on ice. There were famous entrepreneurs throughout these decades, but the mythology increasingly rang hollow. Instead there was collective achievement and sacrifice, including political movements like women's suffrage, and the birth of a military industrial complex that would invent the terrible and wonderful, from hydrogen bombs to Tang. This era belonged to the corporation, to Ford, IBM, GE, Westinghouse, and Bell Labs; teams of professional managers in crisp suits and their scientific methods for improving efficiency and performance. Innovation was the purview of university research departments and corporate campuses. Entrepreneurs were cast as loners and misfits.

The roots of the current entrepreneurial myth began on those campuses, especially at Stanford. In 1939, Frederick Terman, the dean of Stanford's engineering school, encouraged his students Bill Hewlett and David Packard to start their electronics business in a garage near campus (HP was Silicon Valley's original startup), and in 1951 Terman helped create Stanford Industrial Park, leasing university land to young high-tech firms, whose work was often funded by the Department of Defense. Many developed Cold War technologies in radar and aerospace, including computers and the silicon semiconductors that powered them, which gave the region its famous nickname.

By the end of the 1970s, Silicon Valley's culture was changing from one built around teams, research, and government contracts, to a place increasingly focused on individual entrepreneurs. As it did, Silicon Valley's startup myth emerged. That myth's central promise was that anyone, regardless of their background, could invent the future and be rewarded for it, if they had the right invention or ideas and the strength of character to see it through.

The hero of that myth has different names, but he shares the same characteristics. He is a singular brilliant individual, with the power (alone) to invent and inspire, a willpower to make the impossible possible, and a bit of an antisocial streak. He is the lone genius. The creator. The founder. The model for all other entrepreneurs out there. He is a he. He is young. He is a misfit. He went to Stanford or another top university, but didn't graduate. He doesn't care about the rules. He has something to prove and zero deference to those who stand in his way.

According to journalist Adam Fisher, author of the oral history *Valley of Genius*, the prototype Silicon Valley entrepreneur was Nolan Bushnell, who cofounded the video game company Atari. "He was a pop cultural entrepreneur," Fisher said. "The first entrepreneur out of Silicon Valley who actually affected and wanted to affect the culture. Before that Silicon Valley was making parts for the war machine and was dominated by guys with pocket protectors and short-sleeve button-up shirts and crew cuts working out of the NASA base." Bushnell changed that. Not by developing the most powerful technology, making the most money, or outlasting the competition, but by creating *Pong* and *Pac-Man*, giving us a reason to actually care about computers.

There are many entrepreneurs who have fallen into this heroic archetype in the four decades since Bushnell came around. These titans include Microsoft's Bill Gates, Oracle's Larry Ellison, and Amazon's Jeff Bezos, whose fortunes, inventions, and impact on technology, business, and day-to-day life are immeasurable. But the church of the Silicon Valley entrepreneur is dominated today by the holy trinity of Steve Jobs, Elon Musk, and Mark Zuckerberg.

Jobs: "The searingly intense personality of a creative entrepreneur whose passion for perfection and ferocious drive revolutionized six industries: personal computers, animated movies, music, phones, tablet computing, and digital publishing," wrote Walter Isaacson in his relentlessly bestselling biography *Steve Jobs*. Jobs, the Silicon Valley kid that was Bushnell's protégé, who dropped acid, ate wildly restrictive diets, and combined hippie counterculture attitudes with Japanese aesthetics to personalize the computer. Jobs, who emitted a "reality distortion field" that convinced people to do the impossible. Jobs, who became the first genuine celebrity of Silicon Valley, with four movies made about him. The guy who got fired from his own company, returned to bring us the iPhone, died, and was reborn as "the greatest business executive of our era," to quote Isaacson. Black turtleneck. Loose jeans. Round glasses. Gray New Balances. Steve Jobs: the entrepreneur's messiah.

Musk: "The most daring entrepreneur of our time," according to Ashlee Vance, bestselling author of *Elon Musk*. "He's the possessed genius on the grandest quest anyone has ever concocted." Musk, the peerlessly brilliant inventor who personally made ecommerce possible (PayPal), revived the electric car (Tesla), and reignited the space race (SpaceX). Musk, who wants to take us to Mars, have us zipping underground in hyperloops, and save humanity. Musk, the media darling who inspired Robert Downey Jr.'s *Iron Man*. Musk, who is so efficient with his time that he slept beneath his desk and pees in three seconds flat. Musk, whose rabid fans (dubbed Musketeers) personally attack his critics online, and get his face tattooed on their bodies. Black t-shirt. Tight jeans. Hair that has magically grown back. Elon Musk, the patron saint of serial entrepreneurs.

Zuckerberg: The dorm room hacker who commanded legions to "move fast and break things." Zuckerberg, the programmer who ushered in the social media age and a wave of startups that chased it. Zuckerberg, the socially awkward, quasi-recluse. Zuckerberg, the billionaire in his twenties who sought to change philanthropy, education, communications, and the world. Zuckerberg, the antihero of the *Social Network* movie, who made a generation believe that a billion dollars really is cooler than a million dollars. Zuckerberg, who said, "In a world that's changing really quickly, the only strategy that is guaranteed to fail is not taking risks." Zuckerberg, who connected the world, at the cost of our privacy, and democracy. Jeans. Sneakers. Hooded sweatshirt. Mark Zuckerberg, the prophet of disruption.

How many aspiring entrepreneurs have cited at least one of this holy trinity as their hero? How many have copies of their biographies on their slim bookshelves? How many style themselves in their image, from their mannerisms and extreme diets, to their dress and conduct, berating employees, breaking norms (and laws), and casting themselves in their mold, in order to play a role they believe they need to?

"More crimes have been committed in the name of Steve Jobs than anyone in the Valley," said Kent Lindstrom, the former CEO of Friendster who hosts the Silicon Valley podcast *Something Ventured*. "To extract pieces of his personality—'I yell at people because Jobs did or wear black turtlenecks'—is insane," he said. "I met Steve Jobs. You're no Steve Jobs."

Leslie Berlin, a historian who oversees Stanford's Silicon Valley archives, noted that the myth of the lone genius entrepreneur was a purposefully created one. Most digital technology companies and their inventions are the product of group efforts across industries and borders. But savvy PR firms, journalists, and the public found it easier to associate complicated, disparate technology with the face and personality of a single individual. "The Horatio Alger thing is key," Berlin said, over lunch in Palo Alto. "The notion of an individual striving to be rewarded just fits perfectly."

The entrepreneurs who rise from the Valley's floor to the top of the public's imagination tend to share similar characteristics: They appear accessible and relatable, even if they are actually supernaturally intelligent and socially awkward; they are young, because youth and beauty and a whiff of scandal are a magnet for attention; and they are rich and famous. "That's the big difference," Berlin said. "Entrepreneurs here used to be highly successful *businesspeople*, including Steve Jobs before he left Apple the first time. By 2011, when he died, he was a celebrity. That didn't used to exist. No one put posters of Gordon Moore [Intel's founder] on their wall," said Berlin, causing me to instantly recall the big poster of Jobs my old roommate Adam hung above his bed, how Musk dates actresses and rock stars, or that Zuckerberg once made a guest appearance on *Saturday Night Live*.

More than build technology, mythmaking is what Silicon Valley does best. It tells stories about commerce and science. The people there aren't just engineers and executives; they are dreamers, visionaries, and thought leaders . . . something you can be, too, if you just start up. When venture capitalist Tim Draper created a private college teaching entrepreneurship south of San Francisco, no one batted an eye when he named it the Draper University of Heroes. But like most good stories, Silicon Valley's fable of entrepreneurship is largely a myth.

"The Jobs/Musk model is taken to represent the category, when in fact it's a very very small subset," said noted venture capitalist, economist, and Cambridge professor Bill Janeway. "Most of the people who generate reality distortion fields are so divorced from reality they fall off their ass."

And yet Silicon Valley's startup myth persists, because it's irresistible. We love the story of the wunderkind, inventing the future in their dorm room. In her book *Valley of the Gods*, Alexandra Wolfe chronicled the first class of Peter Thiel's eponymous fellowship, which coerced bright young minds under twenty to defer college, move to Silicon Valley, start a company, and become the next "boy CEO." Its first celebrity was James Proud, a dough-faced British lad who pitched an asteroid mining operation, then blew through more than $40 million to create a sleep tracking machine that never went anywhere, even though the company was valued, at its peak, at more than a quarter of a billion dollars. "The young, aspiring entrepreneurs were seduced by the lifestyle, by the oddity of it all," Wolfe wrote of the Valley's startup scene. "They were the new waiters and waitresses on Sunset Boulevard trying to win Oscars in Hollywood."

The result is often a homogenous culture ripe for parody, which a show like HBO's *Silicon Valley* nails so perfectly. "There's a hive mind mentality," said Matt Ruby, a comedian who cofounded the software platform Basecamp and now skewers Silicon Valley's startup myth through Vooza, a fictional startup. Ruby saw a cultlike mode of thinking, acting, and living in the "startup ecosystem" in the Bay Area and beyond. Young tech company founders dressing the same (Allbirds sneakers, tight jeans, and a t-shirt, hoodie, or Patagonia zip-up with their startup logo printed on it), eating the same weird diets (Soylent meal replacement shakes and "brain hacking" cocktails of supplements and microdoses of psychedelics), living together with other founders, going to Burning Man together, then using the same word salad to pitch similar companies to the same pool of venture capitalists, combining the same technologies and markets with a slight twist ("It's an AI powered e-scooter blockchain solution driven by big data"). They did this because that is what the myth dictated entrepreneurship looked like, but it all added up to something that was so derivative, Ruby saw it as contrary to the spirit of genuine entrepreneurship. "Anytime you've got a mass of people who completely agree with each other on anything," he said, "well, that is the opposite of innovation or being counterintuitive."

Just as surely as it was for the robber barons a century and a half ago, most of Silicon Valley's startup myth was rooted in astronomical wealth. Steve Jobs became a household name after Apple's record-breaking IPO, Elon Musk was the same after his PayPal payout, and that was before Mark Zuckerberg broke the bank. "When you get a twenty-three-year-old becoming a billionaire, the culture snaps its fucking head," said Fisher. "It's an impossible, rags-to-riches story." But each year it gets retold with a new overnight sensation: Uber's Travis Kalanick, the Stanford alumnus who formed Instagram and Snapchat, and on and on, until you have a collection of names whose rapid catapult into the top 0.1 percent of global wealth forms the characters in an impossibly compelling fairy tale. Who could resist that?

Perhaps the story that best captures the seductive power of Silicon Valley's startup myth is that of Elizabeth Holmes, whose scam blood testing company Theranos raised more than $700 million from investors before collapsing. Holmes is infamous now, a cautionary tale about the gap between the myth of entrepreneurship we want to believe and the reality that underlies it, but what stood out for me as I read journalist John

Carreyou's book *Bad Blood* in my Palo Alto Airbnb was how skillfully Holmes sold her nonexistent technology to the world since dropping out of Stanford at nineteen, based on nothing but the entrepreneurial myth everyone wanted to hear.

Holmes worshipped Steve Jobs from a young age and modeled her life on his. Carreyou claimed that Theranos workers could pinpoint which chapter of Isaacson's biography she was reading based on the period of Jobs's career she was impersonating, down to the black turtleneck, the design of her "mini-lab," the choice of Apple's preferred ad firm Chiat\Day, the diet of green drinks, and the way she tore into people who "failed" her. A few saw through Holmes's charade, but for wealthy investors, ranging from top venture capitalists like Tim Draper, business moguls including Robert Kraft, Carlos Slim, and Rupert Murdoch; corporate partners such as the Cleveland Clinic and Walgreens; and nearly every global media outlet that placed Holmes's face on magazine covers, what they saw in Holmes was everything they had been taught to see by Silicon Valley's startup myth. President Obama even appointed her a global ambassador of American entrepreneurship.

When Theranos came crashing down, the world was aghast. How could this happen? How did so many bright, successful people fall for this con? But when you think about it, Holmes delivered exactly the product she promised: not pinprick blood testing, but the heroic entrepreneur we all wanted. Innovative. Young. Attractive. Bold. Unapologetic. In that respect, Elizabeth Holmes succeeded beyond her wildest dreams. Jennifer Lawrence is cast to play her in a film adaptation. She even won the Horatio Alger award. Ragged Dick would have been proud.

"EVERYONE KNOWS SOMEONE WHO IS being an entrepreneur at Stanford," Aggarwal said, as we met up with Chizewer outside the student union building the day after Fan's lecture and walked over to a career fair set up nearby. Companies big and small were lined up in small booths and tents around the paths near the campus bookstore. Chizewer and

Aggarwal planned to walk around and ask companies about any internship opportunities and gauge their potential interest in Scheme.

"Come on," Aggarwal said, "let's split up and start taking down names to contact later."

Chizewer approached a tent for Robby, a company making a small self-driving delivery robot, which was founded by Stanford graduates who had gone through Y Combinator, the pioneer of startup incubators, where young entrepreneurs receive office space, advice, and guidance from seasoned investors, in exchange for a piece of their company. He began asking the founder about the internship process at the company. "What's the interview like? Where do you find candidates? How big is your team?" The man asked Chizewer why he wanted to know all this, and he explained that he and his friend were trying to solve recruiting problems for companies.

"What kind of problems?"

"Internship problems," Chizewer said, with a hopeful smile.

"What's the name of your company?"

"Scheme."

Oh, the man said, we'd already done work like that with another company. Chizewer kept the smile up. "Cool!" he said. "Well, do you have a contact?"

Scheme wasn't the first company working on campus internships. Part of the reason for coming today was to learn just where Scheme could fit into the market, but it was difficult. Chizewer and Aggarwal didn't yet have business cards (though they had printed a few t-shirts), and once people found out what they really wanted (and that they weren't engineering PhDs), they either brushed them aside or mocked them outright.

"Oh great!" a man who ran a chip company in Southern California told Aggarwal. "I was just looking for someone to disrupt the recruiting process . . . hahaha!" Interns cost more than they were worth, he said. It was glorified babysitting.

"Well, we focus on project specific, nontechnical roles," Chizewer said. "Our thesis is that small company internships can be valuable."

Later, back at Starbucks, the two of them talked about what they had learned. "I think we validated some parts of our process," Aggarwal said, "but I think we need to focus on a pivot to consider after this."

"Honestly," said Chizewer, "maybe we look beyond Silicon Valley. Beyond startups and Stanford, to other companies and even community colleges. Not elite jobs." Every type of business could benefit from summer interns. Just imagine what an accounting student could do to help a local restaurant owner clean up her books. Scheme could democratize the internship beyond the top schools and companies, so that every student had a chance to learn and every business got the help they needed.

If Chizewer and Aggarwal needed help with Scheme, they had limitless resources at their disposal. Stanford offered dozens of programs in entrepreneurship, from summer certificates to graduate degrees, in areas as diverse as journalism, environment, engineering, law, and medicine. There were campus incubators and accelerators where students could gain office space and advice from seasoned founders, various Stanford venture capital funds available to invest in their companies, and even something that described itself as "an incubator for incubators." Students could join a growing number of entrepreneur clubs to suit every potential interest in the topic, gaining access to like-minded peers, professors, and outside contacts, including one that was only open to students who had already created and sold a company worth $1 million or more. Or they could live in the entrepreneurship-themed eDorm, which opened in 2012, attending regular lectures and helping their neighbors with their startups. Other students went further, starting business with their professors, many of whom were successful entrepreneurs outside of campus. A student could spend their entire time at Stanford taking classes, attending lectures, and going to meetings on entrepreneurship, and they would never exhaust all the options the school offered. And if that didn't satisfy them, they could put their studies on hold for several years, without penalty, to pursue their startup full-time.

Surprisingly, this focus on educating the entrepreneur is a relatively new phenomenon, not just at Stanford, but at universities around the world, which have done more to propagate the startup myth than almost any other institution, with real consequences in academia and beyond.

The formal study of entrepreneurship in America began in 1947, when a professor at Harvard Business School named Myles Mace created a course called "The Management of New Enterprises," because he wanted to help GIs returning from overseas to start companies. "Mace said, 'We need to teach these guys how to make a living,'" said Howard Stevenson, a professor emeritus at the Harvard Business School, who helped pioneer its modern program on entrepreneurship.

At the time, entrepreneurs had a stigma around them. "This was the era of riding the escalator up as far as you can go and living on that floor until you retire," said Stevenson, and Harvard Business School's curriculum focused on training professional managers for corporations. Since business schools had tight relationships with large corporations, who funded them, provided them with research, and gave jobs to graduates, the notion of studying what amounted to small businesses was a nonstarter. Entrepreneurs were characterized as disruptive and deceitful loners, misfits, hustlers, and nobodies . . . think Willy Loman in *Death of a Salesman*, a schmo who failed to make it into respectable corporate society. Others said teaching entrepreneurship was impossible, because entrepreneurs were simply born with innate personality traits.

"When I began studying entrepreneurship in the late 1970s, my colleagues said, 'You're basically studying people in polyester suits. Going into entrepreneurship studies will ruin your career,'" said William Gartner, a professor at Babson College, outside Boston, a school that devotes itself exclusively to entrepreneurship. "'There's no money there. Nothing to study.'"

Things began to shift around the middle of the 1980s. Economically, the United States was cycling through recessions, and the cultural grip of the once-indominable American corporation was slipping, as inflation, competition from Japan, and a sense of stagnation took a toll. This coincided with the first big tech startup boom, built around the personal computer, and the rapid success of companies like Microsoft and Apple, driven by a new species of founder. President Reagan cast Silicon Valley's digital entrepreneurs as America's "pioneers of tomorrow" in his 1983 State of the Union address. Universities suddenly woke up to realize that wealthy entrepreneurs had money and might be willing to fund the education of future entrepreneurs.

As resources grew, the field of entrepreneurship studies increasingly embraced Silicon Valley's startup myth and wove it into their core. A key shift was in the academic definition of an entrepreneur, from Richard Cantillon's broad example of someone who bears a risk in return for a potential future reward (which could encompass any small business or self-employed individual), to something narrower. The field found its intellectual anchor in the writing of Joseph Schumpeter, an Austrian political economist and failed banker, who eventually taught at Harvard, until his death in 1950. Schumpeter's core idea was that the entrepreneur was capitalism's key change agent, a "Man of Action" rather than a "Static Person," who breaks out of the equilibrium with tremendous energy, to create "new combinations" of ideas and inventions that drive economic development to new heights. But it was Schumpeter's theory of Creative Destruction, which he arrived at near the end of his life, that forever shaped the study and perception of entrepreneurs.

"This process of Creative Destruction is the essential fact about capitalism," Schumpeter wrote in his seminal 1942 work, *Capitalism, Socialism, and Democracy*. The entrepreneur's role was "to reform or revolutionize the pattern of production by exploiting an invention or new commodity, or producing an old one in a new way, by opening up a new source of supply of materials or a new outlet for products, by reorganizing an industry and so on." Creative Destruction was driven by innovation. Innovation brought turbulent change, establishing new winners and losers, but ultimately pushed everyone forward. The entrepreneur's ideas didn't matter. What mattered was action, or as Schumpeter put it as eloquently as Elvis, "getting things done."

The tidal change to this definition of an entrepreneur was monumental. It shifted the paradigm from ownership and risk, to one that was process oriented. Entrepreneurship was now focused on innovation and disruption, therefore anyone who did that was an entrepreneur, including teams of managers and researchers earning salaries in large corporations, who bore little personal risk, but reaped the rewards nonetheless. The entrepreneur became an exceptional, visionary individual, and this excluded most of the people who had previously considered themselves entrepreneurs.

"Schumpeter provided heroes," explained Louis Galambos, a business historian at Johns Hopkins University. "We want to have heroes and leaders who inspire us. Something powerful professionally, but also powerful in a public way." Schumpeter's ideas, which really only gained widespread traction in the 1980s and 1990s, blended together very neatly with neoconservative ideas in economics. "Thatcher, Reagan, the whole Chicago school . . . Schumpeter fits strongly within that," said Galambos. Schumpeter's theory quickly gained traction as a perfect way to explain and define why entrepreneurs mattered . . . but only certain entrepreneurs. The entrepreneur worthy of study was not a mere shopkeeper or the owner of a large regional cement company. They were exceptional visionaries, capitalism's best and brightest, whose daring actions had profound consequences that ultimately made our lives better. He cemented the myth.

The study of entrepreneurship at universities all over the world has since exploded. In 1985, there were around 250 courses on entrepreneurship offered at American universities. By 2008, there were more than 5,000 courses offered. That number today is exponentially higher, to say nothing of its growth globally. Entrepreneurship studies have grown from a maligned outlier to a field of study that produces a constantly growing trove of research (over 15,000 papers written a year, according to Google Scholar), into every single conceivable aspect of entrepreneurship, from papers questioning the right conditions in a particular Iranian city to spur entrepreneurs to build a water park, to a much publicized study out of the University of Colorado, that showed people infected with toxoplasma, a mind-controlling parasite found in cat feces, were more likely to start businesses than those who weren't infected. I shit you not.

Before you reach into the litter box for a taste of inspiration, you should know this boom is not without criticism. Being such a new discipline, a lot of entrepreneurship education falls short, amounting to what MIT's Bill Aulet called "Clapping for Credit" in a *Bloomberg Businessweek* article: students sitting in class, listening to a wealthy, successful entrepreneur tell their life story and then left to draw their own lessons on how to apply that to their ventures. A lot of the teaching around entrepreneurship is prescriptive, with a focus on the steps needed to launch and grow a successful company laid out in various methodologies, such as the Lean Startup, based on the bestselling book by Eric Ries (who had dropped out of Yale to start a similar company to Scheme). The result, too often, is a formulaic, step-by-step approach to entrepreneurship and what it means to be an entrepreneur.

This frustrated Aggarwal and Chizewer to no end. "I mean, so much of entrepreneurship is intangible," said Aggarwal the night after the career fair, when we all went out to a packed Indian restaurant in downtown Palo Alto.

"All you get from the university is: make a pitch deck, make a business plan, don't give up, and so on," said Chizewer, describing his experience with Stanford's entrepreneurial education so far. "Everyone said the same thing: work hard, failure is inevitable and it's good for you, and it all worked out. I think it's good advice in a vacuum, but simply telling people to persevere through failure is not necessarily helpful."

"I want to hear a lecture from someone who failed," Aggarwal said. "I want to hear about them starting a company, and it crashed, and why. We get that in one-on-one interviews with people, but not in class." They had the same experience at Startup School, a program run by the incubator Y-Combinator, which Scheme had been accepted into weeks before. That morning, the two had gone to Y-Combinator's San Francisco offices to hear a lecture by Patrick Collinson, the CEO of the mobile payments company Stripe. "He didn't talk about luck," said Aggarwal, "or factors that led to his success that were out of his control. He said how Stripe took two years to launch, but then said, 'Oh, but you should launch as fast as you can.' That doesn't help us."

"They all try to fit into this model of what Y-Combinator and Stanford say takes to make a successful startup," said Aggarwal.

"Out here, the path to entrepreneurship has become standardized," said Chizewer.

As the startup template spread out beyond Stanford and Silicon Valley, it set the bar for what entrepreneurs were worthy of study, what version of entrepreneurship was worth teaching, and where financial resources should go to support entrepreneurs. New schools and think tanks of entrepreneurship were almost exclusively focused on the startup model. Universities and governments set up incubators and innovation zones, furnished with the same open concept furniture, color schemes, and exposed beams found in San Francisco startups, and made sure everything culminated in press-ready Demo Days, those beauty pageants of the startup world where one entrepreneur after another gets up onstage in front of a room of investors and journalists and tries to sell them on how their idea will change the world in five minutes.

Silicon Valley's startup myth venerated the act of starting up more than anything that came after that. The curriculum looked at entrepreneurship as a process of starting a business, financing it with outside investment and rapidly growing it to the maximum scale possible. Other forms of entrepreneurship, such as lifestyle businesses, or those based around slow growth and self-funding, were scarcely touched on, if at all. I asked Irv Grousebeck, the man who established the Stanford Graduate School of Business Center for Entrepreneurial Studies back in 1985 (he is also a successful businessman who owns the Boston Celtics), whether this model presented an unnecessarily slender version of the wider entrepreneurial experience.

"Absolutely," he said, "but that's not our consequence. It's not part of our job." Stanford's Graduate School of Business was a training ground for the world's top MBA students. Despite its clout and wealth, it had limited resources and time to teach them. It needed limits, and that didn't include someone "taking over their mother's dress shop," he said, dismissively. Stanford wasn't selling any one thing to entrepreneurship students; not a model, not a message, not a prescription. Its graduates had gone on to start all sorts of different businesses, ranging from Schumpeterian disruptors in technology to ice cream companies. "I'm not teaching cost accounting in Indiana," he said. "I'm teaching entrepreneurship in Silicon Valley. Fall off a log out here and you'll become a hero! The environment dictates that."

Over the week I spent interviewing students and faculty at Stanford, many were keen to stress that the actual number of students who were actively starting companies while at school was small, likely less than 5 percent. But the aura they cast and the way the school glamorized and promoted that made entrepreneurship seem outsized on campus. "Yeah, I think infatuation is a big part of this," said Chizewer, "but these worlds definitely meld here." Their professors regularly bragged about how successful they were as entrepreneurs, even if those claims were greatly exaggerated, as if justifying their presence. "Departments here that are world renowned (like psychology, which is number one in the world) are looked down on and mocked by students," Chizewer said, echoing what Debra Satz, the dean of the arts and science faculty, told me about dwindling enrollment in liberal arts, "because they're not linked to entrepreneurship," in the way business, engineering, or computer science was.

The lines between school, work, students, and faculty had already blurred beyond recognition at Stanford. Students regularly co-invested in companies with their professors or appointed them as paid advisors to their boards. Numerous Palo Alto venture capital firms deployed student "scouts" on campus, who hosted free drinks, dinners, and even performances by comedians like Trevor Noah, in order to source potential investments from their classmates. Some venture capitalists flew promising student founders to Las Vegas for a weekend of partying. Chizewer and Aggarwal did their best to keep Scheme and the rest of their lives at Stanford separate, but it was hard to escape the scene. "Entrepreneurship is an addictive feeling," Aggarwal said. "People can feed off that. It can be all the social energy you need."

Several months before I visited them at Stanford, Aggarwal and Chizewer were already talking about the fundraising road ahead for Scheme. First they would get seed funding from angel investors to build out the platform, then use the validation from early customers to start pitching venture capitalists (VCs) for the next stage of funding. The two were getting no shortage of introductions to VCs from friends, professors, and mentors in the business (by this point, they had brought on two cofounders to help build the company; one worked nearby, and the other lived in China). Still, they wanted to take their time and get it right. I pointed out that Scheme wasn't an actual business yet. It had no customers or users or revenues. In fact, they had no idea what they would charge clients or when they would even charge them. What mattered was the idea and getting it funded.

A month later, when we spoke, Chizewer and Aggarwal were working on raising $50,000 to get the business off the ground. A month after that and they were already pitching to VCs, while being advised by another veteran venture capitalist. The advice was typical: they had to show how they'd acquire clients and validate their assumptions. But most important, they had to think bigger . . . not just Stanford and internships at startups but a market potentially worth billions. So they were telling investors that millions of American businesses would pay for facilitating internship placements for millions of students, making it potentially a $100 million business annually. All of this was theoretical and based on the rosiest possible scenario. By the time we met in Palo Alto a few weeks into their junior year, Scheme had still placed just one student at an internship.

Venture capital and venture capitalists are at the core of Silicon Valley's startup myth and are one of the most problematic aspects of it. The venture capital–funded model of entrepreneurship has become so dominant in the technology business, as well as other businesses that are increasingly copying its tactics (food, retail, consumer products), that the language, methods, and metrics of entrepreneurship are increasingly standardized along the narrow lines of what VCs want to see. For the VC, fundraising is everything. It is the means of output and the measure of success. Fundraising is validation within the industry, in the press, with competitors and customers. Around Silicon Valley and in the world that emulates it, talk about raising money ("We're raising, are you raising? How much are you raising? How much did you raise? From who? At what valuation?") is far more prevalent than talk about the underlying business or technology. And for an entrepreneur who steps onto this ride, the time they spend raising money is often vastly greater than the time they spend building the actual business they're supposed to be raising it for.

"Venture-funded entrepreneurship is the perfect bliss point for entrepreneurship: the fundraising, the ambition theater, the validation of egos, the hero worshipping we do around a certain kind of entrepreneur . . . each of those elements intersect at bliss point," which is the valuation around the latest funding round, said Bryce Roberts, a venture capitalist who runs the funds Indie VC, and O'Reilly AlphaTech Ventures from Salt Lake City. "It's a sugar high. It's the junk food of entrepreneurship. It wears off quickly."

The problem, according to Roberts and a growing chorus of skeptics in the industry (including many current and former VCs), is that fundraising is actually a terrible metric for entrepreneurial success. It has nothing to do with how well a business is run, how much revenue it generates, or the profit it makes. It is entirely about how well the founder can convince others to give them money. There's an element of Ponzi scheming to this. The more money an entrepreneur raises, the higher their company's valuation, which helps the VC fundraise more money from its own investors, pushing the entrepreneur to raise more money to increase their company's valuation, to deliver a better return for the fund. Theranos raised $700 million and was valued at $10 billion, without ever making a working product or a single dollar of revenue, and that was not just seen as normal but as an astounding success until it was exposed as a fraud. Of the dozen top unicorns (companies valued over $1 billion) expected to go public in 2019, just one was profitable. Not Uber or Lyft, WeWork, Spotify, Snap, or Dropbox. Each one lost more money than the other and yet was heralded as the greatest business success in a generation. This is the entrepreneurship myth we are venerating and the fundamental problem with the VC's role at the center of it.

"If your customer is a VC, what you're peddling is a business plan that you're trying to monetize," said Tim O'Reilly, a famous entrepreneur, investor, and writer in Silicon Valley. He predicted this will only worsen if the most egregious myths of Silicon Valley's startup model continue being perpetuated: that people have to raise money from investors to be an entrepreneur, that money raised is equivalent to success, that you don't have to make a profit, and the only thing that matters is an exit. "That's not going to end well."

Venture capital remains a crucial source of funding for entrepreneurs developing advanced ideas and technology that will take years to pay off, such as biotech cancer treatments or microchip designs. The problem is that venture capital has become a sort of game, and if you learn how to play it, you can raise free money, succeed or fail, and do it over and over again. Ideas in the VC game are less passions and more schemes. Entrepreneurs and VCs will chase a trend for six months, then move on. This is how you get companies like Juicero, which made a fancy machine that basically just squeezed juice boxes into cups ($120 million raised over four years), and innumerable ill-fated copycat ideas chasing the same pool of money, from meal kit delivery services and social media platforms to electric scooters and smart watches. The commitment is short term, because the expectations are as well. This is rote, soulless entrepreneurship.

"The craft has become 'starting up,'" said Roy Bahat, who runs Bloomberg Beta, the venture capital arm of the financial information corporation. Define a market segment, pour money into it, and capture a monopoly as quick as possible. In essence: a land grab. "Silicon Valley tradecraft is labeled as technology, but really it's about growing really really fast," without constraints or regard for the consequences.

Those consequences were seldom acknowledged amid all the rapturous praise for Silicon Valley's startup myth, but they formed the heart of what troubled me about that myth's domination over the culture of entrepreneurship. The first consequence was the very independence that defined an entrepreneur's soul. "What's the point of being an entrepreneur if you can't work for yourself?" asked Jason Fried, the CEO of the

Chicago web development software company Basecamp and the author of several bestselling business books, including *ReWork*. "The moment you take money from someone else, you work for them." Basecamp was privately held, financially viable (tens of millions of dollars in profits generated annually, according to Fried), and innovative (it created the standard web design software Ruby on Rails), yet it had achieved all of this without a cent of venture capital funding. "We generate our own money," Fried said. "We sell a product for a price, and people pay for it." It astounds him that he's seen as the outlier, when the reality is that his business is no different than the vast majority of companies out there in the global economy. Doing the work. Getting paid. Not thinking about the next round or an exit.

The second problem was how Silicon Valley's startup model is plagued by inequality. Most VC funding goes to male, white founders who went to Stanford or Harvard. The reason shouldn't be shocking. Most venture capitalists in America are also white males who went to Stanford or Harvard, came out of the same industry, play by the same rules, and reward the same behavior. Female entrepreneurs received just 2.2 percent of venture capital funding in 2018, around the same percentage as visible minority founders. The vast bulk of funding goes to companies based in the Bay Area, then New York, Boston, and a handful of other cities. Even Seattle, home of both Microsoft and Amazon, received a piddling 2 percent of VC funding in 2017. For an industry that loves to criticize the East Coast elite, Silicon Valley has managed to innovate itself into a more powerful and unequal version of that elite, swapping Brooks Brothers suits for Patagonia vests.

Third, the startup myth's rags-to-riches heart is largely as hollow as Horatio Alger's. The reality was that many of the startup entrepreneurs in Silicon Valley were far from bootstrap pullers, putting it all on the line. Many dabbled in startups because it was a relatively risk-free path to the top and a way to get even richer quicker. If they failed, then the money lost was mostly that of investors and rarely dipped into the personal wealth of founders. No one was losing their home. The adventure would be a great story about the virtue of "failing up," startups looked good on a résumé, and they could easily get a job somewhere great with their Ivy League degree. Even Chizewer and Aggarwal had secured paid internships at Goldman Sachs and Accenture for the next summer, in case Scheme didn't take off.

"It doesn't matter if we take a résumé hit," admitted Aggarwal of the relatively low risk he and Chizewer took on while starting Scheme as Stanford students. "It's not even close to an even playing field." When Chizewer heard Maureen Fan tell a couple hundred of Stanford's hopeful entrepreneurs to work outside the system, do what they wanted, and not follow rules, he shook his head in disbelief. "You can't do that without some serious privilege," he said.

"Every single VC says, 'Raise a seed round with friends and family,'" Aggarwal said. "Well, you can only raise that if your friends and family are rich!" Already the two had spent $4,000 of their own money (which they made by coaching debating, tutoring, and with summer jobs) on building the platform. Both felt a growing fear as their costs grew, while that first dollar of revenue seemed months away. But still, they would be fine.

Then there was the problem of venture capital's disproportionate influence and inflated importance. For all the mythology surrounding it, venture capital financing for entrepreneurs remains an exceedingly rare phenomenon. In 2018, for example, there were roughly nine thousand investments made by venture capitalists into businesses in the United States, which sounds like a lot, until you realize just how small that number is. At any given time there are more than thirty million businesses operating in the United States, and US venture capital investments (including both those invested in early-stage startups and more established companies) represent less than half a percentage point of GDP . . . a drop in a bucket. In other countries, it is vastly less.

In 2017, Professor Howard Aldrich, a sociologist from UNC Chapel Hill, and Martin Ruef, of Duke, released a paper that showed that despite the fact that barely a fraction of a percent of companies in America received venture capital funding, and fewer still made it to a public listing on the stock market, papers about entrepreneurship that focused on these two topics increased dramatically from the 1990s until the present . . . in some cases making up nearly half of the published articles in some entrepreneurship journals.

"In academia, where research time and funds are limited resources, far too much effort is devoted to understanding the handful of business startups that experience high growth or public offerings; and far too little effort is devoted to understanding the millions of startups that struggle alongside them," Aldrich and Ruef wrote. The balance had tipped far out of whack with reality.

Aldrich compared the entire practice to the field of biology and asked what would happen if half the biology papers published each year were about elephants, rather than the 99.9 percent of other species—from ants and fleas, to plankton and microbes—that constitute biodiversity on the planet. "It's an incredibly stupid model to push this as a paradigm to entrepreneurship," Aldrich said.

In 2013, the nonprofit Kauffman Foundation (which has done more to promote entrepreneurship education, advocacy, and venture capital in America than any organization) published a report, noting the danger of a creeping imbalance between the entrepreneurship that was being taught and promoted (the startup myth) and the reality on the ground. "Educators worry that the discipline already may have narrowed its mission and brand more than is truly necessary or desirable," wrote the report's authors, "by defining success in the framework of startups and venture capital, rather than in the framework of life enhancement." In essence, the report was calling for a return to the soul of the entrepreneur.

Over the year I spent speaking with people in the world of technology startups and entrepreneurship studies, I encountered a growing chorus of voices, including experienced founders, professors, and even well-known venture capitalists who had also begun questioning Silicon Valley's startup myth, the model it perpetuated, and the problems that model created. Some were busy experimenting with alternative ways of building companies, including forms of financing different from venture capital, which made room for more inclusive and diverse entrepreneurs.

"The business model is the message," said Mara Zepeda, who ran the community software platform Switchboard and launched a movement with other largely female, largely minority founders of technology companies called Zebras Unite in 2017, which promotes alternatives to the classic Silicon Valley startup myth. "If startup culture values hyper growth, exits, and profits above all, then you get qualities—hero worship, zero sum gamesmanship, an erosion of democratic norms—that amounts to a culture, which multiplies over and over again, like a cancer."

The founders who were reaching out to Zepeda saw entrepreneurship as something so much more than what this narrow culture presented. For them it was inherently personal and also vastly more diverse, both in the background of its entrepreneurs and in the journey they took along the way. This was the entrepreneurship I recognized in myself and the entrepreneurship I would seek over the rest of my research as I traveled beyond Silicon Valley.

It was one that I even recognized in Aggarwal and Chizewer as I watched their experience building Scheme and struggling with the bigger questions that their new venture brought out. After a summer of endless pitch meetings with venture capitalists around San Francisco and Silicon Valley, Chizewer and Aggarwal were growing hesitant about the startup myth's promises. The venture capitalists they spoke with were wildly inconsistent. One day they would have a meeting with an investor who would immediately dismiss Scheme as impossible, then six months later that same VC would reach out and ask how they were doing, then go silent again for several months. It seemed like these VCs were chasing deals at random, on a whim, with no real sense of the business Scheme was trying to build.

"I think that's the problem with the mindset out here," Chizewer said, as we met up for a coffee between classes one afternoon. "Validation comes from money. But that doesn't validate your product. That just validates someone has a positive experience with you. What we realized is that investors are hesitant, and should be, to dump money on something that has no product validation."

"It brought us back to the level," Aggarwal said. "We pretty much decided we're not going to raise money until our product launches. We are going to focus on actually getting clients."

What had begun as a frustration had given birth to an idea, grown into a business, and thrust two people who had barely entered adulthood into the world of entrepreneurship. In the months they'd been at it they had learned a ton: how to build a database and write a business plan, pitch to investors, research a market, and collaborate with friends and strangers. They'd foregone sleep and parties and the last truly free years of their young lives, pursuing something that was bigger than them, not so much for the gold at the end of the rainbow (because, to be honest, even they weren't sure it was there), but for something else . . . the deepened sense of friendship that working together as cofounders of Scheme had given them, a value they hoped to provide to students and customers, and the new sense of purpose a startup brought to their lives. Their experience illustrated something essential about entrepreneurship: that the real heart of the project was in the people bringing it to life, the relationships they formed, and the struggles they went through. The romance of the startup myth, along with the huge sums of capital flowing all around them, made this hard to see, or at least hard to focus on for long. But there were moments when Chizewer and Aggarwal seemed to grasp it.

They took their first check from a venture capitalist right near the end of the school year. It was inevitable, probably. The culture around them pushed them to do it, and the money in hand was hard to ignore. Ultimately, it was hard to say: Would they come to regret selling a piece of their business, or would they become two of Silicon Valley's next heroes? Either way, launching Scheme had given them a sense of what entrepreneurship was like: stimulating, social, fun, all-consuming. They knew the challenges that lay ahead and went on undeterred. They had a taste for entrepreneurship now. There was no turning back.

PART II

STARTING

CHAPTER 2

Starting Over

ARLY IN THE summer of 2017, I was walking around my neighbor-hood in Toronto, when I saw the bright yellow sign I had been expecting: COMING SOON: SOUFI'S, FROM SYRIA WITH LOVE. Ever since Canada began admitting Syrian refugees at the start of 2016, I figured it was only a matter of time before a wave of Syrian food businesses began appearing in my hometown. Soufi's was the first green shoot of the latest emerging community of immigrant entrepreneurs.

In a city like Toronto, where more than half of the residents are born in another country, immigrant entrepreneurship is inescapable, especially in the enclaves that sprout up on certain streets and neighborhoods. The hustle of the barbers, reggae shops, and sidewalks perfumed by the smoke from jerk chicken cooking up on Eglinton west; the tumbledown postwar strip malls packed side by side with Punjabi jewelry stores, sweet shops, and colorful fabric outlets in Brampton; steamy Russian banyas in nondescript buildings in Mississauga; a tiny pocket of East African butchers on one corner of Thistletown; and the gigantic Chinese mega malls of Markham, selling everything from hand-pulled noodles and Maoist texts to condominiums and luxury cars, in just one of half a dozen Chinatowns around the city.

The first business I hit when I walk up my street is a fruit store, run by a family from China, next to a sushi place run by a Korean family. The neighborhood is officially Little Italy, but it was Jewish before that, and now it is mostly Portuguese in flavor. Each group left its mark on the commercial landscape, like Grace Meats, the local butcher shop that sells warm fresh ricotta and spicy capicola salami along with latkes and challah bread. Just today I discovered that the French café by the library is now a Venezuelan coffee shop selling Chilean empanadas. These are just the visible business, to say nothing of the Polish carpenter who built our closets, the real estate investor from Amsterdam ten houses away, and the New Yorker who runs a growing software startup on the corner.

If the Silicon Valley entrepreneur is driven to start up, the immigrant entrepreneur is determined to start over. Immigrants leave behind homes and history, families and friends, careers and reputations, businesses and assets, and trade it for an opportunity to begin anew.

The immigrant entrepreneur has its own heroic mythology, particularly here in North America. "It is a proud privilege to be a citizen of the great Republic, to realize we are the descendants of forty million people who left other countries, other familiar scenes, to come here to the United States to build a new life, to make a new opportunity for themselves and their children," said President John F. Kennedy, shortly before his death. "That is what this country has stood for for two hundred years, and that's what this country will continue to stand for."

Those rosy sentiments have waxed and waned with different politicians, as America and Canada have welcomed some groups of immigrants (Christian Europeans) over decades while refusing others (Jews, brown-skinned people, Asians). But although nativism has recently reared its ugly head in the United States and across much of the Western world (and is growing in Canada), the core mythology around the immigrant entrepreneur remains strong.

In the United States, as well as other wealthy countries, immigrants tend to be more entrepreneurial than the native-born population. In 2016, Sari Pekkala Kerr, a Finnish labor economist, and her husband, William Kerr, a business professor, published a paper for the National Bureau of Economic Research, which tried to quantify this phenomenon. They found that while immigrants tend to make up just 15 percent of the US population, their share as the percentage of entrepreneurs has grown remarkably, from 17 percent in 1995 to 28 percent in 2012. In Canada, immigrant entrepreneurs look statistically similar to entrepreneurs born here. They experience no greater rates of entrepreneurial success or failure than the average, and they form all sorts of businesses, from unincorporated one-person operations cleaning houses or gardening to complex corporations that do everything from owning fleets of dump trucks to managing hundreds of millions of dollars in investment funds. Last year, a study by Statistics Canada showed that companies owned by immigrant entrepreneurs accounted for a quarter of all net new private sector jobs, even though they represented just 17 percent of firms.

But while the economic output of immigrant entrepreneurs is often used to frame the discussion around them, the reason I am interested in them goes far beyond money or the number of jobs they can create, compared to native-born entrepreneurs. For me, the immigrant entrepreneur represents the fundamental hope that all entrepreneurs experience, deep in their souls, that they can build a new life and identity through a business, regardless of their past. That the entrepreneur can always start over.

SINCE THE FIRST PROTESTS BEGAN against the dictatorship of Bashar al-Assad in the spring of 2011, Syria quickly dissolved into a bloody and complex civil war that reduced the country's cities to rubble, killed more than half a million people, injured countless more, and sent more than five million Syrians into exile. In September 2015, a raft carrying Syrian refugees capsized in the Aegean Sea, and a photographer captured the lifeless body of three-year-old Alan Kurdi washed up on a Turkish beach, instantly personalizing their plight. This prompted many governments, such as Germany and other European nations, to admit them as immigrants.

When the Canadian government of Prime Minister Justin Trudeau and his Liberal Party came to office in the fall of 2015, it quickly got to work fulfilling a campaign promise to accept a significant number of Syrian asylum claimants. Canada sent staff to refugee camps to vet applications, created programs where individuals and communities could privately sponsor Syrians (my synagogue sponsored a family, as did some friends), and pledged to resettle twenty-five thousand Syrians in Canada by the end of the year. The first Syrians landed at Canadian airports at the start of 2016, with Trudeau there to personally welcome them to their new home. They quickly became a *cause célèbre*, with the obligatory footage of Syrian children trying ice skating rounding off the nightly newscast for weeks.

Months later, as the presidential campaign of Donald Trump moved from a quirky sideshow into the White House, Canada's acceptance of Syrians took on a new significance. Trump had promised a total shutdown to Muslim visitors to the United States, with sharp curbs on all forms of immigration. US refugee resettlement dropped from one of the highest in the world to one of the lowest, topping out at just over 18,000 resettled in America in 2019, the lowest level since 1977. Just a handful of these were Syrians, owing to Trump's ban on immigrants from Muslim majority nations.

By the start of 2019, more than 60,000 Syrians had been resettled in Canada. It was inevitable that a number of them would soon find themselves becoming entrepreneurs. For Syrian immigrants here, entrepreneurship was not simply an economic issue. It was a stepping-stone into a new life, made possible by culture, skills, resources, and most importantly hope.

Soufi's opened for business in August of 2017. The restaurant was small and bright, with roll-up windows that opened onto the busy sidewalk of Queen Street and an interior tailor-made for Instagram, complete with white subway tiles, vintage photographs of Syrian markets highlighted with bright colors, a chalkboard menu, and a selection of bric-a-brac items; including instruments, red fez hats, plants, Turkish coffeepots, and family pictures. The smell of yeast, sumac, and za'atar hung in the late summer air. The slogan I'd seen on the window before it had opened, *From Syria with Love*, was now written on the menu board in big letters, as well as the door, the takeout menus, and the bright yellow T-shirts the staff were wearing, punctuated by a heart.

Soufi's was a simple restaurant: a small menu of options geared to takeout, no waiter service, and a few scattered tables. A young man with a shaggy beard and tremendous head of hair under a Toronto Blue Jays hat was staring dreamily into the distance behind an espresso machine, while a young woman with a big smile (his younger sister, it turned out), came up to greet me. "Hi," she said. "Welcome to Soufi's. I'm Jala."

Jala Alsoufi was just twenty-three years old and had graduated a year before from the University of Toronto with degrees in architecture and psychology. She had arrived on a student visa in 2012, while her parents and two brothers followed her three years later. The Alsoufis were not refugees. The family was originally from Damascus and Homs, in Syria, but since 1995 they had been living in Jedda, Saudi Arabia, where Jala's father, Husam, a civil engineer, had been managing a beach resort on the Red Sea that he partly owned. Though trained as a graphic designer and a social worker, his wife, Shahnaz Beirekdar, had not worked in a decade, partly because of Saudi Arabia's conservative attitudes around women and partly because their affluent life (luxury cars, domestic help, private clubs, a yacht) was so easy there. Jala, her older brother Alaa (still staring into space from behind the coffee machine), and a younger brother who was still in high school mostly grew up in Saudi Arabia, though they spent summers back with relatives in Damascus and Homs.

No one in the family had been back to Syria since the war began, but that conflict had made their life in Saudi Arabia precarious. Though Husam had been working there for twenty years, it was impossible for the family to ever obtain Saudi citizenship, which meant that they could theoretically be sent back to Syria anytime. Husam was accepted to Canada as a skilled immigrant, and once the family arrived in Toronto, he started talking about entering the city's hot real estate market, buying and renovating and reselling homes. He was just waiting for his partners in Jedda to send him his portion of equity in the business he said they'd owned. It never happened.

"Once my dad moved here, his business partners stabbed him in the back," Jala said. "They refused to give him his shares in the company." Because foreigners have few rights in Saudi Arabia, there was little Husam could do about it.

The family's options were limited. Husam's engineering degree from Syria was not recognized in Canada, and Shahnaz was still learning English. Jala watched as her father's frustration with his Saudi partners grew, and their savings dwindled. She had already been accepted to a master's degree program, but she began talking with her parents about opening up a restaurant. Despite the hundreds of Lebanese falafel places, Israeli restaurants, Afghan bakeries, and other Middle Eastern foods available, Syrian cuisine had no face in Toronto. The influx of Syrians had not only given their culture an elevated profile in Toronto, but a growing market of potential customers continued arriving at the airport each day. Didn't they talk about how much they missed that food? Weren't they always so disappointed in the manaeesh flatbreads they occasionally found and the sweet cheesy knafeh desserts that fell flat when they tasted them?

"We saw something lacking that was branded as a Syrian restaurant," said Jala. "We wanted to highlight the Syrian cuisine, which had gotten lost in the shadows of a general 'Middle Eastern' cuisine. This would be a strictly Syrian restaurant." They could do it together! Shahnaz was a great cook and could develop recipes, Husam understood the hospitality business and always wanted to own a restaurant, Alaa was personable and could deal with customers, and Jala was interested in marketing. It would get them out of the house. It could grow into a chain of restaurants. It would be fun!

"Why not?" Husam recalled saying with a shrug, as he smoked cigarette after cigarette on the restaurant's back patio. "At least until I get my money from Saudi Arabia."

The family got in touch with a real estate agent (coincidentally, my brother-in-law) and looked for a spot in the trendy Trinity Bellwoods area. The rent was high, but Jala didn't want to open up a restaurant in a strip mall outside the city core, in a neighborhood with other Arabic immigrant businesses. "We didn't just want to focus on Syrians or Middle Easterners," she said. "We wanted to open downtown, to share the culture and atmosphere of Syria with people from all around the world."

In the months leading up to the opening, Husam would walk around the house at 7 a.m., shouting, "Wake up, Soufis! Time to get to work!" Jala got her friends from college to help design the interior, and everyone in the family pitched in with the construction, working fifteen-hour days for months. It was exhausting but also exhilarating. "It was not easy," said Shahnaz, especially compared to their previously cushy life in Saudi Arabia, but she was incredibly proud of what they had accomplished together so far. "Here, I'm involved in everything," she said with a smile, as Jala translated. "But I'm happy."

The menu at Soufi's was built around two quintessential Syrian street foods: freshly baked manaeesh flatbread topped with a variety of ingredients, from sujuk (spiced ground beef) to crumbled halloumi cheese with braised, lemony spinach with sumac; and knafeh, a warm dessert of gooey cheese and phyllo strands, scented with rosewater and soaked in syrup. Shahnaz had created the recipes based on those in her family, in old cookbooks, and what she learned from watching YouTube videos. Jala even developed a vegan knafeh, called "banoffeh," which was made with coconut caramel, bananas, and tahini and inspired by her love of banoffee pie, a 1970s-era dessert that is a portmanteau of "banana" and "toffee." The Alsoufi family hired young Syrian refugees as cooks.

The city's food lovers who had been anticipating this wave of Syrian restaurants looked to Crown Pastries, one of the first Syrian food businesses to open in recent years, for a tantalizing preview of what was possible. The small bakery in a strip mall, wedged between a Subway and a halal cheesesteak shop in the eastern suburb of Scarborough, had opened in 2015 and was consistently cited as the best source of Syrian sweets in the city. Their beautiful pastries greeted anyone who entered the bakery and stretched the length of the place: piles of baklava in various shapes and sizes, from cigars piled like log cabins, to triangles stacked into pyramids; birds' nests of swirled noodles with whole pistachios nestled in the center like eggs; custard-stuffed semolina and sweet cheese dumplings called halawi jibben; and chocolate mafroukeh, which were dense chocolate brownies covered in a storm of pistachios, almonds, and cashews.

Crown Pastries was owned by Rasoul and Ismail Alsalha, brothers from Aleppo, a city that was being systematically reduced to rubble when I first met them during the war's peak. Their grandfather had operated his own bakery, called Jamal, since 1980, where Rasoul had worked, learning the delicate art of stretching phyllo and balancing butter and nuts with the right sweetness. "That's the key with Syrian baklava," he told me. "You are supposed to taste the butter and nuts. It's not as syrupy and sweet as the Lebanese or Greek kind." In 2008, their grandfather passed away, and when his uncle took over the family bakery, Rasoul decided to strike out on his own.

"I felt I wanted my own thing," he told me, sitting with his arms crossed, as he often did, at one of the few tables in the small shop. "That was my dream. To open a bakery." Rasoul had stubble, thick black eyebrows, closely cropped styled hair, and the strong arms of someone who wrestled dough. He carried himself with a quiet, reserved demeanor. Rasoul opened the original Crown Pastries back in Syria with a friend, during the summer of 2008, in the heart of Aleppo's old city, investing $20,000 in the business. He was just twenty-one at the time. The business did okay, but it was hard to get the attention of customers when you were just one more baklava shop in Aleppo.

Ismail was nineteen at the time, studying in London, when something happened to the family that neither of the brothers would speak about. The war was still two years away, but whatever the threat was, it was dire enough that within two weeks the entire family ended up boarding a plane to Toronto and claimed refugee status in Canada. "We just wanted to get out somewhere safe," said Ismail, who has a wide smile, is slightly taller than his older brother, and wears his hair cut short at the sides. They arrived with nothing but their clothes and twenty dollars in Rasoul's pocket. The bakery had been left to his partner in Aleppo. "It was brutal," Rasoul said, when I asked what it was like to abandon Crown Pastries overnight, "because that thing was a dream you're building." Ismail immediately entered school, studying hospitality at a community college, while Rasoul went out and found a job at a Lebanese bakery to support the family.

"Within one week I had a feeling," Rasoul said. He knew he would reopen Crown Pastries in Toronto. It was just a matter of time. He didn't talk about it for a year, even to Ismail. He just put his head down and worked his butt off, waking at 5 a.m., commuting two hours each way on public transit, rolling out sheets of phyllo dough, brushing, folding, and baking all day for minimum wage, returning home, eating quickly, and passing out in exhaustion and frustration. "I know my skills," he said, "and I work honestly, but the salary I was getting wasn't fair."

Rasoul was told it would be years, even decades, before he could save enough to open a business, buy a house, and get settled, but he could only defer his dream for so long. The war had destroyed his past. "Everyone we knew was either killed or moved," Rasoul told me. Aleppo's Crown Pastries had been abandoned to rubble. He had no choice but to plant that dream again. In 2015, with $25,000 saved and an equal amount borrowed against his credit card, he reopened Crown Pastries in Toronto with Ismail. The place was as faithful a re-creation of the original as possible, right down to the layout of the cases, the mosaic tiling at the entrance, and the golden crown that was its logo.

I asked the Alsalha brothers what it had felt like to wager the tenuous life they had built up in Toronto and open the bakery. "It feels awesome," Rasoul said. "I felt like my dream started to come true." Ismail looked at his brother, almost scolding, and reminded him of the stress they experienced during those early months; sleeping three hours a night, dealing with permits and construction and endless expenses and headaches. "When you open a business, you put all of your past, future, savings, and credit in one spot," said Rasoul, spreading out his hands to sweep in the entirety of the small bakery. "All your life. It feels horrible. It's all here."

"This business is like our baby," Ismail said, patting his brother on the shoulder. "It feels like part of the family."

Crown Pastries wasn't the only Syrian food business that had been reborn in Canada. Isam Hadhad started Hadhad Chocolates from his Damascus kitchen in 1986, growing the company into one of the largest producers of chocolate in the Middle East. In 2002, Hadhad opened a massive factory to meet the growing demand for exports to foreign markets, including Europe. But it instantly came to an end in September 2012, when a Syrian government air strike blew up the factory. No one was killed or injured in the bombing (the work day had finished minutes before), but the business was completely destroyed.

"The war ruins everything," said Tareq Hadhad, Isam's son, who is a trained physician. "It doesn't ask if it's one side or another." The family stayed in Damascus for six months after the bombing, feeling like "fish in the ocean," with no idea where to go or what to do. Everything was in Syria: their past, their people, their investments, their lives. "We felt it was our land and our country and the war would end soon," he said. "We tried our best to stay in Syria." One day, Tareq and his brother were walking home when a rocket struck right near them. Neither was injured, but both men stood up amid the rubble, ran home, gathered their family, and said, "It's not time to do business . . . it's time to survive." The business was dead. But they could live. They escaped over the border to Lebanon.

In 2015, private sponsors brought them to Antigonish, Nova Scotia, a town with fewer than five thousand residents. The Hadhads assumed they'd eventually move to Toronto, or at least Halifax, but the warm welcome they got from the community, including support for housing and even winter clothing for the children, made them want to give back.

The only way they could was to make chocolates, so that's what they did. "People brought us here to build something. It's disgraceful to leave them and go somewhere else. The town needs physicians, but at the same time they need current jobs," said Tareq, when we spoke by phone. "We didn't want to come here to take anyone's job. We didn't need support from the government. We came here with skills and experience and we can build it ourselves. We just needed an open door."

What began as a side business in their home kitchen in 2016 quickly expanded into a small factory at the center of town. They called the business Peace by Chocolate, because peace was what they cherished the most. "Without peace you can't build a business," Tareq said. "We know how to lose millions, what you built your whole life, in a second. That's it. That's the fragility of peace. That's the treasure." By 2018, Peace by Chocolate was rapidly expanding its sales across Canada, producing three million chocolates a year, and employed thirty-five Antigonish locals in its factory. In the first two months of 2018, they sold as many chocolates as all of 2017 and began exporting to the United States. A Canadian astronaut had even brought one of their chocolate bars onto the International Space Station.

Wherever they ended up in Canada, Syrian entrepreneurs seemed to be cooking and selling food. You had the Shahba Shawarma food truck in Calgary, Middle East Café in Saint John, Newfoundland, Pistachio Catering in Vancouver, Oasis Mediterranean Grill in the small city of Peterborough, Ontario, and the Damascus Café & Bakery in the northern mining town of Sudbury, to name a few. I was surprised to find a Syrian family at a farmers' market in the tiny town of Meaford, Ontario, in the summer of 2017, selling meals from a folding table. Al Sheayer Catering was run by two brothers and their wives, who cooked Syrian classics including grape leaves rolled around spiced rice and smoky eggplant baba ghanoush. The first summer I saw them, only one of the women spoke basic English, and their handwritten signs were hastily scratched out from a Google translation. The following summer they offered more dishes, displayed in their own packaging, and had a broader menu. One of the brothers explained that they now worked several farmers' markets and catering jobs a week and would soon leave their day jobs to open a restaurant.

Wherever Syrian immigrants had landed, the same story played out. There were Syrian restaurants, grocery stores, catering companies, and specialty food shops popping up in every corner of the world, from Cincinnati to Stockholm, São Paulo, and even Gaza City. In Germany, where more than a million Syrian refugees had arrived since the start of the war, they had opened every conceivable type of food business, from simple shawarma and falafel spots to elaborate restaurants run by former Damascus celebrity chefs. One Syrian cook even opened a soup kitchen to serve the German homeless.

The biggest concentration of these entrepreneurs were in countries that bordered Syria, which housed the greatest number of refugees from the war. In Amman and Istanbul, Ankara and Beirut, and even Baghdad, Syrian entrepreneurs were selling food to their fellow refugees as well as locals. Nowhere was this more visible than in the giant Zaatari refugee camp in Jordan, which at its peak housed more than 150,000 displaced Syrians and became the country's fourth largest city. The dusty grid of tents and shacks, spread out on an arid desert plain, was plagued by the problems typical of refugee camps: crowding and squalor, crime and despair . . . but it bustled with entrepreneurship. Zaatari boasted its own commercial strip, nicknamed the "Shams-Elysees," a riff on the famous Parisian shopping street that integrated the Arabic name for Syria. A resident could buy pretty much anything they wanted on the Shams . . . TVs and satellite dishes, computers and mobile phones, clothes and beauty products. But the majority of its vendors sold food, from pizzas and kebabs, to fresh produce grown in greenhouses that refugees had cobbled together in the camp.

"We call it survival entrepreneurship because of the nature of the crisis at the beginning," said Ozan Cakmak, who managed the United Nations response to the refugee crisis in Turkey during its peak from 2016 to 2017. "You're forced to leave Syria. You don't have time to take your credentials. No one knows what you've done in your country. There's judgments against immigrants and refugees in every country.

You need income. You have skills. People have similar tastes, and so you do what you can to make a business out of it."

This entrepreneurship is neither planned nor is it often even sanctioned, legally speaking. Though some UN programs and NGOs help refugees start businesses in the camps, most simply pop up one day. "You can see signboards in Arabic advertising baklava or other foods," said Cakmak. "It's a quick, low-hanging fruit to enter there." No one is building these businesses to get rich or with help from investors. They are purely for subsistence, because no one intends to stay a minute longer than they have to in a refugee camp, and most of these businesses are sold to the next group of refugees who take their place.

For many immigrants, the need to secure some form of financial survival is the prime motivator of their move into entrepreneurship and is referred to as a *push* factor. Unlike the pull of an entrepreneur pursuing an attractive idea they simply cannot pass up (a romanticized core of the startup myth), a push to entrepreneurship is driven by necessity, often by a lack of better options, a problem that plagues immigrants. Immigrants are more likely to be unemployed in their first ten years in Canada than the rest of the population. A government report in 2013 showed that more than a third of recent immigrants to Canada were living in poverty, particularly in immigrant-heavy cities like Toronto and Vancouver, where half the population is foreign-born. That applies even when immigrants are college educated, compared to those native-born Canadians with only a high school diploma. Among those who secure jobs, only a quarter of Canadian immigrants are working in the fields they trained in, compared to more than 60 percent for native-born citizens. The problem has become so acute that policymakers have coined a specific term for this phenomenon of squandered immigrant intellectual talent: brain waste.

The reasons why Canada's immigrants struggle to find employment are numerous. Immigrants lack the professional and social networks that native job seekers have, and their knowledge of local markets and practices, not to mention the language, are understandably limited. Many professions are protected by unions and guilds that erect significant barriers to entry. I have two friends who were successful lawyers in Mexico and Israel, respectively, but once they moved here, their prior experience was deemed worthless in the eyes of the Canadian legal industry. Both had to return to law school in their forties at great cost, all while raising young children, only to compete for the same entry-level positions with twenty-five-year-olds. While a shortage of health-care workers continues to plague rural Canadian communities, more than half the foreign-born doctors living in Canada, like Tareq Hadhad, are not practicing medicine. And while some of these highly qualified professionals end up finding work in related fields, you regularly meet engineers, architects, and even ER surgeons driving taxis or operating a restaurant they opened when they discovered all the other doors are closed to them. What is most frustrating is that many Canadian immigrants are granted residency here because of their specific work experience and education back home, only to find out that like Husam Alsoufi's civil engineering degree and twenty years of hospitality experience, none of that matters once they set foot in Canada.

And so immigrants are pushed into entrepreneurship as the best option to start over. This was the case of my family, who came to Montreal in the nineteenth and twentieth centuries from some corner of the long-dissolved Austro-Hungarian shtetl, where they traded tobacco, cut and sewed garments, and scraped together a living in the city's burgeoning Jewish schmatte business. It was what my wife's maternal grandparents did after surviving the Holocaust in Poland. Sevek and Marisha (Sam and Mary) bought a corner store in Toronto and sold whatever they could, then sold that and bought a stationery store, until Sam bought a pickup truck and drove around to farms, buying feathers from goose and duck farmers, before moving on to dealing scrap metal.

None of this was entrepreneurship along the lines of Silicon Valley's startup myth that we glorify, and none of them got especially rich with these businesses. "It was a living," as Mary used to tell me with her Yiddish-inflected shrug. Entrepreneurship is what let them buy a house, clothe and feed two children, take vacations in Florida, and spoil their six grandchildren rotten until the day they died without a penny of debt and money in the bank. In short, entrepreneurship allowed two people whose families perished in Auschwitz to achieve the dream of an upwardly mobile, middle-class life that drives almost every immigrant across oceans.

While immigrant entrepreneurs started every conceivable kind of business, food played an outsized role in the immigrant's journey to entrepreneurship for several key reasons. Everyone needs to eat, and someone who can deliver a more delicious meal has at least a base of success. If there are other immigrants from the same culture, their market has an identifiable starting point. "The food business is quite handy," said Mustafa Koç, a Turkish-born professor of sociology at Toronto's Ryerson University who studies the intersection of food and immigration. "Many of the immigrants who come here are thinking what services they need . . . they are looking at what is missing in their lives and what is easy. What doesn't require millions in investment, and something they can do with a lot of labor? That's when they get into the food business. They know many other immigrants like them seeking culturally familiar food. 'Why don't I open a Syrian grocery?' That's how they start . . . if they pick up, others will say, 'There's money to be made in this area!' Then they open one next to another."

From a personal craving, like Jala Alsoufi's hunger for a proper Syrian manaeesh, or the frustration with the local baklava that Rasoul Alsalha experienced, you have the beginnings of a little Syria. Koç saw this happen all over Toronto, with the European Jews who opened the delicatessens, bakeries, and kosher restaurants that once lined Spadina in the 1940s, the Hungarians in the Annex in the 1950s, the Greeks in the 1970s along the Danforth, the Vietnamese in the 1980s who moved into Chinatown, and on and on. "It is particularly significant with major refugee waves," he said. "They tend to come in huge numbers and they constitute a market. You bring in twenty thousand Syrians to Toronto; you create a market! If you only serve to this crowd, you create a living. It requires basic human skills, tender loving care, and a lot of drudgery . . . these people have a lot of those. The barrier to entry is low."

Within a few years of the first immigrant arriving from a country you have the emergence of an interconnected economy of immigrant entrepreneurs within a community, able to service every possible need of each other's businesses, which increases the opportunities for the next generation of immigrants to become entrepreneurs themselves. New restaurants need specific products, so someone opens up an importing and distribution business. Someone has to build those restaurants and shops, so another immigrant from the community starts a construction company. That leads to a real estate business that sells and leases commercial properties, which needs financing, and since local banks won't lend to newcomers, a pool of loans are set up, helping other immigrant entrepreneurs access working capital. Just as Soufi's and Crown Pastries employed other Syrians, these businesses provide jobs for newcomers, and many of these employees eventually decide they can start their own thing, down the street, in another part of the city, or another part of the country altogether.

"The early pioneers establish the ecosystem for other entrepreneurs," said Jeffrey Pilcher, a professor of food history at the University of Toronto, who spoke with me over a massive crispy dosa at Subiska Foods, a South Indian restaurant in Scarborough, not too far from Crown Pastries. This isn't some romantic process or a particularly charitable one, Pilcher noted. There was rampant exploitation at every turn, typically when more settled immigrants took advantage of naive greenhorns. Sometimes these networks were well-oiled machines, like the brokerage of Chinese restaurants across the United States, run out of offices under the Manhattan bridge, which extended back to smuggling operations in China and took a cut at every step along the way. But more often than not, Pilcher said, the networks grew when everyone benefited. "These diasporic networks look for opportunities and move around. It's a complicated ecosystem that asks, first and foremost, 'How can we as a social unit/extended family, do best?'"

These networks of entrepreneurs extended outward geographically, upward economically, and strengthened over generations, until they played an outsized economic role in many industries and became absorbed into the mythology of that community's rise from outsiders to belonging. Think of the Lebanese and Ismaili shopkeepers across East Africa, the Greek restaurant owners in London, the Gujarati motel owners across the United States, and the Italian real estate developers around Toronto.

At an event for Syrian immigrants in Toronto, I was able to ask Canada's minister of immigration and refugees, Amar Hassen (who had arrived in his teens as a refugee from Somalia), about the value of immigrant entrepreneurs to Canada. "It's really important," he said, "especially the number of small and large businesses started by immigrants here. When you look at studies, it shows immigrants take risks and are eager and keen to establish businesses in Canada." Then, Hassen launched into a well-practiced sales pitch of the government's own programs for tech startups and getting immigrants involved in them.

This is a story that is particularly favored by advocates of skills-based immigration, who love to cite that nearly half of the companies in Silicon Valley have at least one immigrant founder and that Google's Sergey Brin and Tesla's Elon Musk are both immigrants. In the age of ethnic nationalism across the west, it can be tempting to make the argument for immigration on the basis of money: that we should let in immigrants because they start businesses, create jobs, and effectively make us more money than they cost to integrate into our society. But there's something crass about this. The people who want to shut out immigrants aren't doing so because of rational economic arguments about the labor market supply. They're doing so because there's something they don't like about *certain* groups of immigrants, who typically look different than them, worship a different god, and speak a different language. Most people call that racism.

Immigration is more than just a unit of economic output, and immigrant entrepreneurs shouldn't be judged on their ability to create more jobs than native-born entrepreneurs or act as a fertile solution to ageing populations in wealthy countries. Immigrant entrepreneurship is fundamentally a process of human transformation and empowerment, which has so much more to teach us about the soul of the entrepreneur than making money. And that process starts with the entrepreneur's ability to transform herself into something more than life's circumstances have thrust her into.

"It's a social need as much as economic," said Vivek Wadhwa, a successful software entrepreneur and academic, who speaks and writes about immigrant entrepreneurship in Silicon Valley as a distinguished fellow with Carnegie Mellon University. Wadhwa had arrived in Cleveland from India in the late 1970s, poor and hungry. He slept at the YMCA and eventually achieved tremendous success, yet that humble start never left his psyche. "It's always having something to prove," he said. "You feel inferior. You get sick and tired of people asking you, 'Where are you from?'" It didn't matter whether you landed in America or Canada, Japan or Tanzania, if you are a foreigner and an immigrant, on some level you are perceived as a lesser human being. "You talk different and look different. And now you have this burning desire in your belly to rise up again and get above that. The risk factor isn't there. You have the motivation to rise up."

Eight months after Soufi's first opened, I stopped by the store and spoke with Jala over coffee and knafeh. She was still the same bubbly young woman I had met in the summer, but as we spoke it was clear she had a lot on her mind. She told me she hadn't been sleeping well, and the pressure of the business increasingly weighed on her. "My dad would tell me to chill out, but I have this alarm ringing in my head that I have to make this work," she said. "For me this business is a fresh start for us as a family. My dad's still living in the past, fighting for his share of his business in Saudi Arabia. So for me, starting this business and making it a success is making up for the loss we already endured.

"The *urgency* is what pushes me," Jala said, emphasizing the word with a startling edge in her usually soft voice. "Making this work is the only option. We had a fresh start, and what sets apart immigrants is coming to a new country, with the new idea that if we work hard and push on, we can make it work. But also, that feeling of loss makes you want to recapture something. I thought that if my parents moved here and we invested just some of our savings in this (instead of all of it), perhaps that would have been less stressful. But our circumstances got us to where we are today. This is not a side project. We don't have another option if it doesn't work out. That's what continues to drive us."

That burning desire was one I encountered with every Syrian entrepreneur I spoke with and the dozens of immigrant restaurant owners from every single corner of the world that I had interviewed over the years, who had left behind certain lives to come to Canada and start over. More than a way to make a dollar, they had something to prove as entrepreneurs, and that need never went away, no matter how successful they became. That was true for Mohamad Fakih, arguably the most famous Arab businessman in Canada, who had transformed a run-down shawarma place into a global empire, boasting more than fifty Paramount restaurants, grocery stores, and other businesses spread across Canada, the United States, Britain, Lebanon, and Pakistan.

When Fakih first arrived in Canada from his home in Lebanon, he found himself shivering in an unheated basement apartment, working at a jewelry store during the day and a donut shop at night. "I cried because it was so cold and I didn't have a proper coat," he said fifteen years later, sitting in a bespoke suit with a Rolex watch on his wrist, and a Mercedes S-Class parked outside. Despite all this success, or even because of it, Fakih still felt he had something to prove. "You have to continually justify to the world your place here. Even after twenty years and more than two thousand employees, I still feel the need to justify my place. To prove that it's worth it," he said. "You lose something when you immigrate. A sense of family, a sense of belonging somewhere. I have to make up for that."

One morning, I visited a tiny business called Zezafoun, a month-old Syrian restaurant set up in an old French café near where I went to elementary school in midtown Toronto. I followed the sound of Arab pop music downstairs to the basement, where Diala Aleid, the thirty-one-year-old co-owner (along with her sister Marcelle and mother Yolla) was chopping onions in glitter sandals, shorts, and a tank top. Both the Aleid parents had been teachers back in Damascus, and the sisters had been working in the film and TV business in London and the

United Arab Emirates when the war began. An older sister already lived outside Toronto, so in 2014 the whole family arrived here and claimed asylum.

Since then, Diala worked on a few TV productions in Montreal as a lowly assistant, at a car dealership as an accountant, and spent many months "sitting at home spending my savings." Her mother, who was an art teacher in Syria, retrained as a hairdresser, but hated the work. The toll of constant rejection, even for the simplest retail jobs Diala was overqualified for, eventually led her to depression. "I finally said, 'This is not going to work. At my age, I can't jump from career to career.'" Diala thought back to her teenage dream of opening a restaurant as a gathering spot for film and culture lovers and realized that dream might have found its fertile soil in Toronto. "It was about time we brought something to the table."

And so was born Zezafoun, the little restaurant named after a linden blossom, where the Aleid sisters and their mother worked all day, cutting parsley and crisping up pita chips for fattoush salad, frying onions to cook with lentils and rice for mujadara, and marinating chicken thighs in cumin, turmeric, and other spices for a baked shawarma that had become their top-selling dish. It was hard, hot work in the tiny restaurant. They used walkie-talkies to communicate between the eight-table dining room and basement kitchen. They lived nearly two hours away in traffic. Money was scarce and the future uncertain, but the family had restored their pride with this little slice of Damascene life they had built here and their rebirth as entrepreneurs.

"An entrepreneur is someone who isn't satisfied with just being," Diala said, stopping briefly to chug water from a plastic container. An entrepreneur had to love to share, because when you open a business, especially a restaurant as an immigrant in a city constantly looking for the world's next great taste, you are putting a new "soul in the town." This is what made immigrant entrepreneurs unique, because that soul was tied into their circumstances. All over Toronto Diala saw brand-new restaurants backed by big money and investors, with million-dollar interiors, that served soulless Instagram food. Meanwhile, the Ale-ids opened Zezafoun with nothing but savings, sweat, and their own identity.

"Doing this from almost nothing, personally, well it brought back my faith in what we can do with talent, passion, and a vision," Diala said, popping a tray of tomatoes stuffed with bulgur, onion, pine nuts, and spices into a small oven with one hand, while wiping her forehead with the other arm. "That to me is the real entrepreneurship: to start some-thing from nothing." Before the business opened, Diala was broke and depressed and wanted to run back to Abu Dhabi and the certain old life she had in the media business. She was paralyzed. And now? "I feel like a renaissance . . . reborn. I am doing something I love. I don't want to go anywhere else! I want to make this better. Now I finally feel settled down, for the first time in years. That's very precious for me."

Upstairs Marcelle was handling the flow of lunch customers with wit, charm, and a fair bit of flirtatiousness. She'd welcome everyone that entered to their "house" and their little "Syria," explain what they made here, why the lentil soup was the best anywhere, and what the pickled stuffed eggplants on the counter were called (makdous). "Do you want kibbeh?" she asked a man in a suit with a bat of her lashes. "I have very nice kibbeh!" When things slowed for a second, I asked her the same questions I'd asked her sister. What did it feel like to be an entrepreneur, especially as an immigrant?

"I feel I belong now," she said. "It burns your self-esteem to be in a new place and prove yourself. But I created my own home now." She wrapped up a falafel and ran out in the rain to deliver it to a nearby store, shouting back, "This is my kingdom and I make the rules now!"

Store by store, shop by shop, bite by bite, the Syrian entrepreneurs I met in Toronto were reclaiming their own version of the Syria they lost. The process of entrepreneurship took disparate individuals and groups, who had been torn apart along religious, ethnic, and sectarian lines, and brought them back together as customers and coworkers. In these kitch-ens, Christians worked with Muslims, Druze and Yazidis with Shias and

Sunnis, urban, wealthy Damascenes with poor, illiterate villagers. One woman, who worked in a collective of female Syrian cooks called the Newcomer Kitchen, told me how cooking meals with the other women there had been the therapy she needed after watching her brother get shot by ISIS.

What the Syrian entrepreneurs were doing with their restaurants and bakeries and food stalls was healing their broken world. To those like Rasoul and Ismail at Crown Pastries, healing came from achieving the highest level of authentic Syrian taste they could manage thousands of miles away. They maintained strict standards and only used the best ingredients, even paying smugglers hundreds of dollars to bring bottles of blood-red rosewater and cardamom-scented coffee beans through Syria's myriad front lines. Everything they built here was a bridge to a broken world, and anything less would be an insult to the memory of the world they'd left behind and would likely never see again, even when the war ended.

This was why Jala Alsoufi and her family made Soufi's so proudly, defiantly Syrian, when they easily could have been another "Middle Eastern" restaurant, serving the Westernized staples—falafel and chicken shawarma—that certain customers might have expected. It was a message of optimism and a way of reclaiming something that had been violently taken from them. "If you asked most people what they thought about Syria, they'd say 'war' and 'displacement,'" Jala said, one warm fall afternoon as we sat chatting with her family on the patio behind the restaurant. "The general attitude toward Syria is negative, which is why we consciously branded as Syrian and were bright and airy. We wanted to show that even if the situation in Syria is very unfortunate, it was important to show Syrian culture, music, art, and food in a positive light."

"It is important to show that we are more than just victims," said Shahnaz, her mother, whose English was now excellent.

One year on and Soufi's was growing, though not yet profitable. "Everyone who said the restaurant business was hard and I should be scared off . . . they were right," Husam said, with a shrug and flick of his cigarette. The fact that Ramadan fell during their first full summer in business really put a dent in sales. Overall, he estimated they had invested close to $325,000 in the business. Still, the plan was always to scale to multiple locations and grow through volume, so Husam wasn't daunted. He had something to prove . . . to the partners who he said bilked him in Saudi Arabia, to his family, to his new country, and to himself. If it failed, he joked that they would buy an RV and the Alsoufi family would drive around the country cooking and camping (his newfound love). When I suggested that they could probably find jobs, Husam laughed out loud.

"A job???" he said, slapping the table, sending cigarette ash flying. "When I came here I didn't think one time to apply for a job!"

"It's a step back to be an employee," Alaa said, as a matter of fact.

"I wouldn't do it unless I absolutely have to do it," Husam said.

This was something I heard many of the Syrian entrepreneurs express, in one way or another. "Our red line is that we don't work for anyone else, not as an employee," said Amir Fattal, who ran a small catering business called Beroea Kitchen with his wife, Nour. Since the moment he left Syria, Fattal was determined to be a self-made man, first setting up hostels and language schools in Istanbul for other refugees and now Beroea Kitchen. He saw entrepreneurship as a nonnegotiable condition of their new life in Canada. "We are not here to work for anyone else," he said. "We are here to develop ourselves. That's what I teach my children: to have their ideas and their business, because when you win you win from your bucket and if you lose, you lose from your bucket."

It made sense. Entrepreneurship, more than anything, represented a level of freedom that was intricately tied to the immigrant experience. When you left the old world behind you lost many things: family, friends, assets, jobs, a past. What you gained was mostly uncertainty. Financially there was no greater degree of success for immigrant entrepreneurs than for anyone else who went out on their own. Most began with fewer resources and connections and knowledge of the local business culture and environment. The odds were often stacked against them, especially during the first few years. And because everything was tied up in their business, it was crushing when those businesses failed.

"When entrepreneurship doesn't work for immigrants, it compounds their alienation," said Lily Cho, a professor at York University in Toronto, who has written about the experience of Chinese restaurant families across the country. "If you don't feel like you have a space, it's much worse when you lose one." Cho knew this firsthand. Her father escaped China's brutal Cultural Revolution and spent his life pursuing a string of unsuccessful ventures, including a restaurant in the Yukon, a jewelry store in Calgary, and a doomed scheme for breeding chinchillas in the family garage. Each time Cho's father failed, it led to depression and a return to the kind of low-wage jobs that entrepreneurship was meant to preclude for immigrants, like the dangerous, exhausting industrial laundromat where Cho's mother still worked in her seventies.

But for most immigrant entrepreneurs, that risk was still worth taking, because the fresh start it promised offered something much deeper than financial gain. I got a sense of what this meant one afternoon, in a small warehouse in the suburb of Mississauga, where I was greeted with a table piled high with raw spiced beef kibbeh, labneh yogurt, shanklish cheese rolled in spices, a stew of sausages, pickles, olives, and other delicious foods laid out by Kevin Dahi.

Dahi was born in a Christian community near Homs and had been living in Toronto for the past decade, working in advertising, but in the past year, he had given up a lucrative job to launch White Spirits, a boutique distillery that made Middle Eastern liquors with Canadian ingredients. His specialty was arak, the anise-flavored brandy consumed around the Mediterranean with mezze feasts like this, which he missed dearly. As we ate and drank, then ate and ate and drank a bit more, Dahi explained to me why he gave up a secure career and certain future to become an entrepreneur.

"I wanted to build something for my kids in this country, so that this is their home," he said. "So they won't think about leaving the country. So they feel comfortable and a sense of certainty here." Dahi looked at the immigrants who had come before him—Italians, Jamaicans, Chinese, Ethiopians—and what Dahi saw were roots sunk deep into the earth. Roots that bound those people's children and grandchildren to this land. "I didn't want to give my kids the option to go back to Syria," he said. "This is where I want to stay. Maybe I will get this place up as a successful business in my lifetime, or maybe my kids will, but they will have something."

Dahi's kids were barely out of elementary school at the time, but he was adamant. "This is about putting down roots! House, school, they're not important. The most important is an income resource. Where you get your money from. If your source of living is here you won't think about leaving." It was something he saw with friends and family back in Syria. Those with businesses on the ground were often the last to leave, departing only once the factory was blown up or taken over, if they were lucky to survive that long. "I don't want to lock my kids here. But this is my way of rooting them."

Syrian entrepreneurs were putting down roots all around the world, regardless of the size of their businesses or ambition. There were women setting up stalls to sell cookies at farmers' markets on weekends, and those who spoke of empires to rival Mohamad Fakih's. In September of 2018, Ismail and Rasoul Alsalha opened their second location of Crown Pastries, near the airport. It was big and beautiful, with architectural details that resembled a grand palace, seating for two dozen, and an expanded menu. Ismail was beaming with pride when I met him there a few weeks after the grand opening. The brothers had finally brought over their fiancées from Turkey, and the two had recently gotten married in a ceremony together, wearing matching midnight blue tuxedos. Nine months later, Ismail's daughter and Rasoul's son were born within twelve hours of each other.

They were now known throughout the Syrian community and the entire city as the kings of baklava. People called them out at the mosque and regularly asked them for advice on starting their own businesses. They were the pillars of a growing community of Syrian entrepreneurs. "I think we're there," Ismail told me, when I asked him whether he felt at home yet. There would be more stores and more opportunities, but it had only been three years since the first bakery had opened ("a long three years"), and in that time they finally felt settled.

"We're married, we have a new business," he said, with his shy smile. "For now, we're set."

The Alsoufis felt the same way. By the summer of 2019 they had begun looking for a second location where they could service their growing delivery business, and were preparing to manufacture a line of packaged products (oils, spices) that they could sell in supermarkets across the country. Husam joked about not even missing his yacht in Saudi Arabia (his new love was riding his Harley Davidson) and was working on launching a separate business in sustainable home design that would tap into his engineering experience. Shahnaz spoke with great pride about getting back to work at middle age, retraining as a cook and an entrepreneur. She referred to the restaurant as her baby.

"We turned a profit. We had regular customers. It really started to be a pleasure. We were finally living our life," Husam told me, sucking deep on his cigarette. "Then it all turned around."

In October of 2019, Alaa attended a protest during the Canadian election outside a campaign event for a far-right, anti-immigrant political party. Supporters of the party and legions of sympathetic trolls identified Alaa in videos and began threatening him, the family, and Soufi's. These threats came at a blistering pace online, over the phone, through the mail, and even in person at the restaurant. The quantity of the hate and the violence of the rhetoric was unceasing. "The easiest word for me is 'nightmare,'" Husam said. "It changed our life completely." After a week of being at the center of a fight between racists and anti-fascists, bombarded by graphic death threats, and fearful for his family's life and the safety of his workers, Husam announced that Soufi's was closing immediately, for good. He papered over the windows, locked the door, and walked away.

The outcry was immediate. Local, national, and even international media picked up the story, and an outpouring of support that vastly outweighed the hatred came flowing toward the Alsoufi family. Hundreds of emails and letters from all over the country and world begged them to reopen, to stay strong, and not let racism win. Flowers, handmade signs, and stuffed animals gathered around the shuttered storefront like a memorial. And then, two days after the spontaneous closure, a surprise announcement: Soufi's would reopen with the managerial support of Mohamad Fakih and his Paramount team, who would help run the restaurant while the Alsoufi family took some time to recover from the ongoing trauma (they would retain full ownership and reap all the profits from the partnership). Fakih told the media assembled in the restaurant at a hastily organized press conference that this was something he felt he had to do, in order to stand up to the same Islamophobic racism he had experienced as an entrepreneur and which he felt could not take root in Canada.

As he stood on the back patio after the press conference, his hands still shaking, Husam Alsoufi confessed that he remained unsure about reopening. The threats were ongoing (Alaa was considering taking a semester off from college for his safety), and he worried about putting the family back into the spotlight. But the nightmare also made him realize that his place as an entrepreneur meant more than just being a business owner. "When we opened, we told people we were giving a piece of home to our restaurant," he said. "Well, this restaurant helped us feel at home. It introduced us to a lot of Canadians. It was a lot of pressure and a ton of work, but we loved it. Why? Because we got to live inside the society. Before this restaurant, I felt like a stranger in this country. We were in the margins. But when we opened this, we started to have real friends in the society we were apart from. This felt really really good. The most beautiful thing about this restaurant is that it gave us a home in Toronto and Canada." He stopped to take another long drag of his cigarette. That sense of home was evident in the letters of love and support taped up on the walls, in the lineup of the reopened restaurant that was now snaking out the door, and in the generosity of strangers, including a neighborhood woman who hosted a feast for Alaa, just to show her support for him. "I am going to fight for that. I'm not gonna hide," he said. "But to be honest, it's really up and down." It made me think of a conversation I had with Jala a year before, when I asked her what it felt like to be an entrepreneur. "I never really thought of myself as an entrepreneur throughout this process," Jala said. In her mind, an entrepreneur was someone who came up with a big idea, like a new app or product. She brought up the trinity of Zuckerberg, Musk, and Jobs, as examples, and said that it felt weird to apply that title to herself when she was just helping her family by starting a business. "Looking back, I do realize we're an entrepreneurial family," she said. "We introduced something new to Toronto: Syrian cuisine and culture." For her, being an entrepreneur was the process of the soul's reinvention that all immigrant entrepreneurs went through: relocating, building from scratch, and starting over, every single day.

"Entrepreneurship is a process, and there's no end to the process," she said. "The results are ongoing."

CHAPTER 3

Life's a Beach

THE ALARM BUZZED next to Tracy Obolsky's head at 4:30 a.m., nudging her awake in the dark. Her husband, Alex Shenitsky, and their pug, Penny, continued snoozing, while Obolsky pulled on her swimsuit and a wetsuit, took a quick hit from the bong in the second bedroom (literally "the bong room"), grabbed her surfboard, and walked out the door. Half a block later her bare feet were touching sand. Small waves were breaking a few hundred feet from shore, as the sun began its emergence somewhere over the purple horizon.

Obolsky paddled out beyond the break, bobbing alone with the seals and dolphins, until a promising shadow beckoned from out at sea. She spun her board toward the shore, taking a few strong, powerful strokes with her arms . . . popping up onto her feet as the ocean unfurled before her, the greens of the murky water now taking on hues of pink from the rising sun.

By the time the sun broke the ocean's surface at six thirty, Obolsky was out of the water, peeling off her wetsuit. A quick shower and bowl of cereal, a kiss to her sleeping dog and husband, and it was time to head back down two flights of stairs with her thirty-pound cruiser bike. Obolsky rode along the concrete boardwalk that overlooked the surf, cruising beside the waves for ten minutes (thirteen if she's skateboarding), until she pulled up at the Rockaway Beach Bakery.

Once inside, Obolsky donned Crocs and an apron over cutoff denim shorts and a tank top and got to work turning on ovens, grinding coffee, and pulling ingredients from storage bins and the refrigerator. As she began the laborious process of rolling, kneading, brushing, and re-rolling croissant dough with endless layers of butter (all that rolling pin work was one reason, besides surfing, that she has the shoulders of a cage fighter), Obolsky turned up the music that played from speakers carved into an old surfboard . . . Bob Marley, Hall and Oates, and a whole lot of Motown. Happy tunes. Drinking cold brew coffee out of a plastic storage jug, Obolsky prepped dozens of baked goods: carrot and bran muffins and various scones, cinnamon buns and fruit pies, quiches, sourdough and focaccia breads, guava and cheese Danishes . . . not to mention cakes and cupcakes, cookies, and whatever else she felt like baking that summer Saturday.

At seven thirty her best friend and occasional "employee" Meredith Sutton knocked on the door. Instantly, the music got louder, and the stories began flying: about the waves, drinking antics, and whatever else passed the time as they shaped dough, cut fruit, made drinks, and got the bakery ready to open. At seven fifty, Tracy walked outside in the sunshine, rolled up the metal grate, and placed a sandwich board out on the sidewalk that said No BAD DAYS above its BAKERY OPEN message. Before Obolsky even stepped back inside, her first customers were waiting. Just another day in paradise.

In Obolsky's case, paradise is Rockaway Beach, the aquatic edge of New York City, a quarter-mile-wide, eleven-mile-long peninsula of cement and sand sandwiched between the Atlantic Ocean and the marshes of Jamaica Bay. If you've ever flown into JFK Airport, it's the first land you encounter, and the jets roar overhead every sixty seconds here. Rockaway Beach is technically part of Queens, but it is separated from the mainland by a series of bridges, so the Rockaways are basically an island.

I first found this place in 2008, when I was living in New York, taking the A train from my apartment in Brooklyn all the way till its last stop, at Beach 90th Street. A two-block walk brought me to the surf shop Boarders, whose gravelly voiced owner, Steve Stathis, rented me a board. I walked another two blocks to the beach, over the boardwalk, and into some great waves, which broke against a rock jetty and peeled along to the left. I went back a few times a year, surfing amid the summer crowds and even on Christmas Day, when I trudged through snowbanks to paddle out among falling flakes.

In those days, the only refreshments available after surfing were a square slice of pizza or a questionable sandwich from the bodega on the corner. But in the decade since I'd first surfed there, especially after the Rockaways were hammered by Superstorm Sandy in November 2011, the area had been radically transformed by a wave of entrepreneurial activity. When I returned in the summer of 2018, I was amazed at how many new businesses lined Rockaway Beach Boulevard. There were restaurants and bars, microbreweries, coffee shops, surf stores, and clothing boutiques, all mixed with the nail salons, check cashing spots, bail bondsmen, and the small businesses that define the entrepreneurial landscape of outer-borough New York City.

Rockaway Beach had been built up by a renewed community of entrepreneurs, but the entrepreneurs in Rockaway were not looking to build huge businesses, change the world, or disrupt industries. Most were not rich, and their success wasn't measured in growth or scale. Rather, these entrepreneurs had gone into business here because it allowed them to build lives around the beach. They were chasing waves, not exits. Rockaway's entrepreneurs had begun lifestyle businesses, because lifestyle was their ultimate goal.

A lifestyle business is a term with many conflicted meanings, but in essence it is a business that operates in order to fund the living expenses and lifestyle ambitions of its owners. The term itself was coined in 1987 by William Wetzel, a professor of entrepreneurship at the University of New Hampshire, who used it to describe businesses unlikely to generate big enough economic returns to interest outside investors. "Lifestyle ventures are usually ventures that are run by people who like being their own bosses," Wetzel told an interviewer once. "But they're in it for the income as well. Indeed, lifestyle entrepreneurs offer a different . . . view of success than those who are mainly after wealth accumulation."

This captures a pretty vast swath of entrepreneurial activity, from part-time sources of income to formally incorporated businesses with dozens of employees. Most businesses are a lifestyle business, from the fruit store at the end of my street, to the landlord who owns their building, the yoga studio upstairs, the companies that supply the store with fruits and vegetables, the trucking companies that haul that produce across the continent, the brokers and shippers and farmers and packers and up and up and on and on, until you really touch the vast majority of actual entrepreneurial activity in the world.

The lifestyle business captures the soul of the entrepreneur's essential hope: To be your own boss. To use your talents as you see fit. To wake up each day and do what you decide to do. To reap what you sow, and build your life around that dream, however big or small it is.

That idea has come under assault by Silicon Valley, a chorus of academics in the field of entrepreneurship studies, and the broader culture, who have declared lifestyle businesses and the entrepreneurs who run them insufficiently ambitious and growth focused, a sap on productivity, and an impediment to what economies truly need. In Silicon Valley's startup myth, a *lifestyle business* is a pejorative, used to dismiss ideas that are not worthy of investment because they lack the grand vision of a truly scalable business. To an entrepreneur pitching a venture capitalist, there is little worse than hearing the phrase "This sounds more like a lifestyle business." It is a kiss of death, uttered with a dismissive tone, with the implied adjectives "shitty little" wordlessly slipped before "lifestyle."

This is a sentiment I encountered many times when I interviewed venture capitalists and academics who study entrepreneurship. As I mentioned, I would start every interview by asking them to define an entrepreneur, which they all did in rather broad terms. But when the conversation evolved, they would invariably dismiss a whole class of small business owners as unworthy of that title. Definitely not a dry cleaner, one said, or a bakery owner, said another, or even someone who owned a "boring box factory" (versus an exciting box factory?). Those weren't *real* entrepreneurs. They were the owners of lifestyle businesses or small businesses or just boring old businesses. To lump them in with exceptional, heroic founders was an insult to the very title of an entrepreneur. What was their value, if any?

The fact that Tracy Obolsky and the other entrepreneurs in Rockaway Beach carved out a little slice of surf heaven in one of the most competitive, expensive cities in the world stands against this. Where the concrete jungle met the beach, and the hustle of New York's streets collided with the hustle for the next wave, Rockaway's business owners were an example of the unsung value of lifestyle to the entrepreneurial experience and the quest for freedom at the core of every entrepreneur's soul.

"HEY TRACY!" SHOUTED A MIDDLE-AGED, heavily bronzed woman, rolling her bicycle into the shop.

"What's up, Martha?" Obolsky said with a huge grin. "How's your week?"

Martha showed Obolsky a dozen stitches on her leg, the result of a surfboard fin slice suffered that morning.

"Oh, that sucks!" Obolsky said, continuing to knead croissant dough. Martha ordered the bakery's signature ham-and-cheese croissant with everything bagel spice and a coffee.

"Have you been out lately?" Martha asked.

"I've been surfing the past five days," Obolsky said. "It's my record for the summer so far!"

Surfers in surf towns basically talk about surfing incessantly. When they surfed, where they surfed, what it was like when they surfed, when they will surf next, and on and on. For the surfers who frequent Rockaway Beach Bakery, that shop talk is just part of the experience. It isn't just surfers, though. Obolsky is the mayor of her little slice of Rockaway Beach and she presides over it with an almost overwhelming cheeriness, greeting everyone who walks in the door with a huge smile and "Hi!"; friendly locals and fellow surfing entrepreneurs; their children (whom she knows by name and welcomes with a Fozzie Bear "Wocka Wocka!" to giggles of delight) and scores of visitors from the city, known affectionately as DFDs, or Down for the Days, who walk in slightly dazed and dressed in expensive "surf" wear from a Brooklyn boutique.

All of them order coffees and bacon, egg, and cheese sandwiches served on homemade scones, snapping Instagram photos of Obolsky's famous croissants, as they sit at a handful of tables. Obolsky designed and built the bakery by hand and decorated it with photos of local women surfing, random thrift store finds, Shenitsky's turntable and records, and a hammock on the big back patio. The whole place is painted a cheery shade of aquamarine, and Obolsky's logo—a woman in a chef's hat surfing a croissant wave—perfectly captures the fun, happy essence of a business, and the entrepreneur behind it, whose life is one big wake 'n' bake ('n' surf).

Obolsky, who was thirty-seven when we met, grew up in New Jersey, the daughter of a stay-at-home mother and a truck driver father, who instilled a strong work ethic in her. Her first foray into entrepreneurship, at seven, was a lemonade stand, but she soon branched out, selling candy her mother bought at Costco for a markup to kids at school, or even slices of a pizza her friends' parents had ordered to random passersby. She also held regular jobs in her teens, including a stint making ice cream.

Obolsky studied fine art in college, with ambitions to become a children's book illustrator, but her attempts at freelance designing fell flat. She missed having a steady paycheck. Instead, she took jobs serving drinks at various shot bars around Manhattan, the types of places where the servers wore skimpy outfits, poured liquor directly into the mouths of male patrons, and danced on the bar. "It was disgusting," she said, "but I'd make seventy dollars an hour, cash." After graduating Obolsky lost interest in art, so she kept working in bars, spending her downtime watching baking shows on television. "I thought 'I can do this!'" she said, and enrolled in culinary school, where she trained as a pastry chef.

Within a year she had met Shenitsky, gotten married in a Las Vegas wedding chapel by an Elvis impersonator, and begun her rise into the elite of the Manhattan restaurant world. Obolsky rotated through a series of high-end restaurants, making desserts and breads for little pay and less credit. "I never made enough money," she said, brushing a glaze on an apricot tart that she was about to place in the oven. "I bounced checks for years. I was so broke. I was slightly taken advantage of for money, but I didn't realize that."

Eventually she ended up at the North End Grille, a popular lunch spot in Manhattan's Financial District. "I was super happy at North End Grille," she said. She was getting tons of press for her creations, like a popcorn sundae, which led to nominations for chef's awards and trips to cook for celebrities. But things changed when the restaurant's head chef left and was replaced by a well-known executive chef named Eric Korsh. "Things got weird," she said. Korsh was abusive, she said, and Obolsky witnessed him sexually harass the female waitstaff on multiple occasions. His behavior caught up with him years later, after he had left North End Grille, when allegations of his conduct were published by the website Eater. Korsh immediately left his next job and issued a quasi-apology for making colleagues "feel badly," but the period began a spiral of disillusionment for Obolsky, which eventually led to the beach.

"Now we're rocking and rolling!" Obolsky shouted to Sutton around nine thirty, as Sutton was replenishing the rapidly diminishing bakery case with whatever came from the oven. On a summer Saturday like this one, the bakery will easily sell out of 150 croissants by lunchtime. "We need more croissants, more drinks, more everything!" Sutton said. The two had met working together at North End Grille. One day, in the restaurant's basement pastry kitchen, Sutton (who grew up in California) told Obolsky that she had gone surfing in Rockaway Beach that morning. Obolsky, who had recently learned to surf on vacation in Costa Rica, didn't even know where Rockaway was, but she was in and immediately told Sutton, "Hey, I wanna surf!"

"We flopped around for a year and a half, clueless about what we were doing," Obolsky recalled. "We'd head out there on our days off or even sometimes before work in the morning and just paddle out, trying to figure what to do when a wave came. We'd be shampooing on the boardwalk, then show up to work and rinse our wetsuits off in the same sink that the prep cooks would wash the fish in. Then we'd hang the wetsuits to dry in the office of the general manager, who asked us what the hell we were doing. But we loved it, and obsessed about surfing, even though we were terrible at it. The commitment was there."

In 2015, the pull of the beach was so strong that Obolsky and Shenitsky moved from Brooklyn to Rockaway. "I was just over it," she said. "Over the hustle and bustle. Over my dog eating chicken bones." They rented a brand-new townhouse apartment a couple hundred feet from the ocean. It was a forty-five-minute commute twice a day to the North End Grille on the A train, but it wasn't terrible. Obolsky would surf in the morning, head into the city, bake all day, and drink a negroni on the subway ride home. Still, her working relationship with Korsh (who mockingly called her "dude") continued to deteriorate. When she asked for a raise, the restaurant offered her a chef's knife.

I don't want a fucking knife! Obolsky thought, asking herself, for the first time, *Do I even want to do this anymore?* She took a job at another restaurant with better pay but longer hours. Now she left Rockaway at 7:00 in the morning and frequently didn't return until 1:00 a.m. There was no surfing, no husband she ever saw awake, no sun or beach or anything she had moved to Rockaway to enjoy. After the first week, she took two days off to surf and was reprimanded for insufficient commitment to her job. "I was never eating, unhealthy, and miserable," she said. "I'd come home crying. Alex would say, 'What are you doing?,' and I'd be too exhausted to answer."

The breaking point came during a big snowstorm. The restaurant was pretty much guaranteed to have a dead night, but as the staff were frantically making plans to get home and pick up kids, the owners informed them that they were doing delivery tonight, and everyone had to work late. "These fuckers didn't care," Obolsky said. "They just wanted to make money." When she heard that the subway had closed, Obolsky flipped out in the kitchen, screaming, "Now I can't fucking get home!" with the unrestrained rage of a good person pushed past her limit. She slept at a friend's house, returned to work in the morning, and finally got home late the following night.

"That was it," she said. "I wanted to be with my husband and I was stuck on a subway, miserable. What was I doing?" she asked herself, of the restaurant business. "The money wasn't that good, especially as a woman."

Spring was around the corner, and Shenitsky, who works in the music industry scouting bands, had been making friends with various bar and restaurant owners around Rockaway Beach, while his wife worked in the city. Whitney Aycock, who owned a pizzeria called Whit's End, told Shenitsky about a shuttered snack shack in the fishing marina. Aycock suggested Obolsky take it over and bake things to sell to the fishermen.

"I was wishy-washy," Obolsky said, citing knee-jerk fears about money and health insurance. "Plus it wasn't even legal, but Alex told me, 'Fuck it! Do it!'" Obolsky began slowly buying mixers and pans and whisks one at a time from restaurant supply stores, carrying them back on the subway. Finally, on June 26, 2016, when she had everything she needed, Tracy Obolsky walked into work and did the one thing that every hopeful entrepreneur fantasizes about doing: she quit her job.

If there is one thing that unites all entrepreneurs, from the poorest to the richest, from the most ambitious startups to the humblest side hustles, it is the conviction not to work for someone else. It often begins as a frustration, grows to a nagging irritation, and by the time they are ready to set off on their own, it has blossomed into a sense of destiny. "The entrepreneurial personality, in short, is characterized by an unwillingness to 'submit' to authority, an inability to work with it, and a consequent need to escape from it," states the 1964 book *The Enterprising Man*, one of the first academic texts on entrepreneurship in America. The primary act of entrepreneurship is one of liberation. Of shaking off the yoke of employment and embracing the freedom of going out on your own.

"For once in my life I was doing something for *myself*," Obolsky said. "They tried to get me to stay, and I was just saying, 'No, no, no, no.' They could have offered me $100,000 and it still would have been no. It was terrifying, but it felt good . . . but still terrifying."

Obolsky described her last day at the restaurant as the moment her life changed. She was supposed to stay through dinner service, but Shenitsky had sent her a message about a party in the neighborhood. So she just untied her apron, handed it to the chef, and told him, "I think I'm gonna go."

"That's it?" asked the chef, staring at her apron with a dumbfounded look.

"'Yeah!' I told him, and I walked out the door," Obolsky said. "That train ride home was more beautiful than ever. The sun was setting over the bay in this gorgeous orange, and I thought to myself, 'I don't have to do this anymore! This is beautiful.'"

The next weeks were far from glamorous. Obolsky and a helper began by digging a four-foot hole for a septic tank in the marina's toxic, refuse-strewn dirt in ninety-five-degree heat. When she finally got the kitchen in the shack set up, the electricity didn't work, and she was forced to bake at home. Still, the fishermen bought her croissants, especially the ham and cheese with everything bagel spice topping that basically built the business.

After half a decade working in chef's coats in windowless basements, "I'd be in a bikini rolling croissant dough, in a shack, smoking a joint." She rode her bike everywhere and never left the peninsula except to get supplies once a week. At noon, a salty old fisherman named "Frank the Fish" would come back with his catch and take Obolsky for a boat ride. The shack had a sunrise view, and she could see the A train crossing the bay, into the city, without her. "I didn't make a lot of money, but I paid no rent, Alex had his job, and it was fun." Entrepreneurship was turning out better than Obolsky could imagine.

Then Labor Day came, and the marina quickly grew cold and quiet. Obolsky realized she would need to move inland if she was going to continue with her business. She found a space and underbudgeted the construction by 300 percent, blowing through more than $120,000 of her life's savings, plus loans and bank financing, to get it rented, permitted, built out, and approved by the city. In the meantime, Obolsky continued selling croissants and baked goods at pop-ups around Rockaway Beach, often at bars or breweries that catered to the surf community, promoting her goods on Instagram. She opened the bakery on a March day in 2017, hardly the height of the season, and yet by 1:00 p.m. she had sold out of everything, filling her register (still a plastic box) with $1,500 in cash.

"I love it," Obolsky said around ten thirty, as the steady stream of weekend customers let up for a rare moment. "I stand in this spot for hours, and I have been doing all of it. Working with my hands, not sitting still. I love the creative aspect of it. I love the challenge in my mind every day and hearing from people how they love the food and the space. Actually, I'm going to take a minute." She stepped outside for a brief second to squint at the sun, wave at someone, and take a breath. "Fresh air," she said with a sigh, before coming back behind the counter to resume preparing for the lunch crowd. "I can't remember if I peed today yet."

THOUGH OBOLSKY'S SUNNY TALE IS appealing, across America and much of the world, the reality for lifestyle entrepreneurs shows a marked decline at a time when entrepreneurship is supposedly blooming. A 2016 report by the Brookings Institute noted that the start-up rate for nearly every single industry (which measures the number of firms less than one year old in an industry) has shrunk across the board since 1979. From agriculture and transportation to retail, finance, and mining, fewer people are becoming entrepreneurs, starting fewer companies each year. In some fields, like construction, there are barely a quarter of the startups there were four decades back. According to a report by the Federal Reserve Board, the share of all business that startups occupied in America went from 14 percent in 1979 to 8 percent by 2016.

There are many reasons for why this is happening, though none of them present a complete answer. The decline in small business startups stems from factors that include the rise of China and other competitive global economies, the price of oil and other commodities, the age and spending power of the Baby Boomers, specific tax policies and regulations for industries, the shifts in where and how people live in communities, and more. But the single biggest factor is likely the increase in market concentration. Since 1989, employment in the largest segment of companies (with more than ten thousand workers) has grown the most, according to an analysis by David Leonhardt in the *New York Times*, while those with four employees or fewer have shrunk the most. These are the supersized firms like AT&T, Walmart, Amazon, Facebook, and ExxonMobil, all of which have merged and acquired competitors ruthlessly and in many cases established complete monopolies over their industries. Because of the network effects, infrastructure costs, and economies of scale these corporations bring, starting viable competitors is simply becoming impossible.

Most advocates of small business in America (classified by the Small Business Administration as those with fewer than five hundred employees, which represents 99 percent of all American businesses) continually point to these trends with alarm, fueling a large part of the investment in entrepreneurship advocacy and education over the past decades. (The story is similar in many other countries, including Australia, the UK, and Japan.) But a growing chorus of voices are now arguing that these trends are not necessarily bad. In their 2018 book *Big Is Beautiful: Debunking the Myth of Small Business*, economists Robert Atkinson and Michael Lind claim that while American small businesses and their owners may be "the most sacred of sacred cows," they are grossly overvalued in terms of their contributions.

The Jeffersonian ideal of a democracy held together by a brave band of self-employed citizens is an antiquated one that needs to be extinguished, they write. Most small firms fail, destroying the jobs they create, and those that survive tend to stay small, employing few people, if any, because their owners want to run lifestyle businesses and are simply not interested in growing larger. Lind and Atkinson present data showing how a big business is more likely to export goods and services, employ more people with better salaries and benefits, positively transform communities with their economic power, innovate and invent. Even democratic measures like civil rights are better advanced by big firms than small ones, they claim, because of their power to influence politics and shape policy through their own actions (by extending more childcare benefits to female employees, for instance).

"The best way to boost productivity is to remove obstacles to the replacement of small-scale, labor-intensive, technologically stagnant mom-and-pop firms with dynamic, capital-intensive, technology-based businesses, which tend to be fewer and bigger," Lind and Atkinson wrote. "If government is to help any small firms, it should focus on the startups that have the desire and potential to get big, not on nurturing Ashley and Justin's efforts to open a local pizza shop." Ashley and Justin, they clarify, are most certainly not entrepreneurs, because they do not fit Joseph Schumpeter's definition of an innovator disrupting an industry. What America needs are more Starbucks, not another Rockaway Beach Bakery.

This also reflects the thinking of Scott Shane, a professor of entrepreneurship at Case Western University, who has argued most vocally for the utility of Silicon Valley's startup model over small businesses. "Most of the impact of entrepreneurial activity comes from the formation of high-potential businesses—the Facebooks and Instagrams and Lending Clubs—not the dry cleaners and clothing shops that dominate government statistics," Shane wrote in 2018's *Is Entrepreneurship Dead?* Creating more venture capital and angel-backed companies and fewer mom-and-pop retail shops is okay for job creation and GDP growth, Shane continues, as "a few extra Facebooks and Googles are probably worth a lot of clothing shops on Main Street because they produce a lot more jobs and economic output."

On the other hand, there is a growing movement of entrepreneurship researchers who see big problems with pushing this increasingly exclusive focus on big businesses and Silicon Valley–style startups (which seek to create big business) at the expense of small businesses. One of them is David Audretsch, a professor at Indiana University, who told me that it comes back to the definition of an entrepreneur. He explained that there are three typical definitions in the scholarly literature. The first is organizational: Is a business new, young, or is an individual self-employed? This definition encompasses the biggest group, including lifestyle entrepreneurs, small businesses, and solo workers and freelancers like myself, my wife, and the rest of my family. The second is behavioral and defined by an individual who is seeking opportunity and acting on it. This definition brings in the corporate entrepreneur, or intrapreneur, and prizes entrepreneurial behavior (new ideas, inventions, etc.) above the creation or ownership of a business. Finally there is the definition of an entrepreneur based on performance: Has this person innovated, and has that innovation led to economic growth or disruption?

Beginning in the late 1980s, Audretsch told me that the latter two definitions, focused on behavior and performance, came to dominate the field, falling in line with a model of entrepreneurship focused obsessively on innovation, growth potential, and scaling up, to the exclusion of anything else. The main problem with this narrow definition of an entrepreneur is how far detached it is from the reality of entrepreneurship on the ground in our communities, where small businesses and lifestyle entrepreneurs vastly outnumber radical innovators.

"We became victims of own success by thinking that this was the only type of entrepreneurship, the only business and social model, and that then became a policy," Audretsch said. "It became a nail and hammer: Give me a problem and entrepreneurship/innovation/growth becomes the solution."

This focus on the startup myth of entrepreneurship has had real consequences beyond academia. As the definition of entrepreneurship shifted to Silicon Valley's, many courses, programs, and practical resources devoted to small businesses and family businesses were cut to make way for incubators, innovation zones, and other programs focused exclusively on nurturing tech startups. Politicians, universities, and others wanting quick results gravitated to the most visible, sexy, and high-profile trappings of entrepreneurship, chasing unicorns at the expense of the rest.

In 2016, Audretsch and three other colleagues published an essay about this called "Everyday Entrepreneurship—A Call for Entrepreneurship Research to Embrace Entrepreneurial Diversity," which argued for reclaiming the field from the focus on heterogenous technology businesses:

"Overall, much of our research continues the highly skewed quest to develop our understanding of entrepreneurship by studying a tiny group of outliers, while frequently ignoring the vast bulk and diversity of what we label 'everyday' entrepreneurship," the paper said. "Not only are the gazelles and unicorns perhaps not as important as we have presumed, but by implicitly defining everyday entrepreneurship as neither important nor interesting we have failed to understand its rich variety and importance."

I asked one of the paper's coauthors, the German professor Friederike Welter, what exactly she meant by Everyday Entrepreneurship (a term one critical academic I spoke with called "a piece of crap"). "We are talking about inclusive entrepreneurship," she said. "If we recognize entrepreneurship as broad as it is . . . and actually recognize that there are different ways to do entrepreneurship, it would be easy." That inclusive look would include mostly small and medium-sized businesses, like the famous German Mittlestand manufacturing companies Welter's research focused on. These firms tended to be small and regional and made everything from pencils and car parts to advanced electronics for medical devices. The Mittlestand companies were the lifeblood of the Germany economy, but because they were not concentrated in Berlin or Frankfurt, they were less appealing than sexy tech startups.

"The venture capitalist can say it's 'just a lifestyle business,'" said Welter. "When you say 'lifestyle,' this in itself isn't saying, 'They don't want to grow.' Well, why should they grow? To satisfy the returns of a VC? Why should he dictate that?" Fundamentally, entrepreneurship was an act of people taking responsibility over their own lives, Welter said, a way of asserting economic and social control of their work and everything that work touched. Almost every entrepreneur wanted to grow their business, but in different ways, at different rates, and for different reasons. Welter and Audretsch stressed that entrepreneurs were not monolithic in their ambitions, and assuming they were was simplistic. They could be innovative *and* independent, community focused *and* high-growth, or a lifestyle business that eventually grew into a multinational corporation. Audretsch recalled meeting two young men in a Vermont gas station in 1982 who told him about the little ice cream company they had in Burlington. The partners were Ben Cohen and Jerry Greenfield, and within a decade, Ben & Jerry's ice cream was known worldwide, culminating in the sale of the company to Unilever in 2000 for $326 million, a result neither man would have imagined when they first began. "Apple started out as a lifestyle business. Facebook started out as a lifestyle business," Audretsch said.

While all entrepreneurs dream of financial success, and many jump in with the conviction they will be the next Steve Jobs, reality seldom turns out that way, and success is impossible to predict. Who knows if the latest pizzeria to open up will become the next Domino's? Or if it's the next regional pizza chain with five locations? Or just a great pizzeria that improves the dinner options in Rockaway Beach? That's the story of the same business, starting in the same way, with vastly different outcomes based on timing, luck, and life's circumstances. While the largest businesses obviously create the most jobs, that is a symptom of their size, not the cause of it. And while politicians love nothing more than announcing a big factory coming to town, bringing hundreds or thousands of jobs in one swoop, that promise carries with it the possibility that the jobs will disappear just as suddenly. As investment 101 teaches, a more diverse portfolio is more stable. The same is true for a local economy.

"I think the realization is becoming more evident that large companies are not going to provide the employment they did in the past," said Mike Herrington, who runs the Global Entrepreneurship Monitor, an organization that compiles data on entrepreneurship around the world. Herrington is based in Cape Town, South Africa, and prior to academia, he was an entrepreneur, starting four companies over his career, including a panty-hose factory that once employed three thousand two hundred people. "Large companies are changing rapidly. More automation is taking place, more technology is taking place, which are shedding jobs. People are realizing they are going to have to provide for their own employment in whatever way that may take." While the data showed that the countries with the most entrepreneurs were the poorest (Madagascar, Cameroon, and Burkina Faso had nearly four times the rate of self-employment as the United States, Japan, and other European countries), the simplified notion that "bigger is better" was a false one.

Herrington cited data from the OECD, a club of the world's most developed countries, showing the average job creation rates for businesses. A microenterprise created 1.5 jobs, a small business could create up to 50 jobs, and a high-tech business up to 250 jobs. "If the goal is to create ten thousand jobs, then obviously the thing to say is 'Let's just forget the small ones and shuttle money into the tech businesses.' That's too simple," he said. "You need a combination of all of them. You can't just generalize. . . . If you can develop another Google, ugh, that's what makes an academic's name, but it's not what makes the world tick. Society can't afford to just have one type of entrepreneurial activity." This was especially true in the developing world, where small businesses contributed an overwhelming share of the GDP, from 60 percent in Herrington's native South Africa, to 90 percent in India. If you are living in the slums of Johannesburg, or even the low-income Averne housing projects a block from the Rockaway Beach Bakery, the ability to create any business that gives you the freedom to pay your bills, support your family, and build a life is transformational. To most people, a lifestyle business is exactly the entrepreneurship they desire.

"While many theoreticians—who may not be too closely in touch with real life—are still engaging in the idolatry of large size, with practical people in the actual world there is a tremendous longing and striving to profit, if at all possible, from the convenience, humanity, and manageability of smallness," wrote E. F. Schumacher in his classic 1973 book *Small Is Beautiful: Economics as if People Mattered*. Schumacher saw work and entrepreneurship not as a process of innovation and creative destruction, but something in line with the Buddhist requirement to seek out a "right livelihood," which brought financial independence and reward, as well as a sense of joy and purpose. This was a basic truth of human existence. "That work and leisure are complementary parts of the same living process and cannot be separated without destroying the joy of work and the bliss of leisure."

Entrepreneurs are rarely just driven by money, because money is always uncertain for entrepreneurs. "The lifestyle business is about control over your time, your boundaries, hopefully your money, but it's really about control," said Morra Aarons-Mele, a self-employed consultant who works on issues related to entrepreneurship (she also coined the term "entrepreneur porn"). "Ultimately I think that's what most people want rather than being a billionaire. Most people want a purpose in their work and control back over their time."

In my wife Lauren's old job as a corporate headhunter, she heard versions of this time and again, from candidates weighing whether they'd take the latest six-figure banking job, even though they knew they would be just as miserable as they were at their current six-figure banking job. What they really wanted was more time for the things they cared about: a business idea, travel, their young family, or finally opening that bed-and-breakfast in the countryside. At the same time, these thoughts were going through Lauren's head. She would stop into coffee shops on the slushy commute to her office, wearing the uncomfortable work shoes she despised, and look at the people there, baking bread or chatting away in the middle of the day, and wonder why she couldn't have that life. Her job was arguably great. She worked five days a week, got paid very well, loved the people she worked for, and never had to put in time on evenings or weekends. But Lauren wanted something that her job could never give her: she wanted to control her life. When and where she worked, what work she did, who she worked with, and even the clothes she wore. She knew she would make drastically less as an entrepreneur initially, but also that she would gain so much freedom, and the tradeoff was one she was willing to take.

Unlike economic data, which is relatively straightforward, tracking the nonfinancial benefits of entrepreneurship is complicated. Typically, researchers rely on surveys of business owners and ask them to self-report levels of things like their satisfaction with work, or with life overall, or health (what one researcher termed "psychic income"). And while the data are far from conclusive, it does appear from various studies that entrepreneurs tend to be more satisfied with their work than those employed by others, even when those employees earn more money.

This was something I spoke about with various lifestyle entrepreneurs in Rockaway Beach, whose satisfaction with work and life came from different sources. For Obolsky, her satisfaction came from surfing, living by the beach, and building a bakery where she completely controls the environment. For Erin Silvers, a dreamy bohemian woman who owned the clothing and jewelry boutique Zingara Vintage, her satisfaction as an entrepreneur was built around her daughter, whom she raised alone. "I am the architect of my own experience," she said. "I have complete freedom and a space that's safe and beautiful in this crazy world." After Silvers moved to Rockaway in 2014, she was able to take her daughter to school and pick her up each day, bring her to the beach, and soak up as much fleeting childhood with her as possible. "My friend recently told me, 'Erin, I don't know anyone who gets to spend as much time with their daughter as you,'" Silvers said, choking up, and going silent. "If I did this anywhere else but Rockaway I'd be more successful, financially speaking, but these things make it worth it here."

Jen Poyant (whom Obolsky praised as "a badass bitch"), ran a podcast studio called Stable Genius Productions, which produced a popular podcast called *ZigZag*, about female entrepreneurs. But while her partner and the rest of the company lived and worked in Brooklyn, Poyant remained in Rockaway Beach so she could spend more time with her son, take him to the beach, and teach him to surf. "Family is a huge part of my life," and the way she ran her business was built around that.

The joy of that daily, monotonous parenting grind, more than anything, was the reason Lauren became an entrepreneur. She was sick of missing the morning drop-offs and pickups. Sick of having to shop for groceries on the weekend. She didn't want to ask permission to go on vacation or take a day off because our daughter was sick. When she became pregnant with our son four years ago, those feelings culminated in her decision to start her own business.

For the past three summers, since she began working for herself, Lauren and I have taken August off, heading up to the country with our kids and parents to go camping, swim, hike, and really just spend time together. Yesterday, I stopped writing this chapter an hour earlier than planned, because it was snowing out and I wanted to take the kids sledding. I could not do that if I had a job. Our two kids suck up an inordinate amount of our time and energy and doubtlessly impact our potential economic performance. But unless we have a mandatory meeting or I have to travel for research or speaking, we are there in the morning to stuff Cheerios into their screaming mouths and walk them to school, there to pick them up hours later, fight them into baths and beds, and kiss their sweet little heads good night.

Having always worked for myself, I honestly find the idea of not having complete control over one's time a foreign concept. "What are you, French?" my friend Steve jokes, replying to my lunch invitation with a picture of a sad salad in a plastic clamshell by a laptop. I'm similarly astounded how some of the friends on my annual ski trip, who are over forty years old, need to ask *permission* six months in advance from their bosses for two days off. When I want to go paddleboarding during the summer with my friend Josh, who operates his own tech support company, we just hit the water. Sometimes we will be paddling around Toronto's downtown harbor, and I will point to the office towers that dominate the skyline and remind Josh that our friends are sitting at their desks, while we are out in the sun. "Do you two even work?" our friend Dan texted us, after Josh sent him a photo of us paddling one random Tuesday morning last July, while Dan sat in the front seat of his car at a highway rest stop, eating a cheeseburger with one hand while he edited a client's contract on his laptop. Of course we work . . . but on our terms.

This sense of freedom can have concrete benefits. One is health. Ten years ago, Amy Febinger was working in Manhattan, producing television and commercials. "I had stomach ulcers from the stress," she told me as we chatted on the Rockaway boardwalk one morning, watching the waves and drinking smoothies. When Febinger took up flower arranging as a hobby and turned it into a side business, she faced a choice.

"Okay," she told herself, "this is when you go for it and build a business, or go back to work and being on ulcer medication." Febinger left a $140,000-a-year job and began scrubbing buckets for a florist, learning the business while splitting piecemeal floral gigs with freelance ad production work. She started surfing in Rockaway and eventually moved there, but kept her floral business in Manhattan and Brooklyn and found herself just as stressed with flowers as when she lived in the city. Finally, Febinger decided to focus on weddings in Rockaway and Long Island, charging more money for fewer events, working out of her house, and taking off two months in the winter, to surf and arrange flowers in Mexico. Febinger's life has been transformed. The ulcers were gone, and though Febinger used to smoke pot to sleep, she never touched drugs anymore, because her anxiety levels were so low.

"Here's the thing: I'm not married, I don't have kids, it's just me," she said. "As long as I can cover my expenses and go on vacations, that's enough. I don't need to make three hundred thousand a year. Why? I don't even have time to spend it." Recently, she had run into a famous florist at the flower market in New York, and Febinger was shocked at how terrible he looked. He told her he was super stressed about his business, which was growing like crazy. "Wow! We got into this business for opposite reasons. I got into this business not just as a living, but to live my life!" Febinger said, pausing to look out at the ocean on a sunny morning, as she sat in a bikini, in New York City. "This is probably the happiest I've been in my life. I'm cool to chill out here in this space for a bit," she said, as a wave crashed. "This is my life."

For lifestyle entrepreneurs, work itself is often as rewarding as the freedom it affords them. Obolsky loves to bake. Silvers loves selling people vintage clothing that brings them joy. Febinger loves arranging flowers. I love interviewing people, because I can have conversations with whoever I want. I hate to use the term "passion" to describe all of this, because it's one that the startup myth has appropriated into the particular oblivion of marketing buzzwords. But it is undeniably an element of what the soul of entrepreneurship is about. After meeting Febinger, I drove down to the leafy, suburban Rockaway neighborhood of Belle Harbor, where Joe Falcone (aka "Joey Clams") was working shirtless in the converted garage behind his mother's house, shaving a long rectangle of high-density foam into a 6′2″ fish-shaped surfboard. A lifelong Rockaway native and surfer, with the Italian-American swagger of a Scorsese character, Falcone began making surfboards as a hobby in his teens, working a variety of jobs in the city—chef, valet, salesman at a surf shop, graphic designer, fashion photographer—until he returned to Rockaway and began shaping surfboards full-time under the brand Falcone Surfboards.

"I wanted to reconnect to the community, and I honestly felt like my life came back to me after being numb," he said. "My heart wasn't into photography, and the conversations I'd have at photo shoots weren't 'nutritious.' I mean people were honestly talking about the Kardashians, and I was just bored." Falcone saw himself as a craftsman, who made surfboards that were tailored to their users and the waves they surfed. "I charge a grand a board and I don't have to make as much as the next guy," he said. "I'm not just pumping out boards to make a quota. At this point in the world it's important to do things with integrity. What I do will live forever. When I die, my boards will be cherished." The work, Falcone insisted, with a dead-eyed seriousness, gave his life purpose. "Nothing fills my soul like this. I'm a toy maker. That's what I do. I do it for people to have fun."

When you work for yourself, the work becomes you. Your ownership isn't just over your business assets and intellectual property, but your reputation, your achievements, your failures, and all that you learn from that along the way. As a writer who has always worked for himself, that is a benefit I rarely acknowledge openly, but it is probably what keeps me writing books, a process fraught with economic precariousness, where the chances of bestseller success are imperceptibly slim, the financial rewards are modest, and the work itself can be torturous. But at the end of the day it is all mine—the shit and the gravy—and more than any money or the thrill I get from seeing my name on another dead tree, this is the benefit I derive from the work.

These benefits are not something all entrepreneurs experience in lifestyle businesses and certainly not consistently. The mythology of the lifestyle business is as strong as the startup myth and equally as fetishized. Blogs, social media influencers, and a litany of authors and experts are constantly telling people to quit their jobs, follow their dreams, live their passions, turn their side hustle into a full-time lifestyle, and do what they have always meant to do . . . all for the price of a monthly WeWork membership.

There are countless consultants, bloggers, and authors who promote the secrets to a life of pleasurable work, with names like the Freedom Entrepreneurs, Freedom Fast Lane, and the Laptop Lifestyle Experts, whose websites are filled with photos of lucky individuals who were once miserable desk jockeys, until they set off on the fulfilling and lucrative life of traveling the world and making money (usually through some affiliate marketing model). The pinnacle of the lifestyle entrepreneurial fetishization is the Van Life movement (#vanlife), an Instagram chronicle of young, attractive couples who travel the world in converted Volkswagen camper vans, posting photos of morning sunrises over California beaches, as he waxes a surfboard (shirtless), and she sips coffee wrapped in a Pendleton blanket (topless).

When I joked to Obolsky about #vanlife, she blushed and admitted she and Alex briefly owned a VW van called Velma. But she knew the type, and nothing grated her more than seeing certain women regularly posing for selfies at the beach, knowing that they were promoting the surf life without actually doing any work to achieve it. Others had been lured out to Rockaway for the season, gleefully opening bars, shops, and restaurants without realizing the gravity of that commitment.

"Go for it! Just open on a Wednesday and the money truck pulls up on a Friday," joked Brandon D'Leo, an artist who left Manhattan to open the Rockaway Beach Surf Club, an "après-beach" bar, with firefighter Bradach Walsh. "The fantasy dries up for most people once January sets in around here." D'Leo confessed that the bar, which was packed when I met him and Walsh there on a Saturday in July, had yet to make as much money as a business as either one of them made in a single year working as an artist or a firefighter.

For most lifestyle entrepreneurs, reality includes the good, the bad, and plenty of the mundane. Steve Stathis, the owner of the surf shop Boarders, which was my introduction to Rockaway Beach years ago, laughed when I characterized entrepreneurship as a lifestyle. Since opening the business in 2004, Boarders had doubled its original size, opening a second location on the boardwalk five blocks away and two other rental outlets on the beach. In addition, Stathis, who got into the business at the behest of his sons after retiring from the gas company, had opened up a bar nearby.

"Now every day I have five operations to run around to," Stathis said, when he popped into Rockaway Beach Bakery one morning, nursing a cold. "Memorial Day to Labor Day, seven days a week." Though he was one of Rockaway's original surfers, Stathis hadn't ridden a wave or even sat on the beach in the past decade. He was too busy. "We're making money. Not making millions of dollars, but we pay the bills and make an income," he said, coughing. I joked that he still had the glory. "Yeah . . . I wash the toilets. I sweep the floor. All the glory!"

What entrepreneur hasn't looked at the modest lifestyle they've built for themselves and wondered if this is all there is? But when I asked them, not one of the entrepreneurs I spoke with either for this book, or in my life, said that going back to a job was a goal of theirs, or even something they would consider doing unless they were absolutely desperate. To most, the idea of being an employee again was traumatic.

Recently, Lauren told me about a dream she had, where she was back in her old job, comparing it to the recurrent nightmare of showing up for a high school exam, naked and unprepared.

In a 2013 study of self-employed individuals in the province of Manitoba, most respondents admitted that as entrepreneurs they worked long hours and didn't make much money, which is typical of the average entrepreneur, who makes less than a similar employee. But the vast majority also said they would not accept a position working for someone else. Why not? One reason might be that after a certain point, money cannot buy more happiness. There have been numerous studies on this, including a landmark one in 2010 from Nobel Prize–winning economist Angus Deaton and psychologist Daniel Kahneman, which found that once American households made more than $75,000 (about $90,000 today), the effect of more money on life satisfaction was negligent. The same effect was true when adjusted for differences in income and expenses, in countries around the world.

And while the motivations of entrepreneurs are wildly disparate and defy easy characterization, an important reason might be the importance entrepreneurs place on freedom. In a 2007 paper titled "Money, Money, Money?," professor Gavin Cassar found that the single most important factor explaining the career choice of nascent entrepreneurs was independence. This is hardly surprising. After all, freedom is the one thing entrepreneurship guarantees, regardless of success, and like all freedoms that people gain, they are hard-pressed to give it up.

There was a time, right before my first book was published, that I thought about applying for a staff position at a magazine or newspaper, to gain proper experience, make connections, and earn a steady salary. What would my life look like now, as I commuted into work in my worn khakis and button-up shirt to sit in a cubicle, making small talk with coworkers, worrying about whether I was making the right impression with my superiors, whether I was taking too long at lunch, or in the bathroom, or trying too hard or not hard enough? Asking permission to do anything consequential. Counting my vacation days or sick days. Not skiing. Not paddleboarding. Not picking up my kids every night because I had to put in a few extra hours at the office, because someone was actually *counting* the hours I worked? How much would I be willing to sacrifice for that? $25,000 more a year? $50,000? To hell with that.

The importance of freedom was shared among the lifestyle entrepreneurs in Rockaway Beach. "These are values we all really understand," said Jen Poyant, when we spoke over drinks at the Rockaway Beach Surf Club. Freedom came with sacrifices. When you owned your business, that business was there day and night, and it didn't take days off. You couldn't simply quit your business. It was impossible to walk away from or turn off, Poyant reminded me, and no one paid you for sick days or vacations anymore. (Obolsky said a weeklong surfing trip to Puerto Rico the winter before had taken a month's worth of work at the bakery to pay off, but it was worth it.) Retirement plans? Ha! Better start saving. "You figure it out," Poyant said, on how entrepreneurs dealt with this balancing act between economic obligations and personal freedom. "You figure out your priorities," and you build your business around that.

Obolsky was clear on her priorities: no chef's coats, no socks, her music, her food, no driving except once a week to get groceries, and business hours that adhered to a flexible, surf town schedule (they actually say "eight to four-ish"). Last February, Obolsky posted a note on the bakery's Instagram feed, with a photo of a surfer riding a tube, saying, "Closing at 2pm today to surf . . . cause YOLO." In the comments, she elaborated that she had closed early for some "Rockaway winter fun mental health," adding the hashtag #livealittle. No requests. No apologies. No permission. Just surf.

Over lunch at a restaurant overlooking Jamaica Bay, a local businesswoman named Galit Tzadik told me that Obolsky was the typical Rockaway lifestyle entrepreneur, living on her own terms and supporting herself with her talents. Tzadik, who had a background in real estate finance, opened her own consultancy in 2015, helping entrepreneurs around the peninsula manage their businesses, plan for the future, and make their businesses more sustainable (she was also the secretary of the local business alliance and a group of female Rockaway Beach entrepreneurs). "Money isn't the end goal for these people," Tzadik said. "I ask them what their end goal is, in terms of the life they want. What's the vision?" Her clients included small contractors and plumbers, baby photographers and personal trainers, home health care workers, retailers and restaurateurs, surf instructors, dentists, doctors, and yoga studio owners, all seeking the "freedom to live the life they want," to take care of their families, and stop living paycheck to paycheck.

Because it was so isolated from the rest of New York City, the Rockaway Beach community was always going to be overwhelmingly one of lifestyle entrepreneurs, Tzadik said. This was a place where the fishermen drank beers with the used car dealers, the bodega owners, and the vendors from the boardwalk each night. It was this same community of entrepreneurs who dug in and rebuilt the area after Superstorm Sandy nearly destroyed it, lending each other spaces and money, pitching in with shovels to dig out moldy stores, setting up a tent to organize relief efforts (as the owners of the Rockaway Beach Surf Club did), or just driving around handing out dry socks, like Joey Falcone. The heart of Rockaway Beach beat in the mom-and-pop businesses that wove themselves together to make its fabric whole again.

"It's an invaluable contribution," says Rodney Foxworth, who runs the national nonprofit Business Alliance for Local Living Economies (BALLE), which promotes small, local businesses and their impact on communities. "They are based in that place. The owners have actual relationships with their employees. They are their neighbors. They work in the same place and go to church and school together. It's very difficult to value or measure that in the typical way. And these businesses are committed to that place." According to numerous studies Foxworth cited, about 70 percent of the economic value a locally based business created stayed in that community, compared to just 30 percent for a business that is owned elsewhere.

In New York City there are nearly a quarter of a million small businesses, which Gregg Bishop, Director of the New York City Department of Small Business Services, confidently called "the economic engine of the city," employing 3.6 million New Yorkers. They provided services from bike repairs and child minding to seven-course tasting menus, pumping untold billions into the economy. "These are businesses who are in business because they just enjoy being in business," Bishop said. "When you think of why people go into business, there's people who do so to sell it . . . that's not these folks." They are looking to build something for the community they are in, Bishop said, and serve their corner of the city with whatever they are selling. But more than that, they were the people who made New York . . . well . . . New York.

"The identity of New York is at stake," Bishop said, when I asked him what the city would be without lifestyle entrepreneurs, who were quickly getting priced out of many parts of New York by rising rents, licensing costs, and other expenses. "When you strip out all our lifestyle businesses, what do you end up with? It's a city that's not exciting. It's a city that could be Anytown, USA, a city that doesn't reflect the diversity of its citizenship, and a city that nobody would really want to be a part of. The reason why New York City is New York City is because that dry cleaner in the neighborhood has been there for thirty years. They know the family in apartment 12D, and know their kids since they were born," he said. "Yes, New York City has Targets and large chains, but you realize the competitive advantage our mom-and-pops have isn't just being nimble and adjusting to consumer behavior, but it's also because they have the right relationship with the neighborhoods they are in."

When Bishop told me this, I thought of the fictional pizzeria run by Ashley and Justin that Lind and Atkinson held out in *Big Is Beautiful* as the opposite of true entrepreneurship and in many ways their poster child for the economic futility of lifestyle businesses. When I lived in New York City, one of the things I loved about the place, which I miss dearly, is the fact that there are Justins and Ashleys (or more likely Sals and Joes) opening up pizza shops every day, all over the city, in a place completely saturated with slice joints. Knowing that you can walk down any single block in that great city and enjoy a multiplicity of pizza slices baked by entrepreneurs is the delicious thing that makes New York City what it is. Could you imagine a New York where your only choice of pizza was between Domino's or Pizza Hut?

BY TWO THIRTY, OBOLSKY STEPPED back to do a verbal inventory of the bakery case: three small focaccia slices, three sourdough loaves, two plain croissants, and one with honey and Maldon salt (my favorite).

She began to prepare croissant dough for the next day, her one day off, when the bakery was closed. (She called it "Sunday," even though it was Monday.) Obolsky planned to sleep in, surf, lie on the beach, and hang out with friends. I asked her something that had been nagging me since I'd arrived in Rockaway Beach. Why not move to California, Mexico, or Hawaii and open a bakery there, like so many other surf bums had done? Why stick it out in gritty, expensive New York on the very day the city delivered a notice that it would be tearing up her sidewalk for the next two months to replace a water main, throwing the remainder of the summer's business into jeopardy? Why not move somewhere with better waves, cheaper housing, warmer, cleaner water, and far less stress? Why build a lifestyle business in a city whose lifestyle defined the term "rat race"?

"My family's from here," Obolsky said, as she worked sticks of butter into dough with her sinewy forearms. "They come out here every few weeks. My kid brother comes to help out here. Plus, the food scene in New York . . . I mean . . . it's New York Fucking City!" Obolsky still earned writeups in publications like the *New York Times* for her croissants and baked goods, which not only drove more customers her way, but fanned the flame of larger entrepreneurial ambitions she harbored. The bakery was a start, but she wanted to expand into a proper production kitchen, bake and sell more products, and eventually start making ice cream again. One day, Obolsky would love to open an old-school soda fountain, with floats and shakes and sundaes . . . really the perfect thing for a beach town.

"Do I want to do more? Yeah, I do, but I'm really happy now," she said. "When things are calm, I'm like, 'Okay, what am I going to do next?' I'm always ready to switch it up and challenge myself."

Four teenagers came in and cleaned Obolsky out of her remaining croissants, leaving only a single loaf of bread, which she put in her backpack to take home. "It's still really hard," she told me, as she walked outside. "Opening the bakery is the hardest thing I've done in my life. Sometimes I wake up and say, 'Ugh, I don't want to go in.' Then I tell myself, 'Oh, you have to ride your bike on a boardwalk while watching the dolphins to the sunny bakery you own . . . *wahh wahh*.'"

"Another week," Shenitsky said, rolling down the metal grates and locking them to the sidewalk.

"Whooo weekend!" Obolsky shouted to the street and walked next door to the liquor store owned by her landlord, Phil Cicia. Obolsky picked up a six-pack of Twisted Tea, the hard iced tea she drinks on the beach, and talked with Cicia about business, his endless struggles with the tax department and the upcoming street repairs that he was dreading. "Hey," he said with a shrug, "it's a living."

The idea that an entrepreneur who makes a living their main goal represents some sort of lesser form of entrepreneurship, that their choice not to grow as big as possible in as little time as possible is some sort of failure and drain on the economy, is a completely false one. Most of us want a good living, and even more than that, a better life, whether we work for ourselves or others. We make choices and sacrifices around the businesses we start, based on the lives we live, the lives we want to live, and the options open to us. Sometimes that means more, sometimes it means less.

Obolsky opened a Twisted Tea, placed it in the cupholder of her bicycle, and rode over to the boardwalk, sipping from the can. She pedaled toward home, watching the waves. Within five minutes of arriving home, she was out the door (following a mandatory bong hit); wetsuit on, board under her arm, heading to the beach. Obolsky paddled into the waves, which were choppy and small, but she surfed them like they were glassy tubes in Hawaii, grinning and fist pumping after each short ride. Friends of hers swam out in the lineup, chatting with Obolsky about the bakery.

Obolsky stayed in the water for two hours, until the sun began dipping behind the apartment blocks, casting a pink glow on the jets taking off from JFK. "Well, I saw the sunset and sunrise from my board today, slept five hours, and worked in between," she said, turning her board to paddle for one more wave. "Not a bad day. Nothing to complain about there," and like that she was up again, shouting, "This doesn't suck!" back to me, in case I'd somehow missed the point.

CHAPTER 4

Bring 'em Up

JESSECA DUPART'S PATIENCE was pretty much spent. What her manufacturer had termed "growing pains" were wearing her down. There was the shipment of Miracle Drops that never arrived at a beauty supply store in Chicago, the furious shop in Oakland that received two orders of Edge Control instead of one, damaged deliveries of styling gels that were returned to Kaleidoscope Hair Products at full cost, and boxes of shampoos that were so chemically pungent, the fumes gave her staff headaches.

Kaleidoscope began as a simple hair salon in this northeastern section of New Orleans, called Little Woods, back in 2012, when Jesseca Dupart was thirty years old, and by the time I visited her six years later, Kaleidoscope was a rapidly growing brand in the African American beauty market. Its hair products sold in salons and beauty supply stores in every state, as well as Canada, the UK, and the Caribbean. All of it

was driven by Dupart's relentless marketing on social media, particularly Instagram, where her handle @DArealBBJUDY was about to gain
its millionth follower.

Dupart stands little more than five feet tall, has big eyes, a wide
smile, and curves that spill out of the outfits chosen to highlight them.
"BB" stood for Big Booty, a God-given asset that Dupart wasn't shy
about deploying in the steady stream of photos and videos she cranked
out around the clock in the service of her business. "If I knew what I was
doing was going to be hair, I probably would have changed it," Dupart
said about the @DArealBBJUDY handle, with a grin. This morning she
was wearing a pair of Adidas workout tights, Yeezy sneakers, and a be-
jeweled T-shirt that said *Pray Girl, Pray*. Her hair was straight and black
(one of many extensions she rotated through each week), and her fingernails on this day were nearly three-inch-long glittering gold, purple,
black, and jeweled talons.

Kaleidoscope's growth had recently exploded, with sales going from
$100,000 a month at the start of 2018, to $1 million by the end of March.
The company in Houston that manufactured and distributed Kaleidoscope's products simply couldn't handle the speed and volume of the
scale, and these problems were irritating Dupart. "We don't have room
for error," she told me, as she sat behind her desk at the company's office, which occupied a few units of the strip mall where her salon had
once been. "A mess-up now costs thousands of dollars, where just a few
months ago it was a few hundred. We went from having a two-day turnover to twelve days," she said, flipping between her two phones and her
computer. "That shit won't work!"

Dupart was conflicted, because the man behind these mess-ups had
been her mentor in the business. He personally convinced her to start
selling products when she was a hairstylist, launching her from one of
the many African American women with a salon in New Orleans, into a
nationally recognized figure in the black hair community, with a rapidly
growing multimillion-dollar business. But now he was on an extended
trip to Africa, and no one was able to help Dupart sort out the growing logistics mess. "I have to do all this—call the shippers, call the box
company—and I see that I don't need him," she said.

Kaleidoscope's demand was growing faster than the company could manage. People would call daily and even show up at the doors trying to buy products that were sold out, including the most popular one, Miracle Drops, which claimed to treat alopecia, hair loss, and other hair damage. "I don't wanna be sold out!" Dupart said in exasperation. "Sold out is missed money!!! I'm flying to Houston next week to sort this out."

In the midst of this, she got a message from her distributor, who was at his hotel in Kenya. Dupart immediately called him. "A lot of errors are looking bad on us," she said, describing the escalating fulfillment issues, "and it's a lot in a very short period of time."

"Well, it's just too many steps going on right now," he replied, explaining how a new partnership with a larger distributor in Atlanta had complicated the process. "We didn't have these mess-ups when we did it ourselves."

"But we're doing triple what we were before!" Dupart shot back, and the conversation quickly escalated in tone, until Dupart was practically shouting at the phone, and they both hung up.

"If he can't contain a small order, that's my concern now. I mean, I'm a loyal person, but if this fucks up, it fucks up for everybody that works here," she said, shaking her head. Dupart paused, took a deep breath, put her hands together in prayer, and closed her eyes. After a few seconds she opened them. "It's my company, and I can't sacrifice my company for someone else. There's too many people counting on me . . . too many."

Those people included her family, friends, and colleagues she supported in various ways and her dozen employees, including a couple who were immigrants from Nigeria, whose three children were playing video games in the back because their school was on spring break. But the most important was the wider community in New Orleans and beyond, who looked up to Dupart as an example of an entrepreneur to follow.

As we walked out to Dupart's Escalade (which was wrapped in Kaleidoscope decals and had a "BB Judy" license plate), a car pulled into the plaza and began frantically honking at her. Four young African American women jumped out and ran up to Dupart, screaming in delight as they embraced her. Pulling out phones for selfies, the women explained in giddy tones how they'd just finished their first year of college in Baton Rouge and had driven here directly after packing up their dorm rooms to meet Dupart. To these women, DArealBBJUDY was more than a larger-than-life figure marketing hair products through hilarious social media skits with celebrities. She was a successful black female entrepreneur from New Orleans, who told other young black women just like her that they too could be entrepreneurs.

OVER THE PAST TWO DECADES, minority women—including African Americans, Latinos, Asians, and Native Americans—have become the fastest-growing group of entrepreneurs in the United States. While the number of businesses owned by white women increased by 58 percent from 2007 to 2018, the number of businesses owned by minority women increased by nearly triple that rate—163 percent—according to a report commissioned by American Express. As of 2018, women of color accounted for nearly half of all female-owned businesses in America, representing nearly six million entrepreneurs, and a third of a trillion dollars in annual revenue. African American women represented 20 percent of these entrepreneurs, growing their numbers at an annual rate of 9 percent, making up the largest segment of female entrepreneurs, after white women. It is estimated that black women open around 550 new businesses a day in America, compared to around 650 for white female entrepreneurs. Black women are the only cohort of female entrepreneurs in America whose rates of business ownership exceed those of their male counterparts. If there is a boom in one cohort of American entrepreneurs that matches the mythology of rising interest in starting a business, then that group looks a lot like Jesseca Dupart.

Part of the growth in minority entrepreneurship is due to the demographic shift around America, with immigration changing the face of the workforce and nation. However, African Americans don't drive that demographic shift in the same way Asian Americans or Latinos do through immigration . . . their numbers as a percentage of the US population are relatively steady. African American women stand out as a group whose entrepreneurial ambitions are backed up by their willingness to put those ideas into action and actually go into business for themselves.

That's the good news. The more complicated news is that black women and other minorities, like women overall, face greater hurdles to becoming entrepreneurs and succeeding at entrepreneurship over the long term. A 2016 Kauffman Foundation report on gender and entrepreneurship found that women are half as likely as their male counterparts to start a new business. Those businesses tend to be smaller on average than male businesses, financed at a lower rate, less profitable, slower to grow, and more likely to be based at home and in female-centric industries, such as beauty. For minorities, the disparity is even deeper. African American female-owned firms generate an average of just $24,700 in revenues annually, compared to $212,300 for white-female-owned firms, presenting a drastic disparity in wealth and opportunity that cuts to the heart of systemic inequality in America.

This, of course, is not merely an economic story but also a cultural one. With a smattering of exceptions, minority entrepreneurs and female entrepreneurs have been left out of the heroic story of modern American entrepreneurship.

"There's explicit classism, sexism, racism . . . every entrepreneur experiences it," said Julianne Zimmerman, the managing director of Reinventure Capital, an impact investment firm based in Boston that targets companies run by minorities. "When I'm speaking I ask everyone in the room to close their eyes and picture a successful entrepreneur," she said. "Then I say, 'Who thought of Tristan Walker, Sarah Blakely, Richelieu Dennis, or Robin Chase?' The room is very quiet. Because everyone was thinking of the same icons: Steve Jobs, Elon Musk, Zuckerberg, Gates," Zimmerman said. "The prevailing simple story is one that gets retold again and again. That's the unconscious bias. None of us is intentionally thinking of excluding those stories. But when we encounter or think of entrepreneurs, we look at what we expect to see. And when we find something that doesn't fit, we have lots of questions."

For investors, whether Palo Alto venture capitalists or loan officers at a New Orleans bank, that bias leads them to ask women and minority entrepreneurs seeking financing for more answers, details, and data to overcome those biases . . . something that white male entrepreneurs are not required to do in the same way. In one study, Harvard professor Laura Huang and colleagues found that female entrepreneurs pitching to VCs were asked more questions about potential risks and losses, compared to men, who got more questions about potential gains. More often, investors will simply find a CEO who fits their expectations of a successful entrepreneur, which is why men continue to receive the vast majority of venture capital funding, perpetuating a vicious cycle that saps opportunity. The Silicon Valley startup model of entrepreneurship produces more Silicon Valley–style startups, reinforcing inequality for entrepreneurs.

"We're dangerously close to having a monoculture within the world of entrepreneurship," said Zimmerman. "A monoculture of who plays. A monoculture of who invests. A monoculture of the kinds of investments they make. A monoculture is always problematic."

Economically this represents a wasted opportunity. "We see for certain that women, people of color, and immigrants are far more likely to start businesses and actually stick with them, than in fact the target demographic among VCs," Zimmerman said.

These entrepreneurs also tend to be more community focused than others. They set up businesses to serve their communities, foster relationships in those communities, and use entrepreneurship to strengthen their communities. For black women in New Orleans's hair and beauty trade like Jesseca Dupart, community isn't just a place where you set up a business. It anchors the very soul of entrepreneurship.

NEW ORLEANS IS A MAGICAL city rich in music, history, and buttery food. But while wealth is apparent in its grand mansions and gilded restaurants, economically, New Orleans remains one of the poorest American cities, particularly in its African American neighborhoods.

Unemployment in Orleans Parish (the greater metropolitan area) is slightly higher than the national average, but as many as half the city's black males are out of work. Considering African Americans make up more than 60 percent of the city's population, these truths inform nearly everything about the shape of entrepreneurship there and its relationship to community.

This makes black women one of the most potent entrepreneurial forces in New Orleans, and for many of them, the hair and beauty business is the path they have chosen to pursue. This isn't surprising, as the hair and beauty industry is one of the most well-defined tracks for business ownership in the African American community nationwide, with more black female entrepreneurs identifying themselves as owners of beauty salons, cosmetics businesses, or other related fields than any other industry by a wide margin.

The historical origin of this goes back to the Antebellum era, when slaves who weren't forced into the brutal labor of plantation agriculture often engaged in subsistence work in cities like New Orleans. Black men would shine shoes, shave, and cut hair, while black women sold food and other goods in the markets and wharves of the city. Slaves were frequently made to groom their owners, as well as other slaves being sold at auction in New Orleans. Most often the money went directly to their owners' pockets, but occasionally some was used to purchase freedom for a slave and their family.

"For slaves, becoming a barber was both a step away from the close supervision of the master and a step toward freedom," wrote Quincy T. Mills in his book *Cutting Along the Color Line*. "Barbering offered free blacks employment without entry barriers or restrictions, and many seized an opportunity to become entrepreneurs. . . ."

After Emancipation, the prospects of freedom quickly gave way to the segregation and restrictions of Jim Crow. Blacks were barred from many professions and trades, banking was effectively closed off, and most white communities across the country simply refused to do business with black entrepreneurs. As African American communities represented sizable markets that white businesses purposefully avoided,

African American political leaders like W. E. B. Du Bois stressed the importance of entrepreneurship in achieving economic and political independence and encouraged black entrepreneurs to build within their backyards. One obvious niche was the hair and beauty business, a market whites had zero interest in servicing.

The pioneering entrepreneur who established the modern black beauty industry was Madam C. J. Walker. She was born Sarah Breedlove on a Louisiana plantation in 1867 to emancipated slaves. By twenty, Walker was a widow with a three-year-old daughter, working as a washerwoman in St. Louis. Dissatisfied with the backbreaking work of scrubbing clothes, Walker put herself through night school and eventually began selling hair products for a local woman named Annie Malone, who marketed creams that would repair the dry, damaged hair that chemical straighteners caused. A rivalry soon developed, as Walker struck out on her own, with the two women establishing competing networks of products, salons, schools, and saleswomen around America and beyond.

Walker quickly became the country's first African American millionaire and star entrepreneur, and she brought her gospel of economic independence to audiences of black women around the world. Her sales conventions and ads in black newspapers featured testimonials from other women who sold her products, claiming things like "You have made it possible for a colored woman to make more money in a day than working in a month in somebody's kitchen." What Walker sold them was nothing more or less than freedom.

"The money and success wasn't enough," said A'Lelia Bundles, Walker's biographer and her great-granddaughter. "Being an entrepreneur and being successful needs to be used towards other ends: political power and providing jobs for other people." Walker's ultimate legacy was linking African American entrepreneurship with a need to serve the community. "I think that probably the hair care products became a means to an end," said Bundles. Walker used her profile to build a political voice for African Americans and women in particular, first within national civil rights organizations (which had relegated women to the sidelines) and then beyond, funding a campaign to lobby President

Woodrow Wilson to outlaw lynching. "Her profile allowed her to be my-
thologized and elevated in the public eye. She was both successful and
knew how to promote her success. It's very much about independence
and about independence from white bosses."

In the century since Madam Walker's rise, the black beauty industry
in the United States has grown tremendously. African American women
alone spend up to $500 billion annually on hair and beauty products and
services (according to an estimate by market research firm Mintel), as
much as three times more than the average white woman, which isn't
surprising, when you witness how even the simplest cut and style for
a black woman is vastly more labor intensive than for a white woman.
Getting a weave is basically a multi-hour surgery involving wigs, glues,
braiding, and stitching. Someone like Dupart gets multiple weaves a
week. The industry today is a mixture of big household names, from
multibillion-dollar brands like Sundial (now owned by Unilever) to
growing product companies like Kaleidoscope, and tens of thousands
of small businesses, ranging from beauty shops and nail salons to individuals braiding hair from their homes, or even on a chair set up on the
sidewalk.

Jesseca Dupart's rise into the upper echelons of this business is
pretty typical of female African American beauty entrepreneurs, especially those I spoke with in New Orleans. She was raised in the city's
7th Ward to a middle-class family. Her beloved father, Jesse, who died in
2011, was an accountant that worked for Shell and a local university, as
well as an entrepreneur who owned a liquor store and rental properties.
Dupart's mother, Evelyn, worked at the post office and had been helping
her daughter with Kaleidoscope's shipping since her retirement.

Like many other women I spoke with, Dupart's love of hair was born
during weekly visits to the salon. "I just liked doing hair and nails and
dressing up," Dupart recalled, as she drove her Escalade on the highway
while simultaneously juggling two phones. "Me and my sister went to
the salon every Saturday. It was an all-day thing. We had long full hair
that wasn't manageable. As a kid you hated the dryer, but there'd always
be people there. Someone would bring in supper plates . . . crawfish or

gumbo or barbecue. I liked getting my hair done. I liked the look after. But more than anything I liked the atmosphere. When you were young it was positive energy."

By seven Dupart was already cutting and styling the hair on her dolls. By twelve, she started braiding her friends' hair after school. Dupart's parents discouraged this; they had high hopes she would become a lawyer or another professional. "Hair wasn't what it is now," she said. "Hair was a hobby." Dupart would sneak friends into her family's house to cut their hair. One time, she hid a girl behind the shower curtain while her mother used the toilet. When Dupart got pregnant at fifteen, her parents let her start charging for her services and transfer to a trade school to study cosmetology. Even though it was far rougher than her gifted high school (drug-sniffing dogs, shootings, and gangs were daily sights), she loved it. "I had a passion for it," she said, especially accounting class. "I loved watching numbers increase."

Dupart worked out of her family's home before and after school, styling the hair of fellow students, relatives, friends, and neighbors, until she built up a loyal clientele. "I didn't just do good hair," she said, "I had good customer service. The customer is always right. But I didn't mind working. I didn't go to parties, or to DJ nights, or second line [Mardi Gras street dances]. . . . I was the one who was there doing your hair. During Mardi Gras I'd work twenty hours straight." By eighteen, Dupart had two children (she now has three) and was making good money, far better than she could have made at the minimum-wage jobs available to her. She soon moved to a beauty salon.

The black beauty business is set up as an entrepreneurial pyramid, and the starting point for many beauticians and barbers is through "booth rent," which is when a salon owner rents a chair to a stylist. Dupart rented chairs at braiding salons, upscale hair care businesses, and even male barbershops. "I'm a girl who can be put anywhere," she said. "I can deal with a ribbing and keep on with my business."

When Hurricane Katrina struck New Orleans in 2005, the city's low-lying African American neighborhoods were the worst effected by flooding, and many residents temporarily relocated to different cities.

Dupart ended up in Houston. She had $20,000 saved from her business but had no access to FEMA funds and quickly spent it covering living expenses for her family. She set up shop in a rented house and began doing hair for other New Orleans exiles, advertising by printing photos at Kinko's of hairstyles she'd done, then pasting them around Houston.

"New Orleans people wanted New Orleans hair," Dupart explained, "and nowhere in Houston did that. We did hard hair!"

What was hard hair, I asked?

"Hair with product in it. Hair that could stand up on its own. Hair that's hard. No one did that ghetto shit there!"

For half a year Dupart lived between the two cities, rebuilding her life and business in New Orleans during the week, then driving to Houston Friday night, to see her kids and cut hair for two days straight before driving back. "It was exhausting," she said. "I love money, opportunity, and growth, but it was exhausting."

By 2007, Dupart had saved enough to open her own business with her romantic partner Ro, which they called RoJes, a barbershop and beauty salon that grew to two locations. This is when she first began to dabble with social media marketing, posting photos and videos on Facebook to draw in business, then hiring local hip hop celebrities, radio DJs, and social media influencers to attend events at the salon. The recession soon hit, and Dupart realized that mixing her personal and professional life wasn't a good idea, as it was affecting her relationship with Ro. She had wanted to strike out on her own since she'd first left home, so she registered the name Kaleidoscope at the end of 2012, because she loved colors.

"I've decided to branch off on my own," Dupart announced in an Instagram post. "God has placed on my heart a phenomenal plan . . . and I'm just executing it." Kaleidoscope salon opened in August 2013, secured with an $1,800 rent deposit (out of her remaining $2,000 savings). Dupart worked tirelessly over the next months to acquire the chairs, sinks, dryers, and other infrastructure she needed and paid for one cut, style, braid, and weave at a time. There was no investor. No bank. No debt. She didn't even consider them. She became an entrepreneur by what she called "grit 'n' gravel."

That December, a stylist left a curling iron on overnight, and the entire salon burned down. Dupart had to rent booths at RoJes to stay in business, even while her relationship with Ro was falling apart. Kaleidoscope reopened in July 2014, and Dupart soon began selling hair products under its brand name. To market these products, which included Sleek Edges (a styling product) and Miracle Drops (a hair repair formula), Dupart got increasingly creative on social media, teaming up with Raynell Steward, a makeup artist who worked at the salon and went by the social media handle Supa Cent, to create funny skits online.

Most were just short videos of Dupart talking, sometimes in the office, sometimes in a car, or at an event. But increasingly there were well-produced, pop culture parodies, including a takeoff on the NWA rap anthem "Straight Outta Compton" featuring all the Kaleidoscope stylists preaching the strength of their "wig game." There was a series of videos called Judy Springer (a take on Jerry Springer), parodies of TLC and Atlanta trap rap videos, and even a trippy remix of the Willy Wonka Oompa Loompa song, with Dupart dressed as Wonka in a top hat, while half a dozen little people dance around her, twerking. As Kaleidoscope Hair Products grew, Dupart started posting videos where she would "run up" on African American celebrities and offer them Miracle Drops. These have included big names like Snoop Dogg, Floyd Mayweather, and comedian Michael Blackson, as well as Instagram celebrities like model/rapper Taylor Hing (aka Chinese Kitty). In addition to this there are thousands of photos of Dupart in every conceivable outfit and situation, from lying in bed in the morning to wearing gigantic ball gowns or fuzzy costumes, to her workout videos and weight loss challenges, and of course pictures of babies, dogs, family, and more dogs. Supa remains a constant presence in DArealBBJUDY's social media feed.

All of this might look like fun, but Dupart's social media presence forms the core of Kaleidoscope's financial success and comes at an increasing cost. Dupart spends most of her time marketing herself and

her business online . . . her phones are rarely away from those glittering nails, and as the production values rise, so do the costs. Celebrities
appear in Dupart's videos because she pays them; a few thousand for
a local influencer, but for someone like Snoop Dogg, it's well into five
figures, paid in cash. When Dupart's accountant inquired about getting
1099 IRS payment forms from one of these recent videos in Atlanta,
Dupart laughed so hard she nearly fell off her chair.

"These are hood-assed niggas!" she told the accountant. "Young
Jeezy ain't gonna sign no 1099!"

As I followed the evolution of DArealBBJUDY's ascent online, what
really struck me was how her social media presence quickly evolved from
selling Kaleidoscope products to a broader forum for inspiring entrepreneurship in young black women. Dupart regularly posted sales figures
and portions of her tax returns, photos of products being shipped and
the operation expanding, and stories about paying off her debt or buying
a new house or luxury car. In each one of these she thanked God but
explicitly told women to trust in themselves and go out on their own.
Dupart was showing other black women that entrepreneurship was as-
pirational, right down to the outfits, trips, cars, and other trappings of
wealth she seemed to flaunt online.

"I define success as how many people you touch," Dupart said, as
we were driving back to the Kaleidoscope offices after meeting the accountant. "Unfortunately, people equate success with money. I bought
a Bentley [a luxury car that costs close to $200,000] not because I like
cars . . . I couldn't care less about them . . . but because it got respect and
people *listened* to me. I got it for the purpose it served. I like the fact that
the money I'm making is very influential. Me doing a skit with Snoop
makes someone who went to school with me say, 'That bitch did it, so I
can, too!' That's New Orleans for ya," she said, as she handed a teller at
the drive-through window of a bank a fat stack of checks to deposit. "I
give ordinary people the game to make money. I'm influential by being
inspiring."

That influence was obvious when you read through the comments of
her Instagram posts:

"real life goals!!! I come on your page just for encouragement…your such an inspiration!!" wrote @shebarber89 when Dupart posted about buying her house.

"Yessssss! This is what the hell im talking bout! 🤷‍♀️💜🖤 *I'm here for this type of boss lady status!!!"* wrote @homes.pho.sale when Dupart posted a photo of her wrapped Escalade.

Even when she shared a $178,182 personal tax bill from the IRS, she got women like @branded_brashay18 saying, *"Even though i know my taxes would look sick* 😬 *I'm ready for my business to prosper! This is only motivation* 🙌*"*

These women saw DArealBBJUDY not as a sex symbol or a style icon, but a brilliant businesswoman who had wrestled success from a hard place. For African American women, one of the most economically and socially disadvantaged populations in American society, there is a burning need to see role models present entrepreneurship as something possible, desirable, and within their grasp. That comes from the tremendous economic success of businesswomen from C. J. Walker to Oprah Winfrey, but also from cultural icons like Beyoncé, who told all the honeys makin' money to throw their hands up and be counted.

"Women are now trying to become a force," Dupart said. "That sense of independence is more important than before. Women are relying on themselves. Women ain't waiting for niggas for nothing!"

Recognizing entrepreneurship as their right was an increasingly important goal for African American women. "We have not been allowed to have," said Elaine Rasmussen, CEO of Social Impact Strategies group, which works to democratize investing and access to capital for entrepreneurs of color and women in the Midwest. "Whenever we have, our shit's been burned to the ground. There is an unconscious fear it may be taken away from you." Reclaiming that economic right began by actively embracing entrepreneurship into the community's identity. "If you walked up to a woman of color or transgender person and ask them how they'd identify with what they're doing . . . many of them don't call themselves entrepreneurs," Rasmussen said, noting how it was regarded as a white word. "I ask, 'Well, what do you call yourself?' They say, it's my side hustle, just this thing that I do. My response back to them is 'Do you have a product or service you sell and get money for it?' Yes. 'Then you are a business.' This is a beautiful thing, a wonderful thing, and you should take ownership of it."

Unfortunately, being a black entrepreneur in America has never been as simple as opening a business. Ownership may be the first step to overcoming inequality, but it is insufficient on its own. There have been overt economic and political barriers that restrict black businesses at every turn and subtler racism that undermines their efforts. During the Jim Crow era, lynch mobs destroyed once-burgeoning hubs of African American entrepreneurship, like the Black Wall Street of Tulsa, Oklahoma, which was completely razed in a 1921 riot. But even today barriers continue to grow. Tennessee recently passed a law that fined hair braiders (an exclusively African American group) hundreds of thousands of dollars for braiding hair without a license, hitting young black women right as they were dipping their toes into entrepreneurship.

Though black women represent the fastest-growing group of American entrepreneurs, they face much higher business failure rates than others. According to data from the US Census Bureau presented in a report by the Center for Global Policy Solutions, in 2012, black female entrepreneurs were the group least likely to have a business with employees. Just 2.5 percent of their businesses did, compared to 11.9 percent for white women and 23.9 percent for white men. Even black men, whose rates of business ownership have declined over the past decade (while black women's grew), still have more than double the number of employees as black women. From 2007 to 2012, during the height of the recession, annual revenues declined by 30 percent for businesses run by black women, more than any other group by a large margin (white women's business revenues declined by 5.7 percent, while black men's business revenues actually increased by 3.9 percent). According to *The Tapestry of Black Business Ownership in America*, a report published by the Association for Enterprise Opportunity in 2016, the average black-owned beauty salon generated just $14,000 in revenue compared to over $56,000 for white-owned salons.

"I don't want to stereotype African American female entrepreneurs, but they are most likely to be frustrated in terms of pursuing their ambitions," says Maya Rockeymoore Cummings, who is President and CEO of the Center for Global Policy Solutions, a D.C. think tank and consultancy she founded. "They are hit with the double whammy of lacking access of capital and the double stereotype of being black and a woman. Both groups have greater barriers to entrepreneurial success, in terms of ability to scale and expand and access capital. That doesn't mean that they don't have ambitions and hopes and dreams," said Rockeymoore. "It just means those are frustrated. The fact that they are most likely to start a business means they are very hopeful. They have a skill, talent, or product idea they feel may be marketable. They are very willing to engage and hang a shingle, but the least likely to succeed."

Of the dozen black female entrepreneurs I spoke with in New Orleans, not a single one, regardless of their financial success, went to the bank for a loan or sought venture capital or outside financing of any sort. That idea was so drilled into their head as inaccessible that it seemed ridiculous to even consider. On the most basic level, this is a missed economic opportunity. Entrepreneurship represents one of the most transformative pathways to creating wealth for African Americans, particularly the kind of intergenerational wealth that can lift families out of poverty and into the middle class. According to *The Tapestry of Black Business Ownership in America*, the median net worth for African American business owners is twelve times higher than black non–business owners. And while white families typically have thirteen times the household wealth than black families in America, when those black households are run by entrepreneurs, the gap is only three times higher. If African Americans and other visible minorities experienced entrepreneurship on par with their share of the population, Rockeymoore said they would create more than a million additional businesses, which could employ nine million more Americans.

"It behooves us to think about what kind of social statement we are making by allowing certain groups of entrepreneurs to succeed while others don't," said Rockeymoore, who thinks popular messaging about seeking venture capital as the ticket to entrepreneurship is "bullshit" for African Americans, who typically have no access to those contacts, networks, and communities of money. As the dismal diversity of the venture capital industry's deals and dealmakers shows, even when they get in the door, black entrepreneurs are rarely given access to them. Without that capital, many African American entrepreneurs were destined to remain in a state of limbo, unable to fully realize their dreams because they lacked the wealth and privilege to take a bigger risk. The irony of all this was often too much for Rockeymoore to witness.

"We came to this country without pay to work," she said, reminding me that the entire community was taken across the Atlantic in chains because someone wanted to make a profit. "We are the only class of people who were once considered capital."

DURING MY WEEK IN NEW ORLEANS, I kept hearing the same word when I spoke about female African American entrepreneurs: community. It was a word I'd heard Dupart use repeatedly, as well as the other salon owners I was speaking with during my visit. It began with the type of business they started, which reflected the needs of the community they lived in. These entrepreneurs build businesses to serve that market, because they were the market. Despite their spending power and the size of the black beauty market, African American women have been grossly underserved by the global beauty industry. Large companies have been reluctant to produce products that cater to the needs of black women, whose skin tones and hair structure are completely incompatible with everything from lipstick shades to shampoos targeted at the white population.

Frustrated by these problems, Kristen Jones Miller partnered with her friend Amanda Johnson to launch Mented in 2017, selling organic lipsticks to match diverse skin tones. Even though Miller and Johnson met at Harvard Business School and had experience in the beauty and retail industry, they faced an uphill battle when raising funding, pitching Mented to more than eighty venture capitalists, who all told them why it couldn't be successful. "Because we are women of color solving a problem of women of color, the rooms we were walking into weren't able to look at the idea in the same way," she said. "I'm not a white guy from Stanford making a mobile app that does blah blah blah. I can't divorce the fact that I'm a woman of color entrepreneur from the fact that I'm serving women of color. That's different from building a business serving everyone and anyone," Miller told me. "I feel like I'm at an extreme advantage compared to my Harvard classmates pursuing markets that don't look like them. They're learning everything about consumers from industry reports and surveys. I'm an expert in being a woman of color and how shitty the beauty business is to women of color. I get up feeling like I'm at an advantage because I know the consumer and problem well."

One afternoon in New Orleans, I had coffee with Niki Da'Jon, who was in the midst of growing her online hair extension business LA Shop Hair Boutique. Da'Jon was twenty-eight years old, wore a necklace with a small gold "Lady Boss" pendant, and was finishing up her MBA at Loyola University, where she majored in entrepreneurship. She told me how she had started the business a year before, following the family path of entrepreneurship (her parents had owned a small tailoring shop that made choir robes but shifted to construction after Katrina). Da'Jon was planning on opening a new kind of beauty supply store after graduation.

The idea came after she was repeatedly greeted with suspicion and hostility at beauty supply stores, something that many black women say is common, especially in stores that are often owned and operated by individuals outside the African American community (Koreans, for example, have a strong presence in the industry). "Why do I not feel valued in my own community, with my own women and store?" she asked. "Why can't there be an African American–owned beauty store? Why didn't the store reflect me? Why is it my demographic that patronizes this store, but doesn't own something like this?" Her idea was to open a beauty supply store that not only welcomed women like her but could serve as a hub for mentoring about topics like self-esteem and entrepreneurship to the young women who came there.

Compared with her MBA classmates, who pitched the type of tech-centric businesses tailored to venture capital, Da'Jon was offering herself up as a model and face in the community. "I want to own this so a little black girl can own something in the community, reflect her community, and give back to the community," she said. "In my community, entrepreneurship is the path forward. [Entrepreneurs] are the hope of the community, because they took in their own hands to better the life of the community. That's especially important in a city with a lot of social assistance. It is not about what someone gives you, it's empowerment."

For the female entrepreneurs in New Orleans's black hair business, empowering the community took many shapes. It was the products and services they made to serve that community, but also the physical spaces of business, which served as what sociologists call "third places": the spots outside of work and home that fulfill the needs of a community to gather, socialize, and forge interpersonal bonds. For African Americans the barbershop and beauty salon have long been that third place. "Part of what a beauty shop represents is physical space under black control," said Tiffany Gill, a professor of history and Africana studies at the University of Delaware, whose book *Beauty Shop Politics* chronicled the evolution of the black beauty salon as a community hub. They are the places where African American women feel most at home, where judgment is withheld, where politics and money and sexuality and any other topic can be freely discussed, and everyone is equal when seated in the stylist's chair.

One of those places was a salon in the city's northeast called Beauty on de Bayou. Located a few blocks from the waters of Lake Pontchartrain, the small, windowless building with its hand-painted signs specialized in natural hair, a subset of the African American beauty market that omitted chemical straighteners and other products meant to "tame" hair, to focus on hair health, curls, and pride. The salon had been opened in 2007 by Dwana Makeba, a woman who held a number of careers over the years, including stints as a professor of African American studies, a tour manager to Harry Belafonte and Tupac Shakur, and a real estate agent. But Makeba always did hair, starting in college, and despite her master's degree, she set up shop in this very poor corner of the city to continue the tradition of her grandmother, who'd owned a salon in the city's 9th Ward.

Makeba, who wore her graying dreadlocks wrapped in a bun, characterized herself as a "culture bearer" as well as an entrepreneur. She saw her primary job as building a safe space for the community, especially after Hurricane Katrina had devastated the neighborhood. "I wanted to be part of the rebuilding process," she said, "to be an anchor in my community." Everyone was welcome at Beauty on de Bayou, and its customers were all treated equally, regardless of whether they were politicians, cops, drug dealers, strippers, teachers, preachers, or their mothers, daughters, or sisters. It wasn't uncommon for a judge, a lawyer, and someone about to stand trial to be sitting next to each other in her chairs. During the 2016 election, Makeba recalled styling a woman who was a Trump supporter, arguing her case to the other women there. "People just said, 'Well, someone has to be on the other side,'" recalled Makeba. "That's the meaning of a safe space. She wouldn't have said that in front of other black women elsewhere."

"Every kind of conversation goes on here," said Aretha, an older woman with a gravelly voice whom everyone called Big Red, as she was having her hair shampooed by one of the stylists. "I mean every kind! Politically, socially, sexually. . . ." Personally, she preferred to talk about football, and the Saints' chances of a Super Bowl appearance.

In the nearby neighborhood of Gentilly, Tanya Haynes credited the dislocation caused by Hurricane Katrina with clarifying the place in the city's fabric of Friends, her well-known salon. "I realized that Friends salon is the hub of the community for women," Haynes said. Friends' clientele were upper-middle-class black professionals who trend conservative in their looks and include the mayor of New Orleans, LaToya Cantrell, who had been elected weeks before I arrived. Haynes does soft hair (unlike the hard styles Dupart does), plays smooth jazz, gospel, and R&B, and doesn't allow children in the shop, so the women can truly be themselves there. These women will linger for hours longer than their treatments require, gossiping, eating meals they bring in, even reading

novels or doing work in the supportive environment Haynes has cultivated. Like Makeba, she never asks twice if someone cannot pay, and
when a customer or their relative dies, Haynes will personally style the
deceased for the funeral.

For Haynes, being an entrepreneur meant you built something "of
your own" in the community and gave that community back the love
it had given you. There was a financial windfall from that, no doubt,
but emotionally the dividends were greater. A few years after opening
Friends, Haynes's son Jared had been murdered in one of the many
shootings that plague the black population of New Orleans. When she
returned to the salon after a month of mourning, customers showed up
in droves, to give Haynes their business, of course, but mostly to hug
and hold her, as she cried in their arms. "That's an amazing thing; the
love of women," she said, tearing up at the memory. "It's not your grandmother, but it feels like Grandma. It's not your aunt, but it feels like your
aunt. It's not your sister, but it feels like your sister." There was no sepa-
ration between business and life. These women were more than customers. They were a real community.

"There's a different kind of burden on black entrepreneurs that
doesn't exist for others," Tiffany Gill told me, "a certain accountability to the community." In her interviews with African American salon
owners across America for her book, Gill came across a common expectation that these women use their businesses, and the money generated
from them, to strengthen the communities they live in. Economically
that meant keeping dollars within the community, supporting local entrepreneurs by spending money at their businesses, and building a truly
communal pot of wealth, one purchase at a time. In turn, these entrepreneurs supported the community by providing goods and services
locals demanded, while doing what they could to offer broader help to
those around them: employing locals, supporting social causes, providing a political voice, even sponsoring the Little League team or Mardi
Gras band.

Jesseca Dupart's ties to her community were strong, and she constantly preached them online, shouting out others who had businesses

nearby, like Supa Cent (who now owned a successful makeup company called the Crayon Case in the same plaza), as well as representing New Orleans and the black women who made it work. "I feel a hundred percent responsibility to the community to make sure we are *straight*," she told me, starting with the fact that she was here for the long haul to build her business. "We probably got a handful of people doing really big shit here. I want everybody to get that. I could move to L.A. or Atlanta, but I wanna stay here so some of that could rub off."

We had just walked into a salon a few miles from her business called Trina Bout That Hair Life Studio, which is where Dupart went to get styled several times a week by Katrina Harris, the owner. The salon was long and bright, and the walls were painted hot pink. Half a dozen women sat in chairs and under dryers, while a TV played reality shows. A young man named David was eating a plate of nachos with his hair in curlers, while someone else's daughter was doing her school homework. Dupart sat down in a chair, and Harris began the two-hour process of applying a new weave to her hair . . . raven black with purple and blue streaks, for an event Dupart was going to later that night. Harris braided Dupart's natural hair into tight rows, applied a glue to the sides and around the scalp, put on a stocking cap, and left that to dry.

"Hey, this hairpiece is too small, it looks like a toupee!" Dupart said, as Harris began stitching the hairpiece around the cap.

"It's not my fault you have a big head!" Harris said and kept weaving.

Dupart wasn't really worried. After all, she had been Harris's boss for two years at Kaleidoscope, giving the younger stylist her first job in a salon. When Dupart closed her salon to focus on hair products in 2017, she encouraged Harris to open her own business. Dupart coached her through the process, helped Harris with finances, and mentored her at every step of the way. Dupart even sent clients her way through social media and was encouraging Harris, who is far more shy than Dupart, to push her online branding to the next level.

Harris's ambitions weren't as grand as Dupart's. Success for her meant being able to live comfortably, to have the time and freedom to raise her ten-year-old daughter, to wake up each day and not have to

worry about money. To be in control of her destiny. The salon had already given her that. "It means a lot to me, pulling up to the doors each
day and seeing my name on the sign," she said, applying more adhesive
to Dupart's scalp, who winced at the glue's heat. "That means everything to me."

David went out and brought everyone back snowballs, the insanely
sweet frozen drinks that are the lifeblood of extended salon sessions in
this sweltering city. As Dupart sipped hers under the dryer, working social media on both her phones, I asked why she helped Harris and others
like her. Especially when the common myth was that entrepreneurship
was a zero-sum game of winners and losers, where competition between
business owners was so fierce, there was no room for helping others,
especially in the same industry and market as you. It flew in the face of
the great heroes of the startup myth—Jobs, Musk, Zuckerberg—whose
ruthless ascents to dominance were littered with those they left behind
in their dust without regard for the consequences.

"The most important thing to protect about the business, no matter
how big I get, is to still be relatable," she said. "I don't want anyone to
say, 'Oh that bitch made it, but left us behind!' Not in a poverty-stricken
city like this one." That meant more than just inspiring other women to
become entrepreneurs via her Instagram affirmations. It meant holding
their hand and acting as a mentor, teaching them about what it took
to succeed beyond the slogans, down to the nitty-gritty of tax strategies, legal liabilities, and marketing budgets. Dupart called it "bringing
people up," which was a term I'd heard other women use around New
Orleans.

Adia Harvey Wingfield, a sociologist at Washington University who
wrote the book *Doing Business with Beauty*, noted that this willingness
in the African American beauty business to help other women become
entrepreneurs is fairly common across the industry and over its history.
She labeled this phenomenon a "helping ideology." "Simply put, owners
placed more value on the ability to help other black women achieve salon
ownership than in the financial gains stylists brought them," she wrote.
"Given the American emphasis on competitiveness, individualism, and

gendered racist messages that exhort black women to see one another as rivals, this ethic is quite remarkable and incredibly noble." When I spoke to Wingfield by phone, she expanded on this, noting that the helping ideology was an antidote to the discrimination African American women faced as entrepreneurs. "It is opening up a niche that allows them to thwart the system" that typically shut them out.

At Beauty on de Bayou, Dwana Makeba was practicing the helping ideology with her stylists, Yonnie "Da Hair Genie" and Morgan "Mo Beauty" Dylan, coaching them in entrepreneurship and even paying for them to attend financial literacy classes. "She involves you," Yonnie said. "She's the salon owner who develops potential. You'd think working under an owner it's just business, but it's more than that." Before working at Beauty on de Bayou, Yonnie had a minimum-wage job at a smoothie stand. Now she was planning to open her own business selling hair weaves. "She brought out something in me that I didn't see in myself," she said. Makeba was setting up a summer camp for young girls, to teach them self-esteem, beauty care, the fundamentals of entrepreneurship, and how to monetize what she called their "black girl magic." "I am a black girl from the 9th Ward," Makeba said, when I asked her why she did this with no clear financial incentive. "Statistically the system is not set up so I can succeed. I have an obligation to reach out to others who look like me, like Yonnie and Morgan, to help them get up."

All around New Orleans, this is what I heard, time and again. "I was put on this earth to help build people up," said Julia Clavo, a model and entrepreneur in the clothing, retail, and cosmetics business, who sold a line of makeup called Spicy Dark. "I'm not chasing money. My ambition is for me and the things I love. I am Martin Luther King and Maya Angelou. They paved the way that we can achieve things to put good in the world. So I *have* to give these girls my knowledge. I'm never too busy to help someone. That's my motto and it's a major responsibility, because if I give out knowledge more will come back to me." Niki Da'Jon told me that entrepreneurship was "the bridge to link who you are with where you're trying to go, with those coming behind you, who don't know how to get there." She was driven to be an entrepreneur to build that bridge.

For Dupart, the helping ideology began at the Kaleidoscope Salon, where she helped her employees like Supa Cent and Harris to branch out on their own. "Supa is the perfect example," Dupart said, noting that her friend now had fame and fortune that rivaled her own. "This girl had no idea she could reach that. When she did, I told her, 'Now that you're here, find ten people and touch them.' Look at Trina . . . she'll be the next millionaire if I push her hard enough. That's why I opened my own shop and pushed them to open theirs. I wanted everyone to eat."

Dupart never imagined she would ever be making millions of dollars a year. She wanted what most young black women in New Orleans wanted: a stable life that she was in control of and a place of her own. But as Kaleidoscope took off, she embraced the money and fame as the best way to bring more women like her up into entrepreneurship. It began organically a few years back, when women started asking her business questions in her social media feed. So she set up a private group on a messaging app, called Judy's Room, where she dispensed advice for female entrepreneurs. She started holding contests on Instagram where the winners were given business coaching sessions and then offered her consulting services by phone, email, and video chat for a nominal fee to other women, posting before and after progress reports of these women's businesses and the revenues they generated year over year.

All of this culminated early in 2018, when Dupart set off on a free lecture series across America called "U Better Get This Free Knowledge Tour." Crowds of women lined up for hours in New York, Atlanta, Los Angeles, Chicago, Houston, Baton Rouge, and New Orleans to hear Dupart speak. More than five thousand people came out during the tour, with venues reaching capacity in every single city. At each event Dupart shared her story and the lessons she learned along the way, from the inspirational ("Pray Through the Process") to the mundane (how to incorporate legally). "My eyes hurt because of the flash from all those pictures with people," Dupart said, but it was immensely rewarding. She pulled up a video of the final event at a church in New Orleans, where she entered in a red trench coat and blond extensions following a second-line brass band, sat on a white throne, and cried.

"When I did my first million, I said, 'I gotta do more,'" Dupart said, "but nothing was more gratifying than that moment, when I could walk into a room with all my peers who wanted to learn something from me, in this city."

A year later, Dupart launched a follow-up tour of ten cities. "THE REASON IM DOING THE CLASS FOR YALL and Giving ALL this game I have away is to build leaders that will build other leaders," Dupart wrote on Instagram when she announced the tour, which sold out all fifteen thousand tickets in five minutes. "Lets create wealth and greatness in 2019. I want us all to be winning." In the comments below, one Instagram fan posted that "She's OUR Madame CJ Walker," which instantly made Dupart tear up (later, she would pose as Walker next to a framed photo of the icon on Instagram, in a wig Harris made). Helping women achieve all she had achieved as an entrepreneur was now her mission. One that she thanked God for daily. "I like to be able to build other [people's] companies," she said. "Your profit is my success, even if I don't see a cent of it. It's real satisfying." In February of 2019, she published a book with her advice on social media marketing.

ON MY LAST MORNING IN New Orleans, I went to City Hall, where Dupart was waiting to receive a citation from City Council for her work in the community. She sat next to her mother and daughter, fingernails tap-tap-tapping on her phones, dressed in a rainbow off-the-shoulder dress, orange Gucci stiletto boots, and a blond extension Harris had put in. As city councillors handed out awards to artists, environmentalists, food truck festival organizers, a voodoo priest, and other community builders, I asked Dupart's mother, Evelyn, where her daughter's desire to help others came from.

"I think she has a heart to see other people succeed as well," she said, noting that it was something they never really discussed openly. She was always generous, but the things she had recently done, including the tour, giving away five hundred bikes at Christmas to children, or simply buying clothes for poor women who contacted her online, pointed to a deeper sense of gratitude driven by her good fortune. "She'll say 'Who am I?' to me," Evelyn said. "She had no formal education or college training, and she's built a multimillion-dollar business. She's that unexpected flower in the desert."

After receiving the proclamation for her work as an entrepreneur and philanthropist, Dupart was approached by Mayor-elect LaToya Cantrell, who told her that she represented the real fabric of New Orleans and the ability to build the kind of "transferrable wealth" in the community that closed the gap of inequality. "When you have women like you as the heartbeat of the economy, demonstrating a commitment to the community . . . well, that keeps the entrepreneurial spirit going and going," said Mayor Cantrell, who told Dupart to reach out if she ever needed anything.

As she gathered with her family in the hallway after, Dupart was flushed with emotion. "That was awesome," she said, wiping away a tear. The night before she hardly seemed to care about the citation— just another event, another bit of content to post on social media—but the city's recognition suddenly sparked a fire in her and deepened her desire to take her commitment to the community to the next level. She and Supa Cent were already talking about a bigger toy drive for Christmas, but now that they had the mayor onboard, why not something huge? Like the Superdome and marching bands and Saints players! And not just toys, but things the community really needed, like toiletries, clothes, and diapers!

You can see the videos and photos she posted on Instagram eight months later. The lineups of thousands of families, the confetti and the marching band, the football players, the piles of toys and household goods, Dupart and Supa posing in half a dozen outfits, including the obligatory Santa hats. They gave away 5,019 toys in an hour, a Guinness World Record, and documented every moment of it for social media (never squander a marketing opportunity). Dupart vowed to go even bigger next year. Her platform was only growing. She had expanded into real estate investing, signed bigger deals with distributors, and was now eyeing national retail contracts. *Forbes* had interviewed her about social media marketing for entrepreneurs, and she had recently appeared on the *Today* show, talking about helping other women become entrepreneurs. Her events took on the tenor of tent revivals, with thousands listening as she preached the gospel of entrepreneurship, concluding with a prayer for their own businesses.

"I wasn't given these blessings just for me," Dupart said, as a young man posed for a selfie with her outside City Hall. "You are responsible as a successful person to pay it forward . . . period! As an entrepreneur I have to tell *everybody* you can do whatever you want." Dupart had no intention of slowing down or settling for anything less than going as high as possible. The community she could affect just kept growing, and there were a lot of women just like her, potential entrepreneurs who didn't even know that it was their time to come up.

PART III

GROWING

CHAPTER 5

Serving and Leading

A DOZEN MEN and a solitary woman sat around folding tables in a conference room by the entrance of the Calvary Church in Souderton, Pennsylvania, drinking coffee and eating bagels and donuts from Wawa, a beloved chain of gas stations. They were employees of NCC Automated Systems, a nearby company that designed and assembled conveyors. At the center of the group sat Kevin Mauger, the forty-six-year-old owner and president of NCC, who was dressed in a blue button-down shirt and jeans. Mauger is slender and of medium height, with slightly curly hair and the faintest hint of a goatee. When the clock hit nine, Mauger stood up with his coffee cup and addressed the group.

"Good morning," he said, making sure to look everyone in the eye. "I do think everything starts with culture." Mauger paused to look around the tables again. "The main point of establishing an ownership culture is to create an environment where people really feel part of something . . . so they can make a difference . . . put more time and passion into their work . . . and so work, for all of us, will become a better place, but only if we can get the workforce into the mindset that they can do great things. Because most of us in the workforce are not in the mindset . . . not engaged."

This group had been selected to establish the culture of the company's new Employee Stock Ownership Plan (ESOP), which Mauger had formally announced a year before, and would eventually shift the ownership of NCC from Mauger to its seventy-five–odd employees. The committee's work was to be entirely employee-owner led, and there were various roles represented here, from assembly line technicians in work boots and bandannas to senior managers in loafers and slacks.

"I believe that when you create something yourself, you believe in that, and make it happen. It's up to you to be smart, and turn the culture into what *you* want it to be," Mauger said, softly repeating, "It's up to you."

This speech could be mistaken for the most generic kind of corporate discourse, but I believed it was something more. In fact, I had driven an hour from the center of Philadelphia first thing this morning to sit in a megachurch conference room to hear it, because I was trying to glimpse a piece of the entrepreneur's soul that is typically private and personal: their values.

Since entrepreneurs wield ultimate control over the decisions in their business, their personal values inform nearly everything about their work, in a way that no company that answers to VC funders or shareholders can: the business they end up creating or running, the products and services they sell, the way they structure that business, who they work with and how they work with them, the way they use money, and what the ultimate fate of their business is over the long term.

Jesseca Dupart's values around community made her use the gains from Kaleidoscope to help other women, while Obolsky's values around lifestyle shaped everything from the flavors of her croissants to the hours of her bakery. The Alsoufi family consciously put their Syrian heritage at the core of their restaurant, because they valued it more than any desire to appeal to the broadest audience, while Nikhil Aggarwal and Andrew Chizewer built Scheme because they deeply believed it could help students who were at a disadvantage.

In recent years, Silicon Valley's startup myth had distorted the perception of an entrepreneur's values. On the one hand, you had the emergence of a highly visible class of social entrepreneurs, with an explicit mission, whose products were essentially selling values. On the other hand, you saw the growing orthodoxy that values should be subservient to growth—or worse, simply marketing buzzwords intended to achieve it—and the only value that truly matters is turning a profit. What brought me to the Philadelphia suburbs was the missing piece in between: a chance to witness how everyday entrepreneurs realized their personal values through their businesses and what that meant for their soul.

NCC AUTOMATED SYSTEMS OCCUPIES FIFTY thousand feet of low-lying, industrial space on a country road, bordered by farm fields, slaughter-houses, and a turkey bacon processing plant. The building is split between a narrow warren of offices and a huge warehouse and shop floor, filled with worktables, giant water cutting machines, welding stations, buckets of small components, sheets of steel and aluminum, and several American flags hanging from the rafters.

"What we do here is simple," Kevin Mauger said, as we walked around the facility in hard hats. "We're taking raw metal and plastic, cutting it, bending it, and building conveyor systems out of it." As Mauger corrected me several times during our tour, a conveyor system is more than a conveyor belt. The conveyor system is the entire apparatus that moves products from one end of an assembly line to the other, often in wild, looping configurations that bend over and under, up and down, and round and round to fit into a facility, like gigantic Rube Goldberg machines. A conveyor belt is just one piece of that; the rubber or metal tread that some goods move along.

If you need something moved across a factory or warehouse in an automated fashion—frozen dinners, ramen noodles, pregnancy tests, prescription lenses—NCC will build you the system to move it. "That includes everything from the conveyor itself, to small machines to do a specific task, like turn a Reese's Peanut Butter Cup in its package around," Mauger said. Food manufacturing and optical assembly made up the bulk of the company's work.

Mauger was not NCC's founder. That was Bob Ryan, who started the company in 1986 after working as a salesman for a conveyor belt company. Mauger grew up nearby and met Ryan by knocking on his door when he was still in college. The twenty-year-old mechanical engineering student had recently found out his girlfriend was pregnant and had started a handyman business to earn cash. "I went from living in a frat house in my junior year of college with forty guys to living off campus with a baby in senior year," Mauger told me, as we sat in his office, which featured several photos of his wife, Danielle, and their three adult children, Philadelphia Eagles paraphernalia, and the usual inspirational office posters ("Rule #1: If We Don't Take Care of the Customer, Someone Else Will . . ."), industry awards, and pictures of Tasty Cakes moving along NCC-built conveyors.

After doing work around his house all summer, Ryan told Mauger to give him a call if he wanted a job after college. "I graduated Friday and came in to work here on a Monday," Mauger said. It was 1994 and he never left. Back then NCC was a smaller company, with fifteen employees and $3 million in annual sales. Mauger described Ryan as a visionary founder, with the charisma of a born salesman, and the shoot-first-and-ask-questions-later management style of one, too. According to Mauger, Ryan's core value was "There's always a way." He refused to tell a customer no, resulting in frequent all-nighters by NCC's staff to realize Ryan's lofty promises. "We fought uphill all the way," Mauger recalled. "We always came through for the customer, but it wasn't easy." For his first fifteen years at the company, Mauger worked every single Saturday and many nights. Burnout at NCC was remarkably high, leading to frequent turnover. "I think that 'Nothing's gonna stand in my way' attitude is an admirable aspect once you've made a commitment," Mauger said, "but it's no recipe for long-term success." Though Mauger loved Ryan and remains close to his family since his passing, he was an example of the values Mauger did not want to embody.

Mauger was a loyal, successful, and largely content employee at NCC who never harbored ambitions to be an entrepreneur. But in 1999, Ryan sold the company to a competitor, in what Mauger described as an "unsuccessful acquisition," and by 2006, NCC was insolvent and millions in debt. Fearing the consequences if it failed, while sensing an opportunity to turn things around, Mauger bought NCC Automated Systems, financing the purchase with a home equity loan.

Suddenly Mauger went from being an employee without one person reporting to him, to the sole owner of the only place he had ever worked. I asked him what the transition to being an entrepreneur felt like. "I was proud of myself," he said, "never fearful, never intimidated, and probably ignorant of all the risks and challenges I'd undertaken. But I was excited for the possibility of the future and to have an impact on that. I was excited to change the culture of the company to one of trust and credibility, but back then, I didn't even know that culture was in the vocabulary. I just knew I didn't like it."

Mauger assembled the company's seventeen employees on the shop floor and made a brief speech announcing the sale. He spoke about the financial situation in vague terms and how everyone had to be more careful going forward. This was a fresh start for NCC. "It wasn't too deep or too visionary," he said. "It was 'Let's get down to business.' Honestly, I wasn't sure what leadership meant."

Mauger approached NCC's turnaround as an engineering project, which could be solved by putting the proper systems, processes, and procedures in place. "I was focused on how to do things, on the technical process," he said. "If we'd continued in that vein, it would have become the proverbial company with me and fifty people helping." Values were the furthest thing from his mind. He dug in, paying off NCC's debt, returning to profitability, and growing sales from $5 million in 2006 to nearly $30 million by 2018. But as the company's balance sheet improved, Mauger sensed something missing. "I realized that I was such a far cry from a leader, it wasn't even funny," he said, reflecting a slow-growing realization that Kevin Mauger actually had no idea what he stood for as an entrepreneur.

THINK OF FAMOUS ENTREPRENEURS, AND their values seem apparent. Thomas Edison valued invention, Henry Ford valued efficiency, while Steve Jobs valued aesthetics. Many successful entrepreneurs have multiple sets of values, contrasting their approach to business with their philanthropy. Andrew Carnegie and John D. Rockefeller were some of the most vicious titans who ever lived, brutally suppressing workers while giving millions to establish vital public services like libraries and parks around the world. Warren Buffett is a market fundamentalist with few moral constraints when investing on behalf of Berkshire Hathaway, yet he is a paragon of personal giving, inspiring those like Bill Gates and Mark Zuckerberg to part with large amounts of their fortunes in the name of charity. Even the Koch brothers, whose money has eliminated pollution regulations and killed public transit projects, give millions to support the arts.

Then there are other entrepreneurs, like the African American hair mogul Madam C. J. Walker, who used their companies to further social causes close to their hearts. Many of these entrepreneurs had values clearly rooted in their religious faith, like W. K. Kellogg, a vegetarian Seventh Day Adventist who created Corn Flakes as a way to promote a whole grain diet (which he believed would help curb the sin of masturbation). But a lot of what we think about today around entrepreneurial values came out of the Baby Boomer generation and the businesses they founded following the counterculture movement of the late 1960s, which sought to marry capitalism with a more altruistic sense of purpose.

A figurehead of this era is Yvon Chouinard, the founder of the outdoor clothing company Patagonia, whose memoir *Let My People Go Surfing* has become a bible for the values-centric entrepreneur. Chouinard was a vagabond California rock climber and surfer, whose business life began in the mid-1960s by making hand-forged rock climbing tools in Yosemite National Park, where he would camp out for weeks at a time under boulders, selling enough tools to buy food, beer, and climbing supplies. Eventually, the company branched out into clothing, until its fleece vests became a uniform for skiers, yuppie dads, and venture capitalists everywhere.

From early on, Chouinard established Patagonia as a company that stood for something greater than its products. "I've been a businessman for almost sixty years," Chouinard wrote. "I've never respected the profession. It's business that has to take the majority of the blame for being the enemy of nature, for destroying native cultures, for taking from the poor and giving to the rich, and for poisoning the earth with the effluent from its factories. Yet business can produce food, cure disease, control population, employ people, and generally enrich our lives. And it can do these good things and make a profit without losing its soul."

Chouinard shaped Patagonia around his personal values, which included a desire to be fun (the opposite of the "pasty-faced" businessmen in airline magazines), a commitment to the well-being of employees (paid well, subsidized daycare and healthy food, flexible time to surf or ski or take care of family), and improving the working conditions along Patagonia's supply chain (fair wages, safe factories). Chouinard's environmentalism is baked into everything Patagonia does: developing fleece made from recycled plastics and switching to organic cotton, starting a repair and buyback program for its products, making charitable contributions to various environmental and conservation causes. The week I was in Philadelphia, the newspaper carried a story about Patagonia donating the $10 million it expected to receive from President Trump's tax cuts back to environmental groups. Far more than the cut and colors of its products or the jagged peaks that adorn its logo, Patagonia is a brand that stands for the values of its creator.

Other companies that symbolize the Baby Boomer generation's progressive brand of entrepreneurial values include the early incarnations of Ben & Jerry's, the Body Shop, and Whole Foods, but there are

countless entrepreneurs who design their businesses as a way to implement their personal values. One of the best known in Philadelphia is
Judy Wicks, whom I spoke with over tea in her historic brick townhouse
packed with art, collectibles, and a pair of friendly dogs. Wicks is nationally known as a champion of local businesses and the founder of
the nonprofit BALLE (you heard from its director, Rodney Foxworth, in
chapter 3), but her journey to values-led entrepreneurship began in 1970,
after she had been living with Eskimos in Alaska.

Wicks and her then-husband Richard Hayne had just moved to Philadelphia, where they opened the Free People's Store, which sold products that appealed to hippies (Bob Dylan records, macramé planters,
vintage clothes, rolling papers). There were free bins for people to swap
goods, bulletin boards to organize antiwar protests and art gatherings,
and the entire shop was tied into the peace movement. "Our values were
baked right into it from the start," Wicks told me. "I mean, our logo was
a dove." Everything was governed by the same antibusiness ethos that
informed Chouinard at Patagonia, with the duo vowing to only take the
minimum profit needed to sustain themselves.

Within a few years, Wicks's and Hayne's lives diverged, as he took
the store in a more commercial direction and pushed her out of the
business and marriage, she says. He eventually turned the Free People's
Store into the global retailer Urban Outfitters, maintaining the trappings of its youth culture (rolling papers, records), while ditching the
anti-corporate values. Wicks eventually opened up the White Dog Café,
which became a pioneer of the local, sustainable food movement, as well
as a laboratory for how she could implement her own values through the
restaurant business.

"From then on, having my work truly reflect what I stand for as a
person became an essential aspect of my career," she wrote in her memoir *Good Morning, Beautiful Business*. "You can find a way to make economic exchange one of the most satisfying, meaningful, and loving of
human interactions." Staff were given regular raises and increasing benefits, and the business became a rallying point for many causes close
to Wicks's heart, from fair trade for the Mexican coffee farmers that

supplied the Café's beans, to local neighborhood preservation efforts, which stopped wrecking balls from demolishing historic homes. She purchased renewable energy long before it became popular, printed menus with environmentally friendly ink, and pegged the ratio of the highest salary at the restaurant to the lowest at 5:1.

"It comes down to decision making," Wicks said, digging her teaspoon into a jar of unpasteurized honey from a local farmer she knew. "Not just the question of 'Does this raise profits?' but how a decision affects neighbors, customers, the environment, and staff. Those questions were always on my mind," and central to her life as an entrepreneur. "To me, my business was the way I expressed my love for the world," she said. "That's the way that a business is beautiful: when an entrepreneur expresses their love for life."

This brand of socially conscious capitalism has become romanticized over the past twenty years or so, as a generation of individuals with strong values began to see entrepreneurship as the vehicle for achieving a desired change, in a way that married the dynamism of business with the broad developmental goals that had previously been the realm of governments and multinational organizations. As organizations such as Ashoka and Muhammad Yunus's Grameen Bank began to encourage, educate, and fund individuals building companies and organizations dedicated to creating solutions for pressing social problems (such as green energy technology or maternal health in a particular community in the Brazilian Amazon), the term "social entrepreneur" began to be widely applied to these ventures. By the 2000s, nearly every university was offering courses, specializations, and degrees in social entrepreneurship.

"It's human nature, like spreading DNA, to spread your values," said Marina Kim, who started Stanford's social entrepreneurship program and now runs Ashoka's programming on university campuses. Over the past decade, Kim has seen tremendous growth in interest from students, schools, and businesses in approaching entrepreneurship from a values-led perspective. "There's something powerful about when you create an organization or a movement. It takes on the personal characteristics of the founder. It's life giving, because you feel you are creating pockets of the world of how you like to position it."

Cheryl Yaffe Kiser, who runs the social innovation lab at Babson College, grew up as the daughter of entrepreneurs in the natural foods business who were driven by their values. Her parents were selling kefir and kamut long before the hippies came around, but something is different today. "We now have front-row seats to a lot of the problems that are plaguing the world," she said. "It is hard to do business as usual and not think about this. It's a narrative that's constantly here. It's not going to go away. It will constantly increase." These systemic problems—health care access, income inequality, climate change—are continually on the minds of her students, who come to her wanting to make a genuine difference in the world. "There is a lot of desire and energy around wanting to start values-based companies, solving problems that are persistent in society," Kiser said, pausing, before rhetorically asking, "When they leave here, is that what they're doing? I'm not sure."

Kiser explained that when social entrepreneurship began emerging as a concept in the late 1980s, it was based on the principle that you could use the agility, creativity, and other advantages of entrepreneurship to tackle systemic issues more effectively than large organizations. The first generation of social entrepreneurs set up nonprofits, foundations, and other noncommercial organizations to tackle these challenges. But after the Cold War ended, neoliberalism took hold as the dominant economic and political ideology, coinciding with the first great startup rush of the dot-com boom. Silicon Valley's mantra to "Change the World" began to be uttered from the lips of every man and woman pitching a company, almost as an oath of tribal initiation.

This shifted social entrepreneurship from a model of service focused on systemic change to one of commerce focused on benevolent consumption. In his book *The Conscience Economy*, Steven Overman wrote that "doing good is the new status symbol," driven by a "global wave of young entrepreneurs who symbolize the optimism for positive change." Welcome to the wear-your-fleece-and-feel-good-about-it lifestyle of benevolent capitalism.

A common version of this too-good-to-be-true practice is called One for One, pioneered in 2006 by the shoe company TOMS. Blake Mycoskie, a wealthy serial entrepreneur, took a break from his latest startup (an online driver education program that promoted hybrid vehicles) to visit Argentina, where he saw children in a village without shoes. "Why not create a *for-profit* business to help provide shoes for these children?" Mycoskie wrote in his book *Start Something That Matters*. "In other words, maybe the solution was in entrepreneurship, not charity." Living on a sailboat in Los Angeles, Mycoskie cooked up a simple formula that would inspire countless startups over the next decade: for every pair of shoes TOMS sold, they would donate another pair to a child in need. This philanthropic bent was the key to TOMS's success, more than the designs of its shoes, because it sold a value, rather than a product.

Other companies that have built businesses around this model are Warby Parker (buy glasses, give glasses), Nouri Bar (buy a nutrition bar, feed a hungry child), Sir Richard's (buy condoms, provide free condoms), Charity Water, and hundreds more. Scarves to women in Afghanistan? Sure. Buy a pair of jeans and clean up the ocean? Go for it! These stories make for great PR, anchoring the websites of these largely ecommerce-based brands, and allow their founders to sit on endless panels at conferences, talking about how they are changing the world, complete with smiling photos of poor children wearing their shoes. These business models also work with the expectations of venture capitalists, because the costs associated with the giveaways are simply a marketing expense tied to growth.

Daniela Papi-Thornton, who has taught social entrepreneurship at Oxford and Yale, calls this phenomenon "heropreneurship," a subspecies of the startup myth focused almost exclusively on the individual as the main actor in social progress. Papi-Thornton came to this realization by being a participant in it during her twenties, when she raised funds on a bike trip to build a school in Cambodia. Only later did she realize what the Cambodian village actually needed were teachers, something she never bothered to ask the locals about. "It's easy to build a building," she said, but real systemic changes . . . the kind that actually have a long-term impact, "take relationships and systems thinking, but also commitment. You couldn't just come in from outside, plop down, and solve a problem." As she began to teach social entrepreneurship this is exactly what she saw: people approaching problems with solutions that made them an individualized hero.

"I call it the Silicon Valley–ization of the social sector," Papi-Thornton said, noting that she frequently has MBA students coming to her saying they want to be social entrepreneurs . . . they just need to figure out the right social issue and business plan first. Many tell her they want to solve a problem in Africa (usually presented as a generic place called "Africa") because it has the most sizzle, when the same problem might be more effectively addressed in their own backyard or by organizations and governments already working in Mozambique or Somalia. "We've done something wrong if it's become a game where you pull an issue out of a box and a business model out of another," she said. "In the social impact world, you have this claim of the impact you'll make, but so many people at the core just want to be entrepreneurs. That's the difference. There's a huge disconnect."

When I set out to start researching how values drove entrepreneurs, these kinds of obvious social enterprises seemed the most popular route to focus on, but I kept resisting them. I would speak with experts on social entrepreneurship or entrepreneurs who had created companies that sold t-shirts to fund eyesight research or made clothes where you could trace the working conditions of their factories, and I felt I was only scratching the surface of an entrepreneur's deeper values. I wanted more.

The last thing I needed was to write about a Kickstarter-funded company in Boulder or Brooklyn, making yoga mats out of recycled water bottles or water bottles out of recycled yoga mats. I didn't want generic hippies or generic yuppies. No Patagonia vests. I was interested in something deeper than boasting about changing the world from a stage. It all felt too cute, too tidy. I didn't think this book could contribute to the truth about entrepreneurship unless I spoke to someone that you wouldn't obviously think of as values-driven: your average American business owner in a competitive industry, ideally a blue-collar one.

Something had to happen, some tangible sacrifice and choice on the entrepreneur's behalf that was driven by their values and went beyond lip service and credos.

This initially brought me to B-Lab, a rapidly growing organization that took the focus on the triple bottom line—People, Planet, Profit—pioneered by companies like Patagonia and Ben & Jerry's, and formalized it into a certified audit process. The organization had approved nearly three thousand designated B-Corporations in sixty countries, including big names like Eileen Fisher and Kickstarter, as well as many smaller firms, who do everything from private equity finance in New York to logging in Costa Rica.

The main difference between a B-Corp and a company that professes values is that B-Corps are legally obliged to change their governance documents to consider the impact of all decisions on stakeholders and not simply shareholders. "It moves beyond mission statements, to legally binding governance and accountability," said Jay Coen Gilbert, one of B-Lab's founders and the organization's managing partner. "It is very different to say 'I care about people and planet' versus 'I am legally accountable to care about people and planet.' . . . That's a major challenge of the source code of capitalism; from only having accountability to shareholders to being accountable to stakeholders."

B-Corp, which is based in the Philadelphia suburbs, was actually the result of Coen Gilbert's and his cofounders' negative experiences as entrepreneurs. In 1993, they founded the basketball shoe company And1, eventually sponsoring NBA stars like Kevin Garnett and Vince Carter. Coen Gilbert and his cofounders donated 5 percent of And1's profits to youth education organizations, improved the company's working conditions at home and in its overseas factories, and integrated environmental sustainability into material sourcing and other components of the business. But in 2005, And1 was sold to a company called American Sporting Goods, whose owner, Jerry Turner, had no interest in continuing with these lofty practices.

"We saw all that get stripped away in the name of greed," Coen Gilbert recalled. "The quote from Jerry when he introduced himself to international distributors about our service mission was 'There's a new sheriff in town,' and he went back to cutting his meat. It didn't have to do with competitiveness, it had to do with his own desire for more. . . . It felt shitty, but it wasn't shitty because we didn't expect it, it was shitty because that was what we could do." The pain of seeing their values tossed in the trash made Coen Gilbert and his friends wonder how they could have made those values stick, even when the business left their hands. The answer was a B-Corp.

Coen Gilbert told me that if someone wanted to understand the role of an entrepreneur's values, they needed to read two crucial essays written in 1970, whose authors lay out vastly contrasting visions for American capitalism. The better known of the two appeared in the *New York Times Magazine* and was called "The Social Responsibility of Business is to Increase its Profits." Its author was the famed economist Milton Friedman, whose rigorous defense of free markets and disapproval of government intervention in business made him one of the most influential economic thinkers of the twentieth century (he received a Nobel Prize in 1976). Friedman wrote that businessmen who believed "that business has a 'social conscience' and takes seriously its responsibilities for providing employment, eliminating discrimination, avoiding pollution and whatever else may be the catchwords of the contemporary crop of reformers," were preaching communism. "Businessmen who talk this way are unwitting puppets of the intellectual forces that have been undermining the basis of a free society these past decades."

Corporations and entrepreneurs were bound to serve their customers, Friedman declared, and more importantly, their shareholders. No one else. Entrepreneurs and executives who used the profits of their business to act like civil servants were fiscally irresponsible and downright dictatorial. "There are no values, no 'social' responsibilities in any sense other than the shared values and responsibilities of individuals," Friedman wrote. A business had one responsibility: to increase its profits.

Friedman's philosophy underpinned the deregulatory regimes of Ronald Reagan and Margaret Thatcher and gave rise to the concept of shareholder value as the principal objective of Wall Street, spurning activist investors to pressure companies for ever-increasing profits, whatever the cost. Moreover, it instilled the notion that business and values were incompatible. The businessman (and by extension the entrepreneur) was to make as much money for shareholders as possible. Anything that detracted from that was a betrayal of America's beating capitalist heart.

While Milton Friedman is less of a household name in Palo Alto than his literary peer Ayn Rand (*Atlas Shrugged* is probably the most influential book in Silicon Valley after *Steve Jobs*), Friedman's philosophy largely dictates the way business is done in that world. A Silicon Valley entrepreneur is practically subservient to their shareholders, because with each round of VC funding, the entrepreneur's ownership, rights, and values are eroded further, while the need to grow at all costs increases.

The essay Coen Gilbert recommended in contrast to Friedman's was written by a little-known career researcher at AT&T named Robert Greenleaf and was called *The Servant as Leader*. As Greenleaf observed the social unrest and student movements of the late 1960s, he was increasingly concerned how institutions like government, universities, and corporations were failing to serve those who relied on them. He called for the emergence of a new generation of servant-leaders to place values at the core of their work.

"The servant-leader is servant first," Greenleaf wrote. "The difference manifests itself in the care taken by the servant-first to make sure that other people's highest priority needs are being served. The best test, and difficult to administer, is: Do those served grow as persons? Do they, *while being served*, become healthier, wiser, freer, more autonomous, more likely themselves to become servants? *And*, what is the effect on the least privileged in society; will they benefit, or, at least, not be further deprived?"

Greenleaf's servant-leader was a human possessed with all the power of free will (both he and Friedman shared an abiding faith in the individual) but also the power of love, trust, empathy, hope, and community. The problems of the world all came down to the failure of individuals to think of others before themselves, to serve before leading, to put their values at the forefront. "All of this rests on the assumption that the only way to change a society (or just make it go) is to produce people, enough people, who will change it (or make it go)."

Friedman's profits or Greenleaf's values? Shareholders or Stakeholders? These questions form a central tension at the heart of what we fight over in our culture every day. And for the entrepreneur, they represent an internal fight for their soul and its values.

BY 2012, KEVIN MAUGER WAS increasingly comfortable as the owner of NCC Automated Systems. Business had nearly doubled since he'd bought the company, and things were running so smoothly it almost felt like a snack cake rolling its way along a well-calibrated conveyor belt. Mauger was financially secure, his oldest kids were off at college, and he had just turned forty. But like most people cresting that proverbial hill, Mauger sensed he wanted more.

"It was just growing up," he said, over lunch at a nearby Italian restaurant. "I started asking myself questions: What is something I'd be proud to accomplish at the end of my life? What do I want to be known for?" In order for NCC to grow, the people there needed a deeper sense of purpose and direction, and so did Mauger. Then, one day, Mauger was attending an industry conference, listening to someone from the Johnsonville Sausage Company give a presentation on leadership. Somewhere in his PowerPoint slides, the man briefly explained the concept of servant-leadership, and a light went off in Mauger's head. "It was something you could get behind," Mauger said, describing this moment as an awakening. "The concept of helping other people is an innate thing that's just fulfilling."

Though the revelation of purpose gave Mauger a strong sense of direction, it was initially just something he thought about. "I wasn't a servant leader. I was a coach. A trainer," he said, noting that most of the values he held came from his high school football coach. Mauger is quiet, somewhat shy, and very private. He admits that he is not one to talk openly about emotions, to brag about accomplishments, or really to stand in the spotlight unless absolutely necessary. "We had always had a set of values, they were posted right there on the wall, and we had people read them out, but they weren't used." But he realized that keeping his values to himself would serve no one. "If you understand what somebody stands for and agree with that, you're more likely to work in sync with them, rather than against them," he said. "That's it. That's values." In order to begin serving others, he had to let them know where he stood.

At the end of 2012, Mauger made his annual speech to NCC employees at the Christmas party, updating everyone on the company's performance and his goals for the following year. In the midst of the speech, Mauger paused and with more emotion in his voice than usual, he told everyone: "As I've grown and developed and thought about my life and business, I've realized that my purpose is to help you all and to create the most positive life possible."

That was it. Mauger didn't elaborate. He was still forming a clearer picture about what his values were and, more importantly, how he would implement them. He began quietly helping employees with personal health and financial issues, like the man whose wife needed a lifesaving operation that Mauger changed the company benefits to cover, or the young man on the shop floor whom he personally brought to rehab. He took joy in the thank-you notes and emails he received from their families (he choked up reading a few to me) but never spoke about this to anyone. Over the next few years, Mauger sprinkled more references about his values into his annual speech and made his first mention of servant leadership in 2015, explaining it briefly. "My job is to provide for you the opportunity to showcase your talents," he said in the speech, "to expand your own horizons and to let you do what you are born, or trained, or both to do."

Mauger's slow realization of his values was hardly abnormal. Few, if any of us, are born with a rock-solid sense of what we believe is fundamentally important in the world. Values are the product of our lived experience. They are shaped by our relationships, circumstances, and the times and places those occupy. Nick Swauger, an NCC production

manager who was first hired by Mauger twenty years earlier, said he saw
Mauger's values slowly emerge over the past two decades, as he realized
his responsibility for something greater than just personal gain. "When
he made those first speeches, the shift in focus was from *me* to *us*,"
Swauger said as we spoke in the church's hallway, after the first day's
ESOP ownership committee wrapped up its work. Jason Link, the company's longtime operations manager, said it was like witnessing someone finding their faith for the first time.

Speeches about values were all well and good, but at the end of the
day they were just words. Nothing really changed at NCC during those
few years. The boss teared up during his Christmas speech and made a
few references to leadership, but on the shop floor and in the offices, the
business of building and installing conveyor systems rolled along. Many
businesses have values posted on walls and websites. Some have five values, others have ten, and a few have dozens. They are typically similar
and include the expected nods to teamwork, service, hard work, grit,
discipline, and so on. Adam Bryant, who interviewed CEOs for the *New
York Times* for many years, told me that typically after listing the fourth
or fifth value, these executives would turn to their assistants with a
blank look, wondering what came next on the list. Values are cheap,
and often they amount to little more than empty slogans, like the beer
company that pays for a progressive Super Bowl ad but does nothing to
change its hiring practices, or the cosmetics manufacturer that slaps
a pink ribbon on its shampoo, while continuing to put toxic chemicals
into products.

At one point, I interviewed an entrepreneur in Chicago with a
metal fabrication business, who had been recommended to me as someone who had built a company firmly around his values. When we spoke,
he rattled off a laundry list of values, but when I asked him to point to
one example of how those values changed the day-to-day operation of
the business, he was stumped.

"Oh yeah," he said, after thinking a few seconds. "We give a bobble-
head each month to the employee who does the best job!"

And?

"And what?"

What else?

"At the end of the year they can win concert tickets and a signed guitar!"

Many entrepreneurs hold personal values and run their businesses as expected. They show up, do their best work, and go home. Nor are an entrepreneur's values necessarily benevolent. As Michael Douglas famously put it in *Wall Street*, greed is a value and a strong one. Milton Friedman's adage to focus on profits above all drives many entrepreneurs and their businesses. But for those who openly profess a broader set of values and commit to living by them, what separates empty rhetoric from genuine values-led entrepreneurship is sacrifice.

Mauger wanted to bring NCC in line with his values, but really had no idea how. Then, one day, he heard a lecture by a man named Ken Baker about Employee Stock Ownership Plans (ESOP). As Baker described an ESOP as a mechanism for growth, as well as a way to spread values through a company, another light went off in Mauger's head. "It spoke to me right away on so many levels: strategic, emotional, financial," he said. "God! There's a million things I don't know, but this is something I really want to know about."

At its core, an ESOP is a specific type of retirement pension plan, which allows employees to gain ownership shares in a company over time. Its roots lie in the cooperatively owned companies of Britain and early America, but ESOPs have been legally enshrined in US law since 1974, and they receive certain beneficial tax advantages over other corporate structures. From an entrepreneur's perspective, an ESOP is a particular form of exit. Rather than sell their company to investors, competitors, or other outside buyers, they sell it to an ESOP, which is set up as a trust on behalf of the employees. Typically the sale is funded with outside debt, which the employees repay over time. Employees are not required to put up cash for the ESOP, but contributions are deducted from their salaries like any benefit plan. Companies with ESOPs include Southwest Airlines, King Arthur Flour, and Wawa, the gas station chain where NCC workers get their coffee each morning.

"I heard all of this and it was *BOOM*," Mauger said, recalling Baker's lecture. "It was everything I was looking for: the power of the team, ownership culture, people feeling like they were part of the company, and that selfless aspect, because of the financial sacrifice."

Mauger eventually met with Baker to learn more about ESOPs and what Baker had done at NewAge Industries, the plastic tubing company his father, Ray, had founded, which he now ran. Baker, who is in his early seventies, is tall, slender, and has the precisely combed hair and confident demeanor of an FBI director. I met him for lunch at the company's facility, just north of Philadelphia, where he greeted me with a salad, a book on the benefits of a vegan diet, and Holocaust survivor Viktor Frankl's book *Man's Search for Meaning*. Before we ate, he led me on a tour of the NewAge factory, which produces plastic tubes of every size, shape, and dimension, from lengths of thick hose for sprinkler systems and smaller ones for McDonald's milkshake machines, to the precise silicone platinum tubes used by biotech and pharmaceutical companies, which were made in double-sealed sterile rooms by staff dressed in head-to-toe protective suits.

Baker began working for his father at six, stapling sales brochures at the dining room table and continued through high school as the factory janitor. After college he helped turn NewAge Industries from a distribution business into a manufacturer. In 1998, Baker bought out his father and brother to become the company's sole owner, starting up the pharmaceutical division and growing NewAge Industries into a firm that did $54 million in sales in 2018 with 165 employees.

Baker's values were based on a strong sense of right and wrong. He once quit a job as a door-to-door encyclopedia salesman, because it required him to be deceptive. "I pay my taxes, don't lie, or cheat. I treat people with respect and don't burn bridges," Baker said. He was not religious but had become increasingly environmentally conscious, converting one quarter of the factory to solar power and diverting all of NewAge's waste to recycling or energy generation. He encouraged healthy eating and exercise and preached to everyone about plant-based diets. "I'm just trying to save the world," Baker said, with a slight smile. "Just trying to keep people alive."

Like Mauger, Baker came to an ESOP through a lecture he attended and instantly thought, *That's it!* At the time he owned only 10 percent of the company, but he set in course a ten-year plan to acquire all of its equity and put the company in a financial position to support an ESOP (which only works if a business is profitable and debt free). "My father thought I had rocks in my head to do manufacturing and double rocks to sell it to employees," he said. In 2000, he hinted in the company's newsletter that he would sell 30 percent of the company to the employees in 2006, which was his way of saying, "Stick around, the party is going to start in six years." True to his word, Baker announced the ESOP in 2006 at an event known as a "reveal" in the ESOP world, starting with 30 percent employee ownership, which became 100 percent employee-owned in September 2019, less than a year after I met Baker.

What drew Baker to an ESOP and what he evangelized about constantly to other entrepreneurs through the Pennsylvania Center for Employee Ownership (an organization he founded) was less about the retirement plan it set up for NewAge employees and more about the way it shaped their culture. "This is an example of shared capitalism," he said, as we went on his daily MBWA (Management by Walking Around) around the factory, stopping to greet every employee by name. "If you look at an ESOP it's not a gift. If employees don't work hard to increase the profitability of the business, then this investment won't grow." Because an ESOP technically turned the people working at a company into its owners, it ideally shifted their thinking to something more in line with the way entrepreneurs saw their business. "The ownership mindset is different than the employee mindset," Baker said. "Owners do things differently, but you don't come out of the womb as an owner."

Baker noticed daily changes in behavior since he began the ESOP, as employees proactively acted in the best interest of the company without managers prompting them. A woman was feeling ill, so her coworkers suggested she move to an easier job that day, easing her burden while safeguarding their group's performance. A forklift driver was spinning in circles for fun, and a colleague upbraided him for mistreating the equipment they both owned a portion of. One employee turned down several thousand dollars to refer friends for vacant positions, because, he told Baker, they were fine friends to go bowling and grab beers with, but he wouldn't want them as co-owners. Baker attributed the company's improved performance to this shifting mindset. Sales were up, mistakes were down, and turnover had never been lower.

Baker was immensely proud of what he had done with the ESOP at NewAge, but his values were constantly being tested. Competitors, investors, and private equity firms were calling daily with offers in hand for the company. Since Baker still controlled the majority of NewAge shares, he held that power. "I could sell this company for a hundred million by five p.m. today," he said. "But why? They'll say, 'Who cares about the employees or the community? Just look at the money.' What private equity does is maximize shareholder value—it's Milton Friedman 101—which is the same thing they teach you in an MBA. Is that what business is about?" he asked me. "No, it's not! A business is a living, breathing thing and you don't abuse it . . . by anybody . . . even the owner. If you abuse it, you kill the golden goose." Before Baker sold his remaining shares to the ESOP, handing employees complete ownership, he was securing B-Corp certification for NewAge Industries, legally binding any future owner (including the ESOP) to the values of all its stakeholders.

Values are relatively meaningless until they are tested. Opportunity has costs, money doesn't come for free, and ideals are easily sacrificed. "When push comes to shove, when the financial model comes into play," that's when an entrepreneur's true beliefs are tested, said Cheryl Yaffe Kiser at Babson College, and the beautiful slogans painted on the wall are revealed to be enduring or hollow. The tie-dye ice cream company sells to a multinational conglomerate. Judy Wick's husband went from a socially conscious, anticapitalist to a billionaire backer of Republican political causes. Google's mantra of "Do no evil" seems quaint now that knowledge of its data harvesting and work with government intelligence agencies and military contractors has come to light, but it shouldn't be surprising, considering that Silicon Valley's startup model prioritizes rapid growth, exits, and shareholder rights above all else. Sometimes an entrepreneur's values fall away during hard times, when money is tight, but more often than not, they are sacrificed slowly, one decision at a time, like a thousand papercuts.

When I asked Mauger about the test his own values faced, when he was weighing whether to convert NCC Automated Systems to an ESOP, he told me it was a simple question of money. Private equity firms and competitors had regularly fielded offers in the neighborhood of $20 million to buy NCC, a substantial multiple on sales. But with ESOPs, the sale to the trust always happened at fair market value, which was determined to be $10 million for NCC, a haircut that Mauger willingly chose to accept. "You're giving that up," he said, of the additional $10 million he left on the table. "So you have to believe in the value of selflessness and teamwork and how these things will chip away at different challenges, and do amazing things for the people you work with every day." Did Mauger have any regrets? "What's several million when I have enough?" he said. He owned his house and a condo in Florida, had plenty of savings for his family and their future, and most importantly, a career he loved, where he remained his own boss (Mauger initially sold 42 percent of his shares to the ESOP for $5 million, with plans to sell the rest over the next decade). "In this case, the impact I could have on this piece of the world is far more than my personal needs."

On May 5, 2017, Mauger gathered everyone on NCC's shop floor. It had been touted as the biggest day in company history, and employees guessed that NCC Automated Systems might be expanding to a new facility, merging with a competitor, or would be acquired by a big investor. Some even hoped Mauger was going to send them all on a Caribbean cruise. There was a DJ, balloons, and a catered lunch, and employees' spouses were invited to attend.

Mauger had been working on his speech for the previous three months and delivered it by heart over forty-five minutes. "I always say that life is sometimes more about the questions than the answers," he began, standing on a stage in a suit and tie. "And I know there is at least one big question about what in the world is going on here. And I promise to answer that today, but it might take me a while to get there." He began with the fact that the most important people were in the room: the people who helped him build up NCC and inspired him daily. Mauger talked about Ken Baker (who was there) and hinted at what he had learned from him. He liked the "essence" of Baker's idea, which was "completely in line with NCC's core values." This new idea would change the nature of the business, from a soloist to a symphony, from a motorcycle to a Dodge Caravan, from a river to a lake. There was another group here who represented a new organization, Mauger said, nodding to friends of his standing in the back, who were dressed in suits, at his request.

But first, Mauger talked about his personal growth through the company. He went back to the speeches he gave over the previous five years, restating the key messages about his values and discovering his purpose to serve. "Today, you will see that I am putting my money where my mouth is," he said. "This isn't just talk." Most companies this size either grew too fast and failed or grew fast until the entrepreneur took a check and was gone. Mauger wouldn't be gone, not yet, but he had sold 42 percent of the company to someone in the room. He took a long pause, as everyone looked nervously at the suits standing in the back.

"Employees please stand up," Mauger said, lifting his hand as if commanding a graduating class. "If you are standing and you are an employee of NCC you are an owner." On command, Mauger's friends began applauding, and the employees, who were now standing there bewildered, also applauded. Mauger walked over and unveiled NCC's new logo, with the line "An Employee Owned Company" boldly written below it, and it began to dawn on everyone just what was happening. Cheering erupted. Some people laughed. Others cried. A few of them (particularly the burliest welders and shop technicians) were speechless.

"People just came up and hugged me," Mauger said, describing that moment as the single proudest accomplishment in his entire life, on par with winning the championship with his high school football team. "There was literally a receiving line, like at a wedding."

Nick Swauger, the longest-standing employee at the company, said he was humbled by the generosity of the act. "It made me feel special," he said. "That I had a new sense of meaning in the company and a new sense of appreciation."

More than a year later, long after the balloons deflated, the hard work of cementing Mauger's values into the culture of NCC was under way. This was the ownership culture piece of the puzzle; the transition from thinking like employees to thinking like owners and the responsibility that entailed. The dozen representatives of the company had been hashing this out all day at the Calvary Church, with help from Matt Hancock, who worked for the Philadelphia company Praxis Consulting Group, which specialized in ESOP transitions.

As Hancock explained, an ESOP was not a magic switch that transformed how a company worked. It was a financial structure and benefits plan, and that's as far as it went for many companies. An ESOP did not automatically give a company values. In fact, plenty of companies we would regard as utterly deficient in values have been ESOPs, including Enron, Lehman Brothers, the Tribune newspaper chain, and United Airlines . . . firms whose ESOPs not only failed to shift their toxic culture, but actually left their employee-owners penniless when the companies failed.

"When you think about it, every action you do affects everybody," said Frank Carpinello, a Harley Davidson–riding shop technician at NCC, during one of the sessions with Hancock. "You own it. To me that feels different, because when you do good, everyone around you earns more." Dane Duncan, one of the newer members of the team, who played in a Christian rock band, said the ESOP made him feel that sharing one's personal values at work was more important, and something about it "compels you to do more . . . that's ownership."

The ownership committee was brainstorming and designing various ways to build and strengthen the culture within the company, from how meetings would be held and awards given out, to which core values they would have input on and how those would be realized day to day. Over the next year, NCC would begin implementing something called the Great Game of Business, which taught open-book management, a method that encouraged all NCC employees to review the company's basic financial results (sales, profits, expenses, etc.) and improve their performance with active ideas and more transparency.

According to Stuart Thornhill, who teaches entrepreneurship at the University of Michigan and previously headed up its center for Positive Organizations, nearly every single measure that matters—health claims, turnover rates, lost time—improved at companies when there was a healthy culture led by values. "Healthy financial results always follow organizational health," Thornhill said. "People get into the zero-sum game idea 'We can't afford to be nice, because it'll cost us,' and research shows that time and again that's wrong. Would we all rather work in a place where we felt we were valued and had community versus only a paycheck? You don't need to think about that too deeply to understand the power involved here." Over the years, various academic studies have shown the potential benefits of ESOPs beyond retirement savings, including improved sales, productivity, employment growth, and decreased layoffs.

One afternoon, I drove up to Princeton, New Jersey, to attend a meeting of the local ESOP association, which was run by Alex Moss, the co-owner of Praxis Consulting, the company that was working with NCC on its ESOP transition. Half a dozen entrepreneurs, owners, and executives of ESOP companies sat around a conference table at a Marriott, ranging from Manhattan insurance brokers to defense contractors. These individuals represented the spectrum of American political and economic thought—from Republican, evangelical Christian, free market fundamentalists to Democrat, atheist, progressive interventionalists— and yet they all firmly believed that sharing ownership of a business was a positive force for change.

"Our company was a hippie company when it began," said Alison Barger, the CFO of Mathematica, a government contractor that focuses on social services, with a mission to help society by improving publicly funded programs that promote well-being . . . the essence of the social safety net most Republicans despise. "They are literally a bunch of socialists, and I have to tell them why profits are necessary," Barger said, of her colleagues. "But that's what makes Mathematica what it is." The company converted to an ESOP in 2005, because its founders worried that a sale to another entity or the public markets would divert the company's vision from being socially driven to profit driven.

Across the table sat Bill Jones, President and CEO of Penn United, a precision manufacturer for the aerospace industry, whose father was one of three deeply religious founders of the company. "I know they wanted to teach people to fish rather than fish for them," Jones said, reflecting the frequently cited parable. "But Dad didn't want to be the one to make all the profit, and as the company grew, he wasn't ashamed to say we should have faith in what we do . . . building with our hands like Jesus, who was a carpenter." The company's ESOP (which Jones thanked Jesus for giving his father the faith to create) was nothing more than a bedrock of Christian values, empowering more than seven hundred employees to be the proverbial fishermen. "The wealth we are creating in everyday people is amazing, not just in families, but throughout a community where they live."

As I drove back down to the northern suburbs of Philadelphia that evening to meet with Bill Stockwell, I began to see how the deeply held values of an entrepreneur—real, meaningful, actionable values—transcended political, religious, or ideological affiliation. Stockwell is a tall, slender man in his seventies with a head of neat blond curls and the rolled-up shirtsleeves of a businessman in a Norman Rockwell painting. His great-grandfather founded Stockwell Elastomerics in a New Jersey garage, and it now makes custom silicon molds for a variety of uses, including switches in electronics, window seals on Boeing airliners, and the bumper pads on SpaceX rockets.

Stockwell had announced the company's ESOP around the same time as Mauger did with NCC. He had arrived at the decision to create an ESOP at Stockwell Elastomerics because he saw how miserable his friends who had sold their businesses to private equity firms or competitors had become. They sat around in Florida, bored out of their minds, and watched powerlessly as twenty-five-year-old management consultants disassembled everything they and their family had built, often destroying the lives of the employees who had built it alongside them. "I've got mine and everyone else gets screwed," Stockwell said, summing up that outcome. "Once you flip the keys, you can't get them back."

I asked Stockwell where his values came from, and like Mauger, he explained how they emerged over time. "I had to grow my own values," Stockwell said. A lot came from the example his father set, especially after Bill took over leadership of Stockwell Elastomerics. Rather than retire, his father returned to the shop floor, so he could teach the next generation of engineers. In the 1990s, as the Cold War defense business dried up, Stockwell was forced to downsize the company, and he also returned to the workshop alongside his father and the other workers. "That time on the floor was the start of my values growing," he said. "Sweating with those guys . . . I depended on them. They depended on me. It was a symbiotic relationship of interdependency. We all had bills to pay and families to feed. We had to figure it out. It was great going through that." Those experiences sunk into Stockwell's head, until they formed into an increasingly clear set of values.

"You realize, it's about more than me. More than 'I got mine,'" he said, describing the dominant ideology that the popular culture depicted as the core of the entrepreneur's soul. "I think that's really affected the United States of America in a very negative way," he said, noting the troubling rise of economic populism on both ends of the political spectrum. "But seeing so many businesspeople take care of themselves, well, I can understand why. It shakes their faith in capitalism. I'm a pure capitalist. But I think capitalism has to extend to the people on the floor. I have ninety-one capitalists here, and the ESOP gives them the opportunity to become something bigger." Not just through a raise or a bonus or the kind of speculative stock options Silicon Valley startups hand out like lottery tickets, but by ownership in a piece of the pie, the ability to grow that pie, and with it, the American Dream.

Stockwell wanted to do everything in his power to help that happen. He had personally financed the company's ESOP, rather than saddling it with debt that employee owners would have to repay, and had also introduced other measures to improve the lives of the company's workers and families, who came from many of the most impoverished neighborhoods in Philadelphia. This included a multidenominational service, whose chaplains visited the factory twice a week to check up on employees' personal lives and those of their families, counseling on everything from substance and spousal abuse to incarcerated children and even suicide prevention. This service was on call twenty-four hours a day.

"Rather than be a business destroyer, I really want this to continue because we are doing good work here," Stockwell said, slapping his hand on the table. "That's where business needs to recognize its value to the community. At the personal level. At the family level. And at the community level. This is just good basic Republican beliefs. Not the Republican Party of now, but its core, which is values based," he said. "We just need to blow some oxygen on the embers."

From fiercely left-wing garden supply companies in Vermont, to blood-red gas field firms in Oklahoma, the entrepreneurs who followed their values into an ESOP were returning to a foundational idea of what capitalism meant. "America was founded on the principle that people who'd never been able to control their economic destiny could do it here," Alex Moss said, noting that what drove most entrepreneurs who converted their companies to ESOPs were two things: a strong set of personal values and also a sense of paternalism that made them want to take care of their employees. These entrepreneurs saw the workers who built their business as a family. Not cogs in the machine or interchangeable units of production in the service of profit, but their own flesh and blood.

As I sat and witnessed one proud businessman after another wipe tears from his eyes when talking about converting their company to an ESOP, the difference between preaching values and living them felt especially stark. These weren't motivational posters or even charitable donations; they were personal ideas about serving a greater purpose than profit. Far more than success or fame or money, this is what drove entrepreneurs like Kevin Mauger, Ken Baker, and Bill Stockwell. They were never going to lecture at social entrepreneurship summits, or market their products as virtuous ways of saving the world. They did what they did because they believed in their hearts and their souls that it was the right thing to do, and as entrepreneurs, they had the power to do it.

"The forces for good and evil in the world are propelled by the thoughts, attitudes, and actions of individual beings," Robert Greenleaf wrote in *The Servant as Leader*. "What happens to our values, and therefore to the quality of our civilization in the future, will be shaped by the conceptions of individuals that are born of inspirations."

CHAPTER 6

Keeping It in the Family

THE TRUCK ARRIVED at the gate of Bodega y Cavas de Weinert, a winery in Mendoza, Argentina, loaded with plastic buckets of just-picked Merlot grapes. It gave a brief honk and the winery's staff quickly unloaded its precious cargo, dumping the buckets into a big metal trough with a giant corkscrew running down its center, which stripped the fruit from its stems and crushed the grapes into a pulpy juice, the first step in making wine. The men at the loading dock worked quickly, with little talk; the fresh grapes had to be crushed and pumped into concrete fermentation tanks before the hot sun of March set them to rot.

Iduna Weinert, the thirty-seven-year-old daughter of the winery's founder Bernardo Weinert and its current commercial manager, walked over to the loading bay when she heard the truck pull in. She greeted the vineyard's owner, Mr. Motta, with the traditional Argentine single-cheek air kiss and the widest smile she could muster and spoke with him briefly about the state of the harvest so far. Iduna pulled a grape from a bin, popped it into her mouth, chewed, and spat it out, complimenting Motta on his Merlot.

"Please tell me we don't have a cabernet with an alcohol of 14 to 15 percent this year," Iduna pleaded with him, recalling how last year, the grapes had much higher sugar levels than they had hoped for.

"No, not this year," said Mr. Motta. "Thirteen-point-five percent maximum."

"Oh, thank God!" said Iduna, kissing him again and walking over to check on the progress of the grape juice in the fermentation tanks.

Though the interaction with Mr. Motta seemed brief, the relationship was crucial to the winery's survival. This harvest, in 2019, was just the second in a row for Bodega y Cavas de Weinert, after a hiatus of several years when the business nearly folded. During that time, the winery's reputation with its suppliers and customers had suffered greatly, and convincing a grower like Mr. Motta to once again sell his grapes to her family business took a tremendous leap of faith. In the two years since she had returned to the winery her father had started, Iduna Weinert had worked with the winery's staff to reopen lapsed export markets, modernize the winery's branding, launch new styles of wines, shift its tourism program to a more high-end audience, and draw up plans for a renovation of the historic property. All of this effort amounted to a single task, taken on with renewed effort every day: to pull Bodega y Cavas de Weinert, Iduna's family business, back into solvency. It had suffered years of decline, as well as a complex tale of fraud that was still weaving its way through the courts in her home country.

A few minutes after Motta's truck departed, an old red Land Cruiser pulled into the property. "Oh," said Iduna, with a bemused grin. "It looks like my parents have come." Bernardo Weinert, who was eighty-seven years old at the time, got out of the driver's seat, opened the trunk, and began directing the winery staff to unload various supplies, while his wife, Selma, who was sixty-nine, took bags out of the car. They looked over and saw me talking with Iduna. I waved and Bernardo began walking over. I heard a voice from the other side of the property and turned to see Iduna's younger brother, André, walking with his daughter across the lawn toward us. I saw the easy smile on Iduna's face harden into a steely grin. "This should be interesting," she said and stood there as her father and brother closed in.

It had been nearly a decade since I had last seen her family at the winery, but her brother greeted me with a hug, and her father (whom I addressed as Don Bernardo, the formal title he preferred) shook my hand and asked whether I was still living in Canada. "Remember," Bernardo said, officially welcoming me back, "you are family."

Only after the various members of the Weinert family walked off did I realize that none of them—not her father, her mother, her brother, or even her seven-year-old niece—spoke to Iduna or acknowledged her presence in any way. It was as though she was a ghost, invisible to anyone but me and the winery's workers. I had been warned that the situation was complicated, and Iduna's return to the winery was far from a simple story of entrepreneurship in a family business, but I had no idea just how screwed up it had all become.

"This is what it is," she told me, shrugging, when I asked what I'd just witnessed. "No one talks to each other."

IN THE SILICON VALLEY STARTUP myth, family is a nonentity. Startups are a one-generation phenomenon, the process of individuals or partners creating businesses, while the family is just something the entrepreneur has at home. Often, family is portrayed as an accessory or an impediment to entrepreneurship, like the first wives of Elon Musk and Steve Jobs, who were cast aside when they were deemed insufficiently devoted to the businesses' demands. Or, the family is there to play the perfect supporting cast to the entrepreneur's success (the lucky second and third wives). Beyond that, the family plays no real role in this myth.

Since Silicon Valley's model places an exit from a business as its immediate goal, this casts the story of entrepreneurship as one with a beginning, middle, and defined end, which occurs in one generation or

less. Against this, multigenerational entrepreneurship is a quaint anachronism, while a family business entrepreneur is a paradoxical term, an
idea completely ill-suited to our dynamic modern economy. What could
be more risk-averse, slow moving, and even anti-entrepreneurial than a
business run by a dynastic procession of genetic descendants, as if entrepreneurship could be transferred somehow by bloodlines?

The reality, however, is that entrepreneurship is firmly rooted in
families. According to the Family Firm Institute, a think tank, approx-
imately two-thirds of the businesses around the world are owned and
operated by families. In America, family firms constitute over half of
the businesses in the country and half of those listed on stock markets. These range from blue-chip multinationals, like Walmart, Mars,
and Fiat, to the proverbial mom-and-pops I have written about so far
in this book, from the Alsoufi family's eponymous Syrian restaurant in
Toronto, to Stockwell Elastomerics, a fourth-generation advanced manufacturing business in Philadelphia.

The wine business is one where family entrepreneurship not
only persists, but remains firmly tied to the industry. Italy's Antinori,
France's Château Lafite Rothschild, Australia's Yalumba, Germany's
Hans Wirsching, California's Wente Vineyards . . . pick up a bottle of
wine from anywhere in the world, and you will often find a product produced by a business that has remained within the same family for two,
four, or a dozen generations. More than its tasting notes or a castle in
Burgundy, the family name behind a winery remains the very essence of
its brand; its lineage of tradition and store of value, a marker of quality,
and the commitment to that over decades and centuries.

Family entrepreneurship may be remarkably common throughout
the world, but it is so markedly different from the standard tale of the
individual founder creating something new, that we often fail to recognize it beyond the first generation or appreciate why it matters. Which
is a shame. Because when we ignore the experiences of family entrepreneurs, we sweep aside some of the most important questions around
entrepreneurship and the two elements of our lives—work and family—
that are inseparable. How do entrepreneurs integrate the needs of their

family with the needs of their work? What becomes of something you create when you are ready to let it go? Who do you trust to take it over? And if you're the one taking something over, how do you make it your own without hurting its legacy or the people who entrusted you with it? These questions are at the core of what owning a business over the long term is really about.

The weight of that legacy was what I wanted to understand. Not just for the entrepreneurs who were working in businesses with their families, but for people like me, who came from a family of entrepreneurs and in some way inherited the desire to live that way. My father is an entrepreneur, his father was an entrepreneur, my mother was an entrepreneur, her father was an entrepreneur, and so on, down to my brother and me, and now my wife, just like her parents and grandparents. Yet none of us worked in the same business or even the same industry. There was a bloodline of entrepreneurship, but it was distinct and separate and seemingly unrelated. I wondered if there was something that transcended generations . . . an inherited sense of the entrepreneurial spirit. What did that legacy look like, and how did it manifest itself in the lives of the entrepreneurs and their families in Mendoza's wine business?

IDUNA* AND I FIRST BECAME friends in 2004, when I was living in Argentina, working as a freelance journalist. I had recently begun writing news stories for the magazine *Wine Spectator* and was ostensibly their South American correspondent, even though I knew nothing about wine. One day, a friend of mine brought me to lunch with Iduna's older brother Bruno, and when I told him that I was coming to Mendoza in a few weeks for the annual harvest festival, he put me in touch with his sister to arrange a visit to Bodega y Cavas de Weinert.

I made a terrible first impression, showing up four hours late after an afternoon of wine tasting with other journalists, quite drunk. The Weinert family had prepared a lavish lunch for me that was now cold,

---

* Because I'm talking about several generations of family businesses, I will refer to many people by their first names throughout this chapter.

but Iduna was all smiles and accepted my apologies with a bat of her hand, as she led me into the giant, elaborately carved wooden doors of the winery to tell me the story of Bodega y Cavas de Weinert. The brick-and-beam winery itself dates back to 1890, when it was built by a Spanish family who opened Bodegas Fontán, which ran until the 1920s. Over the next few decades, the winery passed between owners and frequently sat disused and abandoned, until Don Bernardo Weinert acquired the property in 1975. Bernardo was an unlikely entrepreneur in the Argentinean wine business. A Brazilian of German descent, Bernardo was the son of an entrepreneur who ran a grocery store and dairy factory in a small town. He always dreamed of being his own boss. After dropping out of university and working as a trucker, he started a logistics business that quickly grew to handle freight all over South America. Since Mendoza served as the principal crossing point for freight between Argentina and Chile, Bernardo, who lived in Rio de Janeiro at the time, ended up visiting often for work.

Mendoza is the ideal place for growing wine grapes: the eastern part of the province is flat, dry, and sunny with mineral-rich soil, while in the west, the peaks of the Andes provide a reliable source of water for vineyard irrigation. Though wine has been produced all over Argentina since Spanish settlers and Italian immigrants began cultivating grapes in the nineteenth century, the sector has boomed over the past few decades, particularly in Mendoza, thanks to the success of Malbec, Mendoza's signature grape. Bernardo Weinert noticed that while Chile was exporting a tremendous amount of wine to Brazil, Mendoza exported very little, and he sensed an opportunity. The easiest way into the business was to buy a winery, and though Bernardo Weinert knew nothing about wine, that is exactly what he did.

Partnering with winemaker Raúl de la Mota, Bodega y Cavas de Weinert focused on making a traditional style of wine, aged for long periods of time (two, five, even ten years) in large oak casks. This made the wine stand out, especially as the industry in Mendoza modernized in the 1990s and followed European and American trends to shorter maturation periods in smaller, more intensely flavored barrels of new oak.

Bodega y Cavas de Weinert wines were more mellow and subtle; their flavors were unique and ultimately more traditional than the other wineries nearby. The winery's first vintage, its 1977 Malbec, is still regarded as one of the best examples of the region's signature varietal more than forty years since it was bottled.

Iduna told me all of this as we walked through the winery and descended a dimly lit stairway into the famous cavas (caves), the subterranean cellars that gave the winery its name. Built by European artisans in the nineteenth century, the arched brick cellars were the heart of the winery. They were sufficiently humid and consistently cool year-round, even during Mendoza's scorching summers and icy winters, and they seemed to stretch on forever . . . cellar after cellar, room after room, with vaulting brick arches and ceilings twenty-five feet high. Bodega y Cavas de Weinert aged its wines in huge wooden casks, some as high as fifteen feet tall, and these contained enough wine for more than a million and a half bottles.

Though her father had bought the winery before Iduna and her older brother Bruno were born, the family and his trucking business were based in Rio de Janeiro. Iduna went to a British private school there, and though she speaks with the polished English of international students (as well as flawless Argentine Spanish), she is Brazilian at heart, from her dark complexion (her mother is from the country's tropical north) to her love of the ocean and ability to dance samba late into the night. During her childhood Mendoza and the winery were seen as an investment of her father's, which doubled as a vacation home. "This place is where we came every six months for holidays," she said. "We would stay for a few weeks, but Don Raúl, the original winemaker, was a very serious man, and he didn't like kids around, so we were not involved in the business at all."

That changed in the late 1990s, when Bernardo left the trucking business and the family relocated to Buenos Aires. At the time, Iduna was in high school and dreaded the change, but soon took an interest in the winery. On visits to Mendoza, she hung out in the lab with Hugo Weber, the Swiss winemaker who had recently taken over, analyzing the carefully managed chemical dance of grape sugars slowly fermenting into alcohol. "I loved the lab work," Iduna said. Her father encouraged her to study chemical engineering in college, as a stepping-stone to winemaking, but two years into her degree, Iduna was profoundly unhappy. She wanted to do something different. More than anything, she wanted to go back to Brazil. She dropped out, taught English, lived at home, and tried to figure out what to do next. "I did not want to come into the wine business," she said. "I wanted something else. At least to get a different experience beforehand."

One day, Bernardo invited Iduna to accompany him to New York and help him at a big wine tasting. The winery had always been focused on exports, and the American market for Argentinean wines was quickly growing. Bernardo barely spoke any English, and Iduna could translate for him. Iduna knew nothing about wine, and she was initially turned off by the scene. "Everyone was raving about these wines," she said, describing the insufferably pretentious people she first encountered at the tasting. "I thought, 'This world isn't for me.'"

By chance she met the owner of a small Lebanese winery, whose wines were unique and tied to an interesting story he sold with tremendous panache. "I realized that the wine tasting business was about drama," she said, with a wicked smile. "And I studied drama in high school." This is a massive understatement to say the least. Iduna is a certified drama queen. Her voice booms, her presence in a space is commanding, and she loves nothing more than an audience. At the tasting she invented a character called "Iduna Weinert," an exaggerated version of herself, a cross between a gaucho countess and a fruit-topped Carmen Miranda, who used the strength of her personality to tell the story of her father's wines and help sell them around the world. "Iduna turned into an excellent salesperson," Don Bernardo told me, "especially for the export market."

Back in Argentina, Iduna worked wherever she was needed in the business: filing, translating, helping write promotional material, and so on. She read up on winemaking chemistry and took an introductory sommelier course, as well as classes on export businesses and logistics.

Increasingly, she ran the winery's tastings around Buenos Aires. "I just sort of naturally entered the company," she said, noting that because she was so outgoing, and because females were still a rarity in the business, she quickly built relationships with local and foreign journalists and became the visible face of the family's brand. "I was more of a mascot than anything."

Over time, the family's roles in the business became more defined. Don Bernardo was the owner and president, in charge of the winery's operations (including the taste of its wines) and finances. Bruno, who studied IT and came on board in 2003, was in charge of the domestic market (he and Iduna, while still close, are complete opposites in terms of personality). Iduna took charge of the international market and public relations, and André, who eventually moved to Mendoza, did various work at the winery related to production. Only Selma and Don Bernardo's children from a previous marriage (who lived outside Argentina) were not formally involved in the business.

Iduna worked for a decade out of the company's offices in Buenos Aires. She traveled half the year: to wine shows in Europe, export markets in Asia, then back to Canada and the United States, and on to South America, opening up new markets and expanding old ones. One day she'd be on a riverboat in Baton Rouge, Louisiana, leading a tasting for casino owners, and two days later she would be serving her wine at a banquet in Seoul. She loved the work and was in her element at a tasting or wine dinner, shaking off the stuffy airs of the wine business with her "Iduna Weinert" character. She had a knack for finding other misfits in the business . . . her fellow drama queens. They'd laugh and dance on tables, then go out to eat and drink, making fun of the ascot-wearing, buttoned-up characters they met. I remember seeing her once at a tasting in New York, shouting across the Pool Room in the famous Four Seasons restaurant, pouring wine for an audience who just ate it up.

During these years, Iduna never saw herself as an entrepreneur. "In my mind I was an employee . . . fully," she said. "I told people that 'I work for my father.' But I felt trapped." Her father was the boss and he made it clear to everyone that Bodega y Cavas de Weinert was *his* company, full stop. He consulted with Iduna and Bruno on decisions, but at the end of the day, did what he wanted. Increasingly, this frustrated the siblings, who felt there were serious deficiencies in the way the business was run. The branding had not changed in forty years, accounting was a mess, and there were basic systems for sales, marketing, and database management that Bernardo refused to implement. Slowly, they began to watch other wineries pull ahead of them, especially in the global markets they'd helped pioneer for Argentinean wines. Bernardo was the classic, traditionalist Latin American *patrón* (master). Iduna felt that he ran the business as his personal project. Iduna and Bruno were paid when he felt like it, often only after asking their father for their salaries. "Okay, how much do you want?" their father would ask them, as if they were teenagers requesting an allowance. It was incredibly frustrating.

"It's difficult to see our kids sometimes as human beings," said Wendy Sage-Hayward, a family business advisor and professor in Vancouver, who has worked with a number of clients in the wine business. "We see them as our children. As our projects. Even when children become adults, we see them as our kids. It's very difficult for people to move out of a parent/child dynamic and into an adult/adult dynamic. But also there's so much emotional ownership over a business that they founded that it is difficult to let go and share it. That makes it very hard for the next generation to step in and be seen as a credible addition with innovative ideas. If we can't see strength in our children and let go and invite them to share, we've got a tough dynamic."

When a founding entrepreneur of a business fails to see their children as equals with the vision, ideas, and risk tolerance to continue and build on their legacy, they can cut them off, either by ignoring or downplaying their opinions or keeping important information from them. "The true success of a family business is when we acknowledge that the family business is a system comprised of three parts," said Michael McGrann, who runs a family business consulting firm in Philadelphia called the Telos Group. The three cores of a family business are: the business, the family, and the individuals in it. Many entrepreneurs keep the business separate from their family entirely or compartmentalize it, with limited transparency about the overall state of the business. "If I don't engage my family, I can shut the door to my office and go home," McGrann said, explaining how an entrepreneur often believes that by building a wall around their business, they are protecting their family from it. In the long term, however, this dooms the business and the family because everyone is in the dark, and no barrier can truly insulate a family from its business.

Lauri Union, who runs Babson College's Institute for Family Entrepreneurship and who previously turned around her grandfather's corrugated metal business in North Carolina, said this ultimately led to a loss of entrepreneurial capacity in a family. Deprived of the opportunity to grow, the children in the business feel stifled and suffocated. Their ideas have nowhere to go, and they eventually drift away from the family business. "The younger generation's ability to dream and create is kind of eclipsed by the older generation's desire to retain control," she said. "There's a loss there. How do families think about how to create a better balance? You want the younger generation to be engaged and inspired to create their own vision. When they do that, that is what's going to create the next chapter. If they don't do that because they're boxed in, by the time they're fifty, it's been beat out of them."

ENTERING A FAMILY BUSINESS DOES not automatically make a relation an entrepreneur. Some simply see it as a job or inherited wealth, while others want no part of the business their family owns, regardless of how successful it is. But despite the complexity of mixing family with commerce, many follow their relatives into business because they sense an economic or intellectual opportunity, they feel an emotional connection to the business, or they want to shape a legacy. Legacy is a hefty word, which the wine business values highly. It is why a bottle of Château Lafite Rothschild sells for more than ten times what a bottle of Bodega y Cavas de Weinert does, even though they are ostensibly the same product. But legacy to entrepreneurs in family businesses can mean many different things. "I see legacy as a living thing," said Fredda

Herz Brown, founder of the Family Firm Institute. "I think there are families who see it as a dead thing, but you always change legacy. I think one of the notions about it is that it creates opportunities and burdens. For some, legacy becomes a significant burden." Legacy can be the past and the template for the future, something individual and something collective, a restriction or a liberating force.

As I spoke with entrepreneurs at various family-owned wineries in Mendoza, it became clear how legacy drove each of them differently. For Hernán Pimentel, who ran Bodega Caelum with his mother, Mercedes Diàs, and sister Constanza, their winery was created as a collective family legacy. When Pimentel's parents bought a hundred and fifty acres of land here in 1990, they had no background in the wine business or even Mendoza. They ran a large flour mill in Buenos Aires, but Mercedes was an agronomist with a passion for gardening, and she began growing tomatoes, garlic, and onions on the land. Three years later, as Argentina's wine business took off globally, she tore out all the vegetables and replaced them with Malbec and Cabernet Sauvignon vines, selling the grapes to nearby wineries.

For fourteen years, Mercedes grew grapes for other winemakers, while her children pursued careers in Buenos Aires (Hernán worked at Unilever as an industrial engineer, making AXE body spray). By 2009, Mercedes was divorced and increasingly unhappy in Mendoza. Growing grapes can be a lucrative business, but at the end of the day you have very little control over your product. "When you are selling grapes, the truck shows up without an agreement or a price. They set *everything*, especially when you're growing something high quality. It's not good," Pimentel explained, as we looked out over the family's neat vineyards from the small tasting room of the modern winery. Increasingly, they felt their family's product wasn't being adequately valued by the wineries they sold to, who often blended it with inferior grapes from other vineyards. "The truth of the truth is that if you grow grapes and make your own wine with it, the *only* grape you'll grow is a quality one. But when you're just selling grapes, you care about kilos . . . kilos, that's it."

It became obvious that they should team up to create a winery. The family had grapes and vineyards that were managed by a mother, a son who knew how to build industrial production facilities, and a daughter who had become a sommelier. Mercedes had seeded their collective entrepreneurship by planting vines, and now her children would work with her to make wine from them. "The most important part for us is using our own grapes in our own wines," Pimentel said, poking his nose in an oak barrel to give it a sniff, then shifting his head to place his ear by the hole. "You can hear it fermenting," he said, and I leaned in to listen to the subtle hiss of grape juice being digested by yeasts.

Many people find family businesses suffocating. Imagine being with your parents and siblings and grandparents and children every single day. You wake up with them, drive to work with them, eat lunch with them, attend meetings and travel with them, then go home with them, dine with them, sleep under the same roof with them, and repeat that for the rest of your life. Pimentel went from seeing his sister once a month in Buenos Aires, to seeing her six days a week, all day, and he admits, they get on each other's nerves all the time.

"My mother gave me life and that gives an emotional hit," Pimentel told me, "but the rule here is that we all work as hard as possible. Outside we are mother and son and daughter, but here we are partners. And if my mom comes in and I'm on the computer and she asks me something I know she can find the answer for on a manual on the shelf, I'll say, 'Go over to the shelf and don't break my balls.'"

Despite the daily frustrations and friction, building Bodega Caelum's shared legacy together as a family was ultimately worth it. "It is a question of confidence," he said. "My sister knows me by a look on my face. And I know I can trust her with something a hundred percent. If it's an employee, no matter how well paid he is, I need to think of systems of control . . . for example, managing the cash for wine sales to tourists . . . how do I control that? With my sister, I don't even have to think about that." Same with his mother, whom he trusted completely with the vineyards. That implicit trust gave them all the mental freedom to focus on the work at hand. Everyone's motivations were clear and unified as they built their collective legacy.

For the Weinert family their shared sense of purpose began to unravel in 2010, when Iduna heard that her father had not properly paid the winery's grape growers, yet went ahead building a winery on a vineyard he owned in Patagonia, despite agreeing not to in a previous meeting with her and Bruno. "I said, 'That's it!'" Iduna recalled. "I was done," she said. "It was impossible to represent a company in the world where I don't know what's happening inside of it and didn't like what I found." She hopped a flight to Rio de Janeiro and sent her father an official telegram informing him of her resignation (something required by Argentinean law). Bruno left the business six months later. Neither of them looked back.

The departure was equally frustrating for Bernardo Weinert, who believed that he not only gave his children every opportunity to educate themselves and follow a career they wanted, but to gain a foothold in the winery business and prove themselves through the work they did. "Fathers always have illusions with their kids," he said, noting that it is hard for children in a family business to manage expectations, because they have to work harder and smarter than anyone, just to prove they deserve their job. "You don't just hand out the keys to them," he said, "it's a progressive process." But he also saw increasingly how Iduna longed to be independent, and Bruno wanted to apply his IT skills in a way the winery could never satisfy. Bernardo understood their impatience with the pace of change and acknowledged that his children needed to pursue their dreams, but having them leave the business was a personal blow. "Like all fathers, you're frustrated when your kids can't build their dream," he said. "Family is a very difficult thing to manage. Not all kids will be equal. One will be a leader. Others not. That's the hard part."

Few family businesses succeed into the second generation and fewer still into the third and beyond. The family, the individual, and the business overlap in ways that can be unhealthy, with personal emotions about preferential treatment, sibling rivalry, and love playing out within the economic realities of a business. Often, the founder's children have no interest following in their parents' footsteps, opting for careers in other professions or starting their own businesses.

For all the difficulties, however, the potential advantages of multi-generational entrepreneurship are numerous, too: it can mean lasting economic security and an anchor of a family identity. It can open up choices to new generations that might never have materialized otherwise. For many families in the Mendoza wine business, this is more than enough of a draw.

One morning, I drove an hour and a half south of Mendoza city to the Uco Valley, a region of vineyards in the Andean foothills, to meet two members of the Zuccardi family, who are the standard-bearers of family entrepreneurship in the region. Each generation of Zuccardis has built upon the legacy of the previous one, culminating in their latest (and grandest) winery, Piedra Infinita, a concrete monument to the "infinite stones" of the Andes that opened in 2017, where I met José Alberto Zuccardi and his son Sebastián for a glorious steak and wine lunch.

The Familia Zuccardi business began in the 1960s, when José Alberto's father, Alberto "Tito," came to Mendoza to install irrigation systems for farms and vineyards, bought some land, and began growing his own grapes to demonstrate his technology. José Alberto joined his father's business in the mid-1970s and focused on winemaking, specifically creating wines at a competitive price point with an export focus. He is credited, along with other big family winery owners like Nicolàs Catena, with bringing Argentinean Malbec to the world market. Now in his seventies, José Alberto was proud to talk about how three generations of the Zuccardi family all worked together. He oversaw much of the company's business operations, while his three children had carved out entrepreneurial niches within the family business; Miguel had created a sophisticated olive oil brand, Julia developed the tourism program at Familia Zuccardi's two wineries, and Sebastián, who was in his late thirties, had taken their winemaking to a whole other level. Even José Alberto's mother, Emma, who was ninety-three at the time, still came to the winery every day to work. Bernardo Weinert credited the Zuccardis as the best example of a family business working together within separate channels.

A short man with gray hair, a slight scruff of beard, and a wide smile, José Alberto told me that the difference between individual entrepreneurship and entrepreneurship spread across generations was a question of time. "One generation can build on what the previous generation did, but in wine everything takes a very long, long time," he said. "Nothing takes one year. Five to ten years is short in this business. A family business has the opportunity to invest in the long term. We can commit to develop things as a company that a corporation simply couldn't do."

José Alberto was pouring me a glass of 2017 Concreto Malbec, a wine made from grapes that had been harvested two years before on vines planted more than a decade before that, in a vineyard that had been cultivated for decades, as part of the evolution of a company that was half a century old (yet still considered a new entrant in the global wine business). Winemaking was the opposite of Silicon Valley's rapid iteration and pivots between products and business models and exits. It was like a vine, slowly growing stronger each year, ultimately deepening the roots of the business and the family's entrepreneurial spirit.

That commitment required a steadfast independence, which the family regarded as a core value. A winery owned by a corporation was beholden to its shareholders and to delivering an annual or quarterly return on their investment, which shortened the time frame for any project. Just the day before, a large international investment group paid Familia Zuccardi a visit, with an offer to purchase a controlling stake in the business, likely worth tens of millions of dollars (or more). In an economically uncertain country like Argentina, this was no small thing, but Sebastián had refused to even hear their offer, let alone consider it.

"We don't want investors or outside help," Sebastián told me, through lips cracked by Mendoza's punishing sun and stained purple by wine. "The only thing that matters is freedom." Why? "Because the decisions taken in the family business are not just economic, they are philosophical," he said. "Short-term decisions aren't good for the long term. Our decisions are long-term decisions. Because I'm not the owner of anything. I'm taking care of the legacy of the family. I received something and I take care of it for the next generation."

Didn't an adherence to legacy create companies that were stagnant and resistant to change?

Quite the opposite, José Alberto Zuccardi said. Change was their family's primary goal. Each generation had to provide space for the next one to renew the business in their own way. If that renewal failed to occur, the business withered and eventually died. "When an entrepreneur thinks of things, they need space to develop their capabilities," he said. "My role in my kids' projects is to be a facilitator and an advisor, but really it's to bring those projects to life." José Alberto's parents let him do it by selling their wines globally, and he had done it with his children, most notably with Sebastián's highly ambitious efforts here in the Uco Valley, which had transformed how Familia Zuccardi wines were made.

Sebastián credited José Alberto with offering opportunities at the winery for him and his siblings, but he never forced them to work for him. They came into the business when it called them. Sebastián didn't formally start working with his father until he was in high school, and he wanted to do a project on sparkling wine, which the family didn't produce at the time. "So I asked my dad if I could try it, and he said, 'Okay, from the vines to the market, you grow it and you sell it,'" Sebastián recalled. "So my start in the business was as an entrepreneur, setting up a separate division at nineteen years old with three friends to make and sell this sparkling wine. My parents helped me sell it, opening up their contacts and providing the resources, but this gave me my proper identity within the business from the start."

A few years later, Sebastián was in charge of buying grapes from outside growers and became obsessed with vineyards in the Uco Valley, which are at a much higher elevation than vineyards the family owned farther north. "I told my father, 'The future is in Uco, we need to buy here,' and he told me to start doing my research." Sebastián experimented with different grapes, mapping elevations and cataloging the specific makeup of soils, down to the square meter. What came out of it was Piedra Infinita, a multimillion-dollar winery that completely upended the way the family made wine. Sebastián reversed conventional wisdom, planting new varietals of grapes. Individual vines received different levels of water and different harvest times, depending on their soil composition or exposure to the elements, which he tracked with advanced technology. He certified a big part of the vineyard as organic and fermented the grapes in porous concrete tanks, without artificial yeasts, so the essence of the grape shone through. These wines were interesting, challenging, funky, strange, and expensive, especially in Argentina. In just over a decade, Familia Zuccardi went from selling a handful of wines to offering more than forty different products, and in 2018, Sebastián was named the South American winemaker of the year by the prestigious wine magazine *Decanter*.

"The next generation are more open," said Claudio Müller, a professor of business strategy and family firms just over the border from Mendoza at the University of Chile, who documented how Chilean family-owned wineries were more likely to adopt environmentally sustainable practices in their vineyards than nonfamily competitors. Müller believed that this was a product of the cumulative spirit of entrepreneurship they cultivated. "They can include new technology in the process and adapt better to the market, faster. This can include new grapes, new process like biodynamic/organic growing, and generally the introduction of fresh ideas to the old industry." Fundamentally, it came down to cultivating a sense of legacy with the wider world, which suited a long-term vision, rather than one focused exclusively on profitability above all.

Vikram Bhalla, who runs the Boston Consulting Group's family business practice out of his office in India, has shown that in developing economies, like India and Argentina, family businesses are often more aggressive than others, taking on more debt and pursuing more acquisitions to achieve more growth—demonstrating an appetite for risk that grows with each generation. This came from what Paul Woodfield, a New Zealand academic who researches family wine businesses, called "intergenerational knowledge sharing." Knowledge is cumulative and serves as the base for the next generation's entrepreneurial ideas and the confidence to pursue them.

When Federico Cassone and his siblings built Bodega Familia Cassone in 1999, they did it next to vineyards that their grandfather had bought fifty years earlier. Half a century of inherited knowledge about its vines, soil, and environmental conditions gave them the confidence to try something new and continue taking risks as it grew. A few years ago, for example, Federico decided to try to change the vineyard's soil. "To literally change our *terroir*," he said, describing the process of mulching together eucalyptus bark with organic materials, like fruit stems and skins, to actively alter the family's land in the pursuit of better grapes. They were only able to do this because they already possessed the intimate knowledge of the land. The results, as I tasted in a fruit-forward Cabernet Sauvignon rosé, were incredible. "We did this because *we* believed in it," Federico told me, noting that his family's emotional connection to the business drove their entrepreneurial spirit. "I can tell people these wines are Cassone, because the Cassone family wants them to taste like this. Not because some market asks for them to taste a certain way. No one defends these wines more than us. Nothing is more intrinsic to our family than these wines."

I heard something similar from Lucas Pfister, a young winemaker who managed his family's small vineyard called Finca Sofia, just off the main highway between the Valley of Uco and Mendoza city. Pfister's father, a doctor in Buenos Aires, bought the property in 2004 as an investment, after befriending Bernardo Weinert on a flight. Pfister began to manage the vineyard a few years later, after studying winemaking in Europe and working in Italy, and recently started bottling his own super-funky, minimal intervention wines, crushing the grapes under foot instead of mechanically, to achieve a more natural grape flavor, to showcase the Pfister family's budding legacy, which was rooted in its soil.

"I don't have a vineyard here and another fifty kilometers away," Pfister said, as we drove down the dusty lanes between vines in his pickup to check on the grapes that would be picked in the coming weeks. "I have to make complexity out of this place. What I want are *our* grapes . . . period . . . and for my family, there is enormous satisfaction that I can turn their grapes into my wine. So to take care of that and build on that and maybe one day another generation will continue that . . . well, that's a beautiful thing."

As we drove around the vineyards in the late day sun, Pfister, who was dressed in shorts and a dusty t-shirt, pulled up to a section whose vines were shrunken and sprouting just a few green shoots. He explained how these vines had been recovered after lying fallow for nearly a decade, because Bodega y Cavas de Weinert had stiffed Pfister's father on payment for a harvest, and they couldn't afford to maintain them. He and his father held no grudge against the Weinerts, but Iduna cited this fact as one of the main reasons she left the family business, with no intention of returning.

RIO DE JANEIRO WAS UNDERGOING a tremendous boom when Iduna moved back there in 2010. The Brazilian economy soared, lifting millions out of poverty, and preparations for the Olympics and World Cup injected tremendous optimism and investment into the city. She spent a few months in law school before taking a role with the multinational food conglomerate Nestlé, selling Nespresso coffee products to high-end restaurants and hotels around Brazil. The job was fun, lucrative, and it played perfectly off the skills she had acquired in wine sales. "It was great," she said. "I got a car, a phone, and I was going to eat at the best restaurants every day. Best of all, I got paid on the twenty-ninth of every month like magic . . . *bling* . . . the money was just there in my account!" She spoke with her father almost every day, and he was eager to hear about her success. But when she asked him about the winery, Bernardo simply told her that things were great.

In 2012, during a visit to Mendoza over the Christmas holidays, Bernardo told Iduna and her siblings that he was selling half of his interest in the winery to a successful businessman from Buenos Aires named Miguel López, who was coming for dinner that night. Something about the deal struck Iduna as too good to be true. "This guy shows up at the house, and the second I see him it's so apparent this is such a clear lie,"

Iduna recalled, "but the truth is that there really was no choice." In the two years since she had left the business, Bodega y Cavas de Weinert was in increasingly difficult financial circumstances. Sales to foreign markets were declining, the economic and political climate in Argentina made exporting costly and difficult, and the winery's debts were escalating. López had agreed to come on as a partner and assume those debts, which allowed Don Bernardo to remain in charge of his beloved winery. "I was tired," Bernardo told me, of his motivation for the partnership, which was driven in a big way by Iduna and Bruno's departure. "I looked for a partner to take some of the weight off my back." It was sad, Iduna told me, but there was nothing she could do, and by this time, she was emotionally removed from the business. She returned to Brazil.

After a few years at Nestlé, however, Iduna was bored. The money was good and she had tons of free time to indulge in new hobbies, like running an open water swimming team, but corporate life was predictable, and so much came down to interoffice politics. She missed the personality of the wine industry and, more than that, the personal association with her name and a business. "It was forgotten that I was a Weinert," she said. At Nestlé, she was just another employee.

In 2014, Iduna quit her job to launch Wine Essence, a branding agency for Argentinean and Chilean wineries that wanted to grow in Brazil. Working with wineries, importers, and distributors, she leveraged both her knowledge of the wine business and the Brazilian food and beverage market. "It was really mine!" she said, when I asked what it felt like to finally become an entrepreneur. "For the first time in my life, this was something of my own." Bernardo told me that he knew Iduna would eventually start her own business. Like him, and his father, she craved the independence that only came from being your own boss. Entrepreneurship was inevitable.

FEW MEMBERS OF MY OWN family set out to become entrepreneurs. It just drew us in. We have started companies with employees (sweater factories, hardware distributors) or just struck out on our own as lawyers, writers, and pop-up retailers. "We're the unemployables!" my cousin Eric (who runs an immigration consulting practice) loves to say, but it's true. Those of us who have held jobs in big organizations are frequently quitting or getting fired because the constraints are unbearable. We have too many ideas. Too much of a desire to do things our own way. As the last law firm that interviewed my father told him before he struck out on his own, "You're too entrepreneurial to work here, Sax." They were right. We are the employment equivalent of wild animals, incapable of domestication.

Iduna had unconsciously followed her father's path into becoming an entrepreneur, just as I had, and I wondered whether there was something about entrepreneurship itself that crossed generations, a sort of inherited entrepreneurial spirit that moved through families, regardless of if they shared a business or not.

"There's no tradition in our family, other than the tradition of not romanticizing the past," Sebastián Zuccardi said, when I asked him about this. "Our tradition is doing new things. The tradition in our family is to be entrepreneurs. The energy, what moves us, is always to do new projects." Right now he was working on recovering lost vineyards in the province of San Juan and making a vermouth from scratch. His siblings, his father, even his grandmother, all harbored similar side projects and businesses they were working on, as were other winery owners and entrepreneurs I spoke with. Entrepreneurship, more than anything, was the Zuccardi family's legacy. Not their business, its assets, or the taste of their wines, but the value of being an entrepreneur in its own right. "In our family, it's not a value to be comfortable. It is to be uncomfortable," said José Alberto Zuccardi. "That's not good. That's not bad. It is what it is."

A 2015 paper in the *Journal of Business Venturing* labeled this an "entrepreneurial legacy," a phenomenon where families built narratives around "past entrepreneurial achievements or resilience" to motivate the next generation to become entrepreneurs in their own right. Though the paper focused exclusively on entrepreneurial legacy within the same family business, the concept applies more broadly to people like me, who seem to have inherited some kind of propensity toward entrepreneur-ship. "Family entrepreneurship is actually about the family's legacy of entrepreneurship," said Lauri Union, of Babson College. "It's not neces-sary that the family keeps the same business or expresses entrepreneur-ship in the same way or in perpetuity. The family has an entrepreneurial legacy: people were entrepreneurs in the past, and the family has the desire for their children and future generations to be entrepreneurial." An entrepreneurial legacy was something the descendants of entrepre-neurs were born with, and whatever path they took in life, it remained with them.

"I come from a family of entrepreneurs," said Sofia Pescarmona, whom I met at Bodega Lagarde, the winery she runs with her sister Lu-cila. "When you do new things in an entrepreneurial family, the family sees it as normal, as perfect, never as something bad or weird." No one taught Pescarmona how to be an entrepreneur. Though her grandfather, an Italian immigrant, first bought Bodega Lagarde in 1969, Pescarmona only entered the business in 2001, when she was thirty years old and the winery was on the ropes. She had no experience in the wine business (she'd been working at a giant telecom company in Buenos Aires) and had to learn by doing. "My father tossed me in the pool," Pescarmona said, but she credited the example her family set as entrepreneurs in the construction engineering business they ran in Mendoza with giving her confidence and a tolerance for risk. It fed that hunger for something new and allowed her to succeed.

"Entrepreneurship is a lifestyle," she said, as we walked through the organic vegetable gardens she had planted years before, which provided the fresh produce for the award-winning restaurant she had opened, which was packed with tourists enjoying a long lunch in the shade. "Something about the entrepreneur's lifestyle is the freedom you have. Your kids see this and they look for that in life. To them it all seems normal . . . working nights, working weekends . . . it's just not an issue. When you are an entrepreneur, you're an entrepreneur till three a.m., and it doesn't stop. My kids [who were just entering their teens] see mo-ments of tension in my life. They see the good and the bad."

Over the past year and a half, as my wife, Lauren, began working from home, I wondered what story we were telling our own two children (who were being dragged around Mendoza as I conducted interviews) about being entrepreneurs. What lessons would they eventually take from that? I hoped it was something like the entrepreneurial legacy of my own parents: My mother, who ran a wholesale women's clothing sale out of our home twice a year for two decades with her best friend Paula, which filled our basement playroom with racks of dresses, blouses, and accessories they had bought from suppliers in Montreal. Daniel and I would hide in the racks, as the mothers of our friends walked around in their bras and our mother handled fat stacks of cash as she rung up sales. My father, who proudly told my brother and me about how he came from a humble background and established a law practice serving Toronto's growing Chinese community and later as a private investor, hustling opportunity wherever he could. He loved telling stories about flying to Hong Kong on a moment's notice to get a contract signed, only to end up in the kitchen of a restaurant with his clients, tossing a phone book against the wall at five in the morning to bet on which page it would open on. He shared the good and the bad. The ups of the 1980s and the fizzling of the real estate market a decade later. Deals that popped and those that flopped. He was an open book about entrepreneurship (and continues to be), because he valued everything it gave him, and he wanted us to appreciate that.

"There are some family business leaders that are intentional about talking about their business, how they think about growth, risk, and opportunities," said Michael McGrann, the family business consultant whom I actually first met through my father (who studied family business advising with McGrann). "It is something that can be taught and fomented. It is a mindset."

But despite my father's repeated attempts to teach me specific, highly useful skills in contract analysis, deal vetting, and strategic thinking or to get me interested in following him into law or business, what I have inherited from my father, in the years spent observing him and occasionally working alongside him as he looks at investments, is the love of entrepreneurship. The appreciation of opportunity. The adrenaline thrill that comes with discovering one and the hard lessons when that opportunity does not play out as you expected (which it rarely does). The independence and freedom of being your own boss and how valuable and difficult that is. My parents' entrepreneurial legacy has made me better as a freelance writer, more confident in how I pursue deals, negotiate my contracts, market and network myself, and seek out chances rather than waiting for them to arrive. That is the entrepreneurial mindset: a worldview focused on seeing what is possible and then just doing it.

Of course, there are many entrepreneurs who have no interest in perpetuating that legacy and actively shield their families from their work. My grandfather Stanley Davis might have allowed my mother to visit the warehouse in Montreal where his tool distribution company was based and even to work there one summer, but she was never actively encouraged to take a lasting role in it. My wife's father, Howard, was the second generation in the truck parts distribution business his own father co-owned, but he never talked about his business at home or encouraged his children to take an interest in it. Truck parts were never his passion. He worked there because it was a good financial opportunity, and when he passed away at fifty-nine, his shares were sold to his partners.

In his heart Howard wanted to be his own entrepreneur, just like his wife, Fran. Early in their marriage, they worked together, importing wicker furniture from the Philippines and flower planters from Mexico, which they sold at flea markets around Toronto. As a baby, Lauren slept in a basket under their market stall, but when her sister was born, Howard needed stability and joined the family business. That sacrifice, and the financial security it provided them all, is what allowed Fran to continue her career as an entrepreneur, selling accessories at pop-up markets, and what Lauren believes eventually allowed her to work for herself (though she did work for Fran for two years after college).

"That was his goal all along," Lauren said, when I asked her about this recently. "All of that is possible because of the sacrifices he made."

Howard never pushed his children to pursue stable careers, as he had done. He actively encouraged them to do their own thing, to pursue their passions. The financial security he assured them, even after he died, gave Lauren the confidence to go out on her own as a career coach. When people talk about entrepreneurship and privilege, this financial support is what they mean, and it is something that both Lauren and I had the benefit of, thanks to the sacrifices and success of our parents, who helped us with rent when we were starting out and a downpayment on our home. That privilege is our reality, and while neither of us are particularly proud or ashamed of that fact, we have to acknowledge it with open hearts.

Now the two of us were continuing the legacy of our families together, supporting our mutual ambitions of entrepreneurship with ideas, encouragement, and money when we needed it. When Lauren was working as a headhunter and I was struggling writing books, she was there for me, and now that I am more established and she is starting out, I've got her back. But more than any financial support, it was the emotional support we gave each other to go for it and keep at it that makes us an entrepreneurial family. "If you were just a dude who worked in a bank, I don't think I could have done what I did," she told me, during a rare midweek lunch (sadly, she still eats sardines at her desk). "That gave me permission. You couldn't say no to that!"

IDUNA WEINERT'S RETURN TO THE family business happened in circumstances that moved quicker than anyone expected and with results that few predicted. Since that fateful night in 2012, when López became part owner of Bodega y Cavas de Weinert, the winery quickly fell apart. Although her father was an owner, López had used financial and legal maneuvers to assume total control over the business. He held the position of president, the mortgages for the winery, the house, properties in Patagonia, and even Bernardo and Selma's apartment in Buenos Aires. Under López's direction, Bodega y Cavas de Weinert stopped producing new wines after the 2013 harvest. Instead, the winery got by bottling the vast reserves of wines it held in its cellars. López shipped these wines to warehouses he owned in Buenos Aires, where the wine was sold for cash, which he pocketed. In effect, the business was being drained from within.

"It was so painful," Iduna said. "There were no international markets anymore, the grass wasn't cut, and it got so bad that the winemaker wouldn't come here for more than thirty minutes in a day. I'd visit every year for the holidays because I always felt it was the last chance to see this before it was gone." Still, she refused to get involved. She was happy in Brazil, where her life and business were going well.

But by the end of 2016, when Iduna came back for her Christmas visit, her father was "beaten down" by the way López had conned and manipulated him, and he wanted to salvage something while he still could. Iduna began speaking with different lawyers to see what options her family had. She told me that she did this out of concern for her parents, but there were other factors at play. Brazil had entered a severe recession, and Rio was quickly becoming plagued by violent crime. Iduna's own business was affected by all of this, but as she spent more time dealing with Bodega y Cavas de Weinert's complicated legal issues, her entrepreneurial instincts kicked in. The winery was at rock bottom, but she knew, from the decade she spent working there, what it could still be if the right people were in charge. "I just saw how much potential this company had."

In March 2017, Bernardo Weinert began working with a young accountant and a lawyer in Buenos Aires who specialized in tricky business situations. Nicknamed "the guys" by the family, Antonino Virzi and Leandro Arias saw a potential long-shot around López that was called a legal intervention, a procedure where a court could seize control of a business if it was on the verge of bankruptcy and wrongdoing was proven. They believed the contract with López was largely fraudulent, but since Bernardo had no cash and the winery was already deep in debt, they made a deal with him. If Virzi and Arias won the case, they would be paid with any equity recovered from López. Don Bernardo was excited about the chance to be back in the fight and enthusiastically introduced Virzi and Arias to Iduna. "He saw it as a chance to get the company back," she said, "and a way to get everything this company could do, actually done." Surprisingly, a judge granted the intervention. All shares in the winery were frozen and Bernardo and López were temporarily removed from their roles, while a court-appointed lawyer was placed in charge of the business for two weeks, as he prepared a report to the judge.

Iduna spent those two weeks helping the lawyer and the winery's team prepare the report and quickly realized Bodega y Cavas de Weinert was her future. At the time, she had offers to work for Brazilian coffee companies and other wineries in Mendoza, but the choice was obvious. As quickly as she left Argentina and the winery seven years before, she moved back in force. "We could recover it!" she said, when I asked her what finally made her return. "This place is a Disneyland of the wine business world. And at some point, you have to ask yourself: 'Are you in or are you out?' And this was infinitely more interesting than working with other wineries, selling their wines in Brazil or with Nestlé selling espresso pods," Iduna said, explaining that an entrepreneur, above all else, was someone who relished a challenge. "To me, coming back was about the challenge of recovering this thing." Bernardo recalled warning his daughter that the return was her choice, but one that would entail the sacrifice of the freedom she enjoyed as the owner of her own business to once again work as an employee of the winery (now controlled by the courts), and all the tension that came with that. "She had her dream of independence that goes to her soul," he said, "but I felt good about it."

Over the next year, as the intervention wound through the courts, Iduna worked with Virzi and Arias to try to turn the winery around. Initially her family supported her, but as the intervention neared its end in March of 2018 and Bodega y Cavas de Weinert's ownership was finally going to revert to Bernardo (with López's shares now held by Virzi and Arias), the Weinert family dynamic started to fray. Don Bernardo had assumed that the end of the legal intervention would mark his triumphant return as the boss of the winery he had created and run for more than forty years, but as a condition of his ruling, the judge forbade him from returning as chairman.

"It was very difficult for him to go through with that," Iduna said. "The loss of the title as president was a crush on my father's heart. 'I'm the founder,' he said. 'If I'm not the president then who am I?'" (Bernardo disputed this, saying that nothing changed for him beyond the title.)

Babson's Lauri Union says that this emotion is often the main obstacle that prevents first-generation founders from passing the torch of entrepreneurship to their children, and it is a hard one to overcome. "The definition of *who I am* is the person who created this business. If I'm going to pass that on to the next generation, then who am I now?" she said. "That's mortality." Fredda Herz Brown said that true succession involves an entrepreneur acknowledging that they are at the end of their game. "Giving that up at its very base is accepting where you are in life," she said. "It's hard for an entrepreneur to say, 'I'm now on the downhill swing of my life. I've built this, but now I have to hand it over.'"

Denial was no shield against reality. Mendoza was littered with the abandoned ruins of family wineries that died clutching legacies because they were afraid to take the risks and embrace the change that their founders had once defined themselves by. Sofia Pescarmona saw this every day, in wineries where the founding generation remained stubbornly in charge. "It never works with a figure too strong at the top," she said. "When the tree is too big, it casts a shadow so that nothing grows beneath it."

The Weinert family and business situation only grew more complicated. A few months into the intervention process Iduna began dating Virzi, the accountant who now owned a quarter of the winery with her name on it and was running it day to day (and as its director was essentially her boss). In Argentina, as in many Latin American countries, patrilineal descent is still a common feature of family businesses, and though Iduna's older brother Bruno remained completely removed from the business (and rarely spoke to his parents), her younger brother André still lived and worked at the winery, and the two quickly came into conflict. "The arrival of Iduna created a lot of family difficulty," Bernardo told me, with a sigh. "Her, with her indomitable spirit and style of working, well, it can trip up a lot of people." Considering every family feud has multiple sides and infinite layers, the entire situation was doubtlessly more complicated than how my friend Iduna presented it to me. But the end result was a daughter working in a family business, for a family that no longer acknowledged her presence in any way.

This is the ugly but unfortunately common reality of family entrepreneurship. With emotions, relationships, and long-simmering antagonisms spilling over between the personal and professional, the legacy of entrepreneurship within a family frequently leads to conflict and ruptures of those businesses and families. The wine business is no exception, with public feuds and lawsuits tearing apart legendary families such as California's Mondavi and Gallo dynasties, to name just two. "I never thought it would be this bad," Iduna admitted, when I asked her about this shortly after the awkward encounter with her parents and brother at the winery. "At the start of the intervention my father was happy I'd come back to the company," but now, she felt they saw her as a usurper, executing some sort of palace coup. Her parents even stopped inviting her to Christmas dinner.

"It feels terrible," Don Bernardo said, when I asked him about the family's current situation. "When there's disharmony, the legacy of family and entrepreneurship becomes twisted in that disharmony. And this is the ultimate legacy that matters. Every family has moments of disharmony, and the entrepreneur wants, more than anything, that the family stays together. That they come back together and work together, even if it's in future generations. Sometimes the entrepreneur has time to accomplish this, and sometimes no," he said with a sigh, noting that he was now eighty-seven, and while he was still working with passion, he could not stop time.

"This is my reality. It could be easier. I probably made a few mistakes, but no one knows what's a mistake when you're working to make something grow. Mistakes are only visible in the rearview mirror," he said. He built his winery, he grew it over four decades, and he gave his family the potential to continue that legacy, through education, opportunity, and fostering the value of entrepreneurship he saw as central to his very identity. "I reflect a lot these days," he said, "but what satisfies me is that I did it, and I did my best."

So why, despite all of this, was Iduna Weinert still there when the cost to her personally, and to the family, was so high? Two years after returning she still had no ownership stake in the business (her father had refused to pass on his shares while alive, but she would eventually inherit her portion of them), and though she was paid a salary by the winery, it was far less than she could make if she took a job elsewhere.

At first Iduna told me she worried what would happen to her parents if she left. López's lawsuits were ongoing, and there was a chance they could still lose everything if a court decision went the wrong way. "My parents were going to be out on the streets. What could I do?" I nodded and looked at Iduna, my friend for the past fifteen years, with bare skepticism. "Look," she said, opening her palms, as if showing me she had nothing to hide. "I was already too involved and even though it is personal, the company has been recovering so well, it is just tremendously rewarding to see. The employees, the importers, the grape growers . . . they all trust us now, and we regained that trust with hard work," she said. "Just leaving wasn't going to recover the family relationship. It's irrational, but if we lost everything, I'm going to be blamed anyway. It wasn't a principle thing. I saw an opportunity. I liked the people I was going to work with, and I could do something here."

When she'd returned to the business two years before, there were no exports to foreign markets, except one small Norwegian importer and a wine club in the UK. By March of 2019, the company's wines were once again available in ten countries, based on relationships Iduna had personally repaired one trip and shipment at a time. The winery's lawns were mowed, its buildings were in better repair, and tourists were coming more often and spending more money. Most importantly, Bodega y Cavas de Weinert was making wine again, and its style of traditional winemaking, with vintages aged in large casks, had gone from an anachronism to a resurgent trend in the wine world. By the end of the year

Iduna hoped to have Bodega y Cavas de Weinert in fifteen international markets and launch many more initiatives within the business, including a new restaurant and several lines of entry-level wines.

None of this was done single-handedly, Iduna said. She played a leadership role, but one in a team that was now increasingly professional, with an eye on the next generation of Bodega y Cavas de Weinert, even if that meant a diminished role for the family. The challenges were formidable. Bodega y Cavas de Weinert had lost ten years, and just to recover its previous momentum, the winery needed to grow 15 to 20 percent a year for several years. Already, competitors were swooping around, making aggressive offers to buy out the winery and relieve them of their debt. Change had come, but perhaps too late to renew the legacy.

"My goal is to make this work so that once again we are a player in the wine business," Iduna said. "There's no other project that's more challenging or exciting than this place. We are unique because we produce nothing like anyone else here in Mendoza. It's about this place. If it was some modern winery I'd have said 'Bye Bye' years ago," she said, blowing a kiss into the air. "But this place is special."

That uniqueness, which remained Bodega y Cavas de Weinert's advantage, was her father's legacy, including the very first vintages Don Bernardo had envisioned and bottled some forty years earlier, before Iduna was even born. He was an entrepreneur who had spent his life balancing risk and building businesses, and while Iduna expressed hope that he would be able to enjoy his remaining years fishing in Patagonia and drinking his wine, she was done working for her father. Eventually, she would get a piece of the winery's ownership and continue to build what her father had started.

Silicon Valley's startup myth of entrepreneurship holds that family is something you manage in your off time and don't bring to work, where you are expected to eat cheap takeout and sleep on the office floor until you can achieve a successful exit. These sacrifices are part of that myth and everything it brings with it. The greater truth is that every entrepreneur has the freedom to make those decisions about the intersection of family and work themselves—you can choose to build your business more slowly in order to nurture your children, or you can try to integrate family members into your business, partnering with your spouse or hiring your offspring, with a focus on building something that has no exit, but rather a legacy that will outlast your own mortality.

That doesn't mean that being a family entrepreneur is a free pass to a simpler life or even a better family dynamic. Instead, it means marrying the challenges of work with the challenges of family: a rift between siblings can impact your job, a downturn in sales can ruin dinner, or the failure to reckon with your legacy, and mistakes in preparing it for the next generation, can ultimately tear a family apart. But on the other hand, the Zuccardi family shows what the best version of this can look like: an enduring bond between generations, a shared sense of purpose, and certain freedoms that are impossible any other way.

"I would do it all over again," Iduna told me, when I asked her if she regretted how things had transpired with her family. "I don't regret it at all. I don't feel bad. Actually, I feel really, really good." She was driven by the legacy; of the winery her father built, but also, of a larger entrepreneurial spirit that Don Bernardo Weinert had taught her. "Sometimes I see myself as a reflection of my father," she said. "He used to tell us that 'Life is a jungle, and to survive, you have to do whatever it takes.' . . . well . . . whatever it takes."

CHAPTER 7

A Burrito, Four Beers, and a Roller Coaster

Seth Nitschke bent over bins of small metal parts in the aisle of a Lowe's in Turlock, California, a town in the San Joaquin Valley. It was late in the morning, and this was the second hardware store Nitschke had been to, searching for something to join the wires on a broken livestock fence, with no luck. "Goddamnit," he said. "When you're the owner of a business, you spend one and a half hours chasing down a four-dollar part to get the stupid job done."

Nitschke (pronounced *nitch-key*) had spent most of the morning hauling his cattle trailer across the county. His grass-fed beef business, Mariposa Ranch, was spread between four properties in Mariposa County (where his two hundred–odd cattle grazed in the foothills southwest of Yosemite National Park), the town of Turlock (where he rents a small feedlot, office, and warehouse), and the nearby city of Modesto (where a meatpacking plant butchers and stores his beef). "I spend 30 to 40 percent of my time moving stuff around, without actually making a single dollar," he said, as we got back into his Dodge Ram pickup truck, with his dogs Tag and Bleu yapping in the cab, to visit yet another hardware store. Nitschke said that the daily "commutes" with cattle and supplies from home to office to feedlot to ranches and back added up to four hours of driving a day.

Nitschke is forty-two, lean and compact, with a bristly red beard and mustache. He wears the American cowboy uniform of Wrangler jeans and denim jackets, button-down shirts, a belt buckle that he won judging livestock, and a straw cowboy hat. He jokes that while he's a gun-owning redneck, he's a Californian one, which means he never listens to country music (he worships the Clash), surfs whenever he can, has a wickedly sarcastic sense of humor, and quotes Roman generals and modernist philosophers like Victor Frankel far more than the Bible. He grew up nearby, in an agricultural community outside Fresno, and although his parents weren't farmers, Nitschke gravitated toward ranching in high school, where he judged show cattle for the Future Farmers of America. He studied livestock science in college, where he met his wife, Mica, and worked for four years around the Midwest as a cattle buyer for the agribusiness giant Cargill, sometimes handling four thousand animals in a day.

In 2006, Nitschke returned home to start a grass-fed beef company that began as Open Space Meats and he recently rebranded Mariposa Ranch. At the time, Mica had just given birth to Henry, their first child, and Nitschke used $2,500 of their savings to buy three cows and build a website. Many people believe grass-fed ranching is better for the animals and environment and produces tastier, healthier beef than animals raised in a feedlot. The business model was a fairly simple one, Nitschke said. Cows ate grass, gained weight, and became steak. "I take an animal, pay seven hundred dollars for it, and by the end it's worth four times that."

In the thirteen years since the company began, Henry had grown into a lanky preteen and had two younger sisters, Elle, ten, and Charlotte, four. The business had initially grown steadily, selling meat directly to consumers, butcher shops, and markets around California, as well as large corporate catering companies that provided food to places like Stanford and Google. Despite this promising start, Mariposa Ranch had ceased growing a few years ago, and Nitschke, the cowboy entrepreneur behind the business, was stuck in limbo.

His problems were straightforward. The biggest was land, which Nitschke didn't own. He paid rent to four landlords to graze on their pastures, necessitating a daily shuffling of cattle, horses, equipment, people, and his own ass around the region, taking up time, gas, and energy. "If I lived here, I wouldn't have to deal with this bullshit," Nitschke said, as we drove into one of these properties more than an hour after we left Turlock. He had recently lost the opportunity to buy a ranch, and with the Northern California property market showing no signs of slowing down, his chances to acquire land were diminishing.

Climate change had made farming in the San Joaquin Valley increasingly precarious. It had been six months since it last rained, and the scars from forest fires were visible on the charred trunks of trees around parched pastures. On top of this were the typical gripes of entrepreneurs: the burden of government regulations and taxes, the indifference of politicians from all parties, and the difficulty in finding reliable employees. Over the years Nitschke had churned through salesmen, cowherds, drivers, and a slew of part-time helpers. Most recently, a ranch hand had filled his truck's engine with oil, instead of gas, instantly ruining the vehicle. Nitschke was forced to buy a new truck he couldn't afford.

"This may be dumb cowboy stuff, but at least it's in my control," Nitschke said, as he climbed down into a small creek, where a flash flood had taken out a section of fence the week before. "This is broken and now I'll fix it. I can control that. What's out of my control is the employee who said he fixed it but didn't, because he couldn't get off of fucking Snapchat for ten minutes."

When Mariposa Ranch began in 2006, grass-fed beef was a novelty in America, but inexpensive grass-fed beef was now flooding the market from Brazil, Uruguay, and New Zealand. Well-funded Silicon Valley figures, celebrities, and former hedge fund managers, as well as Nitschke's own brother-in-law, were getting into the grass-fed-beef business domestically, increasing the supply and competition while driving down prices. After his costs, and the half million dollars in operating debt he held in cattle, inventory, and rented land, Mariposa Ranch gave its owner around $30,000 to take home each year. Like many farmers, Nitschke worked another job as a part-time cattle feed salesman to just make ends meet.

"Did you see that article on *Business Insider* about grass-fed billionaires?" Nitschke said, climbing out of the gulley after repairing the fence. "That's because it was never written. Anyone who got in thinking it's a get-rich-quick scheme learned quick." He paused for a second to catch his breath, took his hat off, and wiped his forehead. It was ninety-eight degrees in the sun, and the work was hard, hot, and dusty. "I still don't know if this will work. Thirteen years later and the jury's still out," he said, before declaring, "Let's go for some tacos."

WHEN I FIRST BEGAN THINKING about this book, I wanted to focus on what it meant to be an entrepreneur. Not in an economic sense but something deeper. What did life as an entrepreneur feel like? I knew it was vastly more complicated than the startup myth that had emerged just over the hills to the east, in that other, more lucrative valley. I knew that it was often an emotionally wrenching and permanently transformative experience, a way of working and really of living, whose only certainty was uncertainty. Entrepreneurship was wonderful and terrible, exhilarating and terrifying, soul affirming and soul sucking . . . often in the same day.

I knew all of this because I recognized it in myself, the only person I had ever really worked for. When friends asked me things like "What do you *do* all day?" and "Where do you work?," what they really wanted to know was how I did it. How did someone wake up and go to work for themselves with no promise of success or predictable compensation? What was that like?

Working for myself has always been immensely difficult. It vacillates between the dread of not having enough work and the stress of having too much. Entrepreneurship is a daily experience of going to war with my ego, where I dive into an idea with the utmost optimism in the morning ("This is a brilliant idea!"), only to wrap myself in a blanket of self-hatred by the afternoon ("You are a fraud").

As an entrepreneur, everything is personal and it remained difficult because it was so personal. This unpleasant truth was being overlooked by Silicon Valley's startup mythmaking, which romanticized entrepreneurship and glorified risk-taking with macho slogans about embracing failure, but rarely, if ever, acknowledged the actual human cost of that. This was the difficult truth about what it meant to be an entrepreneur and the real reason, beyond economics, why so few people (one in ten Americans) decide to become one, despite all the glamour associated with it.

I wanted to see the dark side of the soul of the entrepreneur. Not when it was glorious and inspiring, but in those moments that were personally difficult. I wanted to see an entrepreneur face failure . . . not the romantic kind of failure that was supposedly a stepping-stone to success . . . but the real life-shaking threat to one's livelihood and identity. I found that just two hours east of Stanford, in the San Joaquin Valley, among the farmers whose experiences as entrepreneurs were more personally felt than almost any other profession.

"THE SAN JOAQUIN VALLEY IS where a lot of good old-fashioned work shit gets done," Nitschke said, as we sat down at the Oasis, a dusty gas station and market serving sopes, burritos, and tacos. "It's not sexy like L.A. or sophisticated like San Francisco or innovative like Silicon Valley." Nevertheless, the San Joaquin Valley was California's agricultural heartland, growing most of the food the state consumed and exported,

from strawberries and kale, to steaks and almonds. When you drove
down into it, from the foggy coast or the snowy Sierras, it spread out as
an endless dusty brown plain, dotted with green, dominated by pickup
trucks, farm vehicles, and billboards affirming the rights of farmers to
water.

The San Joaquin Valley is a triumph of man over nature, a desert
where rain seldom falls, and light brown dust blankets every surface. It
was brought to life by a vast system of irrigation canals built during the
late nineteenth and early twentieth centuries, which fed the parched,
rich soil and made it a sort of promised land for the poor and destitute
families, like Nitschke's, who fled the dust bowls in the 1930s. Still, despite the economic power of large agribusinesses, the San Joaquin Valley
was plagued by poverty. Cities like Turlock, nearby Modesto, and even
Fresno had shockingly high rates of crime, homelessness, drug addiction, and other social problems. State and federal politicians concentrated their attention along the coast, where the population and money
lay. "We are kind of an afterthought here," Nitschke said. "We grow all
the food but can't afford it. We're a valley of poor people."

The Nitschkes had a spacious home, two cars, three healthy, happy
children, plenty to eat (even if a lot of it was imperfect steaks they
couldn't sell), and enough left over to go to Disneyland or the beach
for vacation. But they were also stuck with a business that was no longer growing and few easy options to change that. When I first spoke to
Nitschke by phone, in July of 2018, he suggested I visit in late September,
when he expected to close on the purchase of their own ranch in Mariposa County, near the Oasis. At $700,000, the ranch was a calculated
risk that Seth and Mica hoped would change things. Owning it would
consolidate their various operations (pastures, office, warehouse, home)
into one location, saving time and money, aligning their family life with
the business, while building equity. Over the spring and summer the
bank had encouraged them to be aggressive, so they rearranged their finances and lives around the impending purchase, renting out the house
they owned in town for the income (moving to a rental on the outskirts)
and pulling the kids out of school in anticipation of their relocation.

Three weeks before I arrived, the bank abruptly changed its mind, denying the Nitschkes their mortgage and the ability to purchase the ranch. "It was a done deal . . . until it wasn't," Nitschke said. "We had a plan, and now it's rather precarious. Because things went the way they went we had a hell of a lot of disruption in our lives." The lease on the rented house had to be renegotiated. The children had to find places at schools in Turlock at the last minute. Boxes had to be unpacked. Even the internet had to be reconnected. Hopes had been dashed. It was back to square one.

"You've been kicked in the balls before, right David?" Nitschke said, when I asked him what it felt like when he heard the news. "It was like that. But falling over, hitting your head, getting a concussion, waking up, and everyone is mad at you."

In thirteen years of entrepreneurship Nitschke had endured plenty of ups and downs. He recalled the first trip to deliver meat to Southern California, when people greeted him at the door with a hug, and then the drive back, when empty cooler boxes scattered all over the highway. "This is never going to work!" he thought, as he dodged cars to gather the boxes. Running a business was riddled with challenges—orders were misplaced, cows got sick and died, accounts suddenly canceled—that fed his uncertainty.

"That thought of 'What the fuck am I doing? This is insane!' . . . you know, that feeling where that anxiety comes home to roost?" he said. "Yeah, I feel that about twice a day." The loss of the ranch was a fresh low for the business, Nitschke, and his family, and he was unsure how to move beyond it. He just knew he had to. He likened himself to a soldier that landed on the beach in Normandy, made it behind a dune, and was now pinned down between the sea and the Nazi machine guns. "You either move forward and go, or sit here and eventually get shot," he said, as we began the long drive back to Turlock. He had too much invested and had worked too hard to give up now. "Losing the ranch doesn't mean it won't ever happen, but it definitely won't happen soon," he said. "So maybe it's saying our life is in Turlock and Dad has to drive an hour to the ranch each day, which sucks, but Dad can hack it."

Hack it. Tough it out. Grind away. Sleep when you're dead. These aren't just the macho terms that ranchers use to describe the determination needed to survive the hard work they do; they are increasingly the mantras of a generation of entrepreneurs. This is what the startup myth perpetuates in stories, keynote speeches, and bestselling biographies of men like Elon Musk who boast about sleeping at their desks, working without vacation, and never ever giving up. Writing in the *New York Times*, journalist Erin Griffith called this growing phenomenon "toil glamour," a work culture where entrepreneurs competitively post enthusiastic slogans on social media about loving Mondays (T.G.I.M!), and coworking spaces cheer their tenants to #HustleHarder with neon signs. In one WeWork, she observed a water cooler, filled near to the brim with grapefruit and cucumber slices, displaying the message "Don't stop when you're tired. Stop when you're done," carved painstakingly out of the rinds of cucumbers, as if someone had specifically asked for the most North Korean–inspired way of displaying the message. "For congregants of the Cathedral of Perpetual Hustle, spending time on anything that's nonwork related has become a reason to feel guilty," Griffith wrote.

In the year and a half since he began his cannabis-focused real estate investment company, I saw this narrative take hold of my brother Daniel. He was constantly on his phone, even during meals, checking email and social media. Though he lives around the corner from me, Daniel was frequently too busy when I invited him to get lunch or coffee or walk one of the kids home. He often told me he had been working till some absurdly late hour the night before . . . 1 a.m. . . . 2 a.m. . . . 3 a.m. "It's called being an entrepreneur, David," he defensively said, whenever I asked him why, an obvious shot at the lazy know-it-all older brother, who was asleep by eleven. Daniel projected this image to others in the competitive Canadian cannabis industry, whose environment was no less young, aggressive, and prone to toil glamour than the startup technology business. "Being an entrepreneur involves both being tireless and constantly tired," he wrote on Twitter after a particularly long night.

The day before that post, Daniel and I were driving an hour west of Toronto to attend the annual meeting of a company our father had invested in. We left at seven thirty in the morning and neither of us had breakfast, but when I suggested that we stop to grab something to eat, he shot back at me:

"There's no time to eat, David! Entrepreneurship is about hunger."

"Not actual hunger, Dan," I said.

"Yes David, actual hunger."

One morning, I met Christopher Oneth for coffee in downtown Turlock to talk about this. Oneth is a therapist who recently took over a counseling practice in nearby Modesto ("Now I'm officially an entrepreneur," he joked). Over the years Oneth had dealt with many entrepreneurs, especially farmers, who came to him with a problem (lack of sleep, trouble with a spouse, substance issues) that was just a symptom of their approach to work. "Every gift we have has a corresponding weakness, but you can get lost in the gift," Oneth told me, as we sat under the shade of an oak tree. "For entrepreneurs, they lose themselves in the job that they do." Losing themselves meant blurring the line between work, family, professional, and personal life. It meant working nights and weekends, always having the phone nearby, always being on call, and always thinking about work.

Firefighters, police, nurses, and doctors also had a tendency to lose their identity in their jobs, said Oneth, but entrepreneurs tended to be more acute. An entrepreneur was a form of identity that inexorably tied up an individual's sense of self with their professional performance. And when the performance didn't match up to the expectation (which it rarely did), entrepreneurs fell into a mental trap and suffered the consequences. "The entrepreneur tends to be a real doer . . . Do! Do! Do!" he said, which led to a bias toward action—the working, hustling, and grinding—which became an emotional crutch to lean on when things got difficult. This set up a vicious cycle, where the entrepreneur's personal troubles led them to lean in to their work, exacerbating stress and exhaustion, worsening personal issues, forcing them to lean further into work. "We're addicted to our own behaviors," Oneth said, noting that bad habits are more powerful than any drug out there. "When I tell entrepreneurs this, they tell me, 'If I stop what I'm doing, then things will fall apart.' They are driven by an unacknowledged fear, because I think people want the glamorous story of entrepreneurship to be true."

What did Oneth tell entrepreneurs who were caught in this loop? "I tell them, 'You will never ever ever get everything done!'" he said. "Because it never ends."

On our long drive back to town I told Nitschke about my conversation with Oneth earlier that day and asked him what he thought about this. "The mental trap for me is that I'm the guy who built it, started it, and funded it," he said. "I know that if I don't hire out staff, all I'm able to do is what I can physically." But letting go was hard, because anytime he had hired others, they let him down. Surrendering control was almost impossible. "You've never had an asshole for a boss until you've worked for yourself," he said with a grin. "My boss is an asshole. A bad communicator and planner who can't get out of his own way, can't get out of the process, and is less empathetic to others. When I said I can tough it out, well, that's not the same thing for everyone else around me."

We pulled up to Nitschke's rented house in the farmland outside Turlock. Tag and Bleu ran around the backyard in circles, while Nitschke kicked aside a few of Charlotte's toys and put his feet up. There were flies everywhere, thanks to the dairy farm across the street and its vast output of manure. I asked what his dream was with Mariposa Ranch. "I wish I could say there was one," he said, taking a long sip from a can of Pabst Blue Ribbon. "The goal now is survival. We're good at what we do, and we can do twice that much with a bit more effort, but how do we get there? We're able to stay in it just enough to be optimistic . . . isn't every entrepreneur a cockeyed optimist? . . . and there's always just enough things in the ether to keep you going. But then you get to the end of the year and look at your finances and say, 'I worked that hard for that much?' How long is that sustainable? It's a hard way to make $30,000."

Just then the dogs started barking and ran to the front gate, as Mica pulled up with the children and a car loaded with groceries. Henry and Elle helped their parents unload the food in the kitchen, while Charlotte strapped on a pair of roller skates.

"Hey Mom, what are we doing this weekend?" Henry asked Mica, who was defrosting a package of Mariposa Ranch ground beef in the sink as she began preparing spaghetti and meatballs for dinner.

"Probably helping your dad do something on the ranch," she said.

"What else?" Henry asked.

"I don't know . . . maybe church," Mica said, putting a pot of water on to boil.

"So, basically nothing new," Henry said.

"Yup."

Out back, Seth returned to his beer as Charlotte skated around. He answered a phone call from a customer and, without looking at any notes, recalled the person's exact order, down to the precise weight of each cut, and arranged delivery. Then he handed the phone to Charlotte on her next pass. "Honey, it's for you. It's the IRS."

Mariposa Ranch was a family business by default, even if the family was not officially part of the company. The children's freshly scrubbed faces were proudly displayed on its brochures and website, posing together and beaming bright, adorable smiles, and in Henry's case, wearing a massive cowboy hat. These were the kind of wholesome, all-American farmers that conscientious consumers of grass-fed beef wanted to buy from. For the first few years Mica had worked with Seth in the office, helping with orders and finances, but as the family grew, she stayed at home to raise the children. Now that Charlotte was getting ready to enter preschool, Mica had recently gone back to college to train as a teacher. But the cheery photos from several years ago obscured the real cost of the business on the family's lives.

I asked Mica about this after dinner.

"It's Seth's baby," she said, of the business. "His firstborn. It's everything for him. He eats and breathes and sleeps it. It defines who he is. It is not an easy road, and we have made a lot of sacrifices to have this business."

What kind of sacrifices?

"Financial, time, our living situation . . . I mean pretty much everything we do is at the whim of the business. I think the business is the rudder of our lives," she said, pushing the remains of her salad around the bowl with her fork. "I mean, we're in our forties now and we still don't own anything. We're really not kids anymore. You see the things we gave up to pursue the dream of the business, and you see the strife it brings. It's cool if you're poor and happy, but if you're poor and pissed off that sucks. And when the kids say, 'We wish you and Dad wouldn't be pissed off,' well that sucks."

Mica did her best to deal with her stress by maintaining a good support system of close friends from her Bible study group and reminding herself that they had begun the business together because they both believed that grass-fed beef was the right way to raise food. For his part, Seth worked out every morning and listened to a meditation podcast. But the costs of entrepreneurship on a family was something Mica was acutely aware of. When she was growing up, her father had owned an environmental consulting business in Los Angeles that ended in bankruptcy. The stresses caused by that failure led to her parents' divorce, and she carried that trauma with her decades later. "I never wanted to be an entrepreneur," she said, "and Seth knew that."

It has long been said that entrepreneurs view their businesses as another member of their family. In 2019, a group of Finnish researchers set out to prove this, comparing the way the brains of entrepreneurs lit up when they spoke about their business ventures and their children. They found the mental bond between an entrepreneur, their family, and their business was pretty much equal. But a business is not a family. It has no feelings, needs no affection, and cannot love the entrepreneur back. Yet a lot of entrepreneurial mythmaking glorifies prioritizing the business above all else.

"If you think of the media image of entrepreneurs: they are these lone wolves sacrificing everything, eating instant noodles, living in apartments with five guys to give all they can, sacrifice everything they can, so they can succeed!" said Willem Gous, a consultant in South Africa, who works with entrepreneurs to give them more control over their lives. "Well, that's not an entrepreneur. The bulk of us have houses, cars, kids. But they romanticize that. Is it viable to live like that? To say, 'Yeah, fuck everything, fuck your wife and kids, they can wait.' No, you can't! You'll never have those kids back again." Christopher Oneth told me that the breakdown of an entrepreneur's relationships occurs when their priorities fall out of balance. The entrepreneur forgets that they are a wife or husband or parent or partner first and an entrepreneur second.

One day in Palo Alto, I had coffee with a software entrepreneur I knew in his early fifties, who was divorcing his wife, splitting with a partner in a fledgling venture capital fund, and recovering from a heart attack. "I lost my family because of the ups and downs, the inconsistency of the highs and lows of being an entrepreneur," he told me. "The latest business was just the dagger, but it was merely the culmination." When business was good, he was constantly traveling, working, and hustling to secure investments and investors, taking time, energy, and attention away from his family. When the business was bad, that led to stress and anxiety, which endangered the family's financial situation. He became so focused on trying to make his business succeed that he forgot to pay his bills and pick up his daughters from school.

The rawness of losing the ranch hung in the air at the Nitschkes' house, like the fine brown dust from the San Joaquin Valley's dry soil, which choked the lungs if you breathed it in too long. Mica and Seth sat at opposite corners of the table. Their body language said everything. Her arms and legs were crossed, and her torso angled away from her husband, who sat slumped in his chair, head hung down into his chest. After a few moments of silence, punctuated by Henry's Xbox banter with an Australian friend on his *Fortnite* squad, Seth began talking about his family, German immigrants who worked the land in Arkansas, fled the dust bowl and the Ku Klux Klan for California, and picked berries in a labor camp. "My family came here as sharecroppers and I'm still a fucking sharecropper!"

Mica made a comment that Seth should maybe think about getting a job he could actually put his energy into. I knew what the suggestion to get a "real" job did to an entrepreneur's ego. It was a hand grenade, and I didn't want to be around when it went off. I had overstayed my welcome in every possible way. The night was over. I thanked them for dinner, got up, and said I would see them tomorrow.

"David," Mica told me as she opened the door. "You picked a really shitty week to come here."

EARLIER THAT WEEK, AS I sat in the church office of a reverend in Turlock, speaking about the advice he gave to entrepreneurs facing challenging times, he said something surprising. The entrepreneur's soul
was frequently lost, but not in the way that most people expected, when
they were facing failure. "I see the isolation of the entrepreneurial spirit
more often when they are succeeding," the reverend told me. "You see it
more in success, because it leads to hubris."

The comment made me think of a conversation I had months before
with Craig Kanarick, a friend whose company Mouth (an online market
for specialty foods) had recently declared bankruptcy. I had invested in
Mouth with my father, but while we began our conversation speaking
about failure, Kanarick reflected on the most difficult times he had experienced as an entrepreneur, during the height of his success in the late
1990s. At the time he was the cofounder of a digital marketing agency
called Razorfish, which grew into twenty-three hundred employees in
nine countries and a market cap of $4 billion at its peak. Overnight,
Kanarick became an entrepreneurial icon of the dot-com startup boom,
profiled in WIRED and 60 Minutes. He had blue hair and wild outfits,
partied with celebrities, and was regularly featured in the society pages.
This outward success hid an inward struggle.

"The journey of the entrepreneur is so bipolar," Kanarick said. "Because while I felt like all those good things were happening, at the same
time I'm suspicious of people trying to rip me off. International travel is
not glamorous at all, I'm sleeping in shitty airplanes and hotels, totally
confused and jet-lagged. I'm dealing with unbearable stress and concern
about the company, employees, and brand . . . what happens if I bump
into an employee while I'm drunk on the street? And, by the way, entre-
preneurialism is a competitive sport. You start the company, compete
against the rest of the world, work to make it successful, but you worry
about competitors and work really hard to try to win! You can become a
little paranoid."

All of this compounded into a pervasive loneliness that hit Kanarick
right when he reached the top. "I had two hundred million on paper

when the company went public," he said. "There was no one I could talk to that about. Who could I? My high school friends? My girlfriend?" At one point, he bought a fancy watch but was too ashamed to tell anyone about it. "I think the loneliness is inherent to being an entrepreneur. You have an ego and think you can solve problems on your own. You can't be an entrepreneur if you're not a little psychotic or egotistical. You have to believe you're right in ways other people don't see, or you can't succeed when people say you can fail." This is the famous roller coaster of entrepreneurship (or, as Nitschke put it, "riding a roller coaster after eating a burrito and drinking four beers"), and every single entrepreneur straps themselves in to ride it, whether they want to or not.

    "The amplitude and frequency of the roller-coaster ride is more intense when you attach your sense of self-esteem to the outcome, but that is a troubling character trait for most entrepreneurs," said Jerry Colonna, an executive coach who founded the firm Reboot, which works with many entrepreneurs and CEOs from the technology industry (Kanarick put us in touch). Colonna had spent the earlier part of his career as a venture capitalist, but when he faced a midlife depression, he realized that he not only wanted to change his own relationship to work but help others change theirs, too. Silicon Valley's startup myth glamorized an entrepreneur's worst habits. "One of the challenges that come from the [startup] archetype is this bullshit belief system that you have to 'leave it all on the field,' bleed to be successful, deplete and exhaust yourself, and that anything less is a source of shame and humiliation. If you do that and fail (like 89 percent of all startups in the first two years), you see it as evidence of your own failings as a person," Colonna said. "Then you sit there and say, 'Who am I?'"

    Colonna rightly diagnosed that this false narrative was something I had lured myself into many times over my own career. "If you only judge yourself as a human being based on whether or not your latest book sells, you are doomed," he said. "You ride the roller coaster. 'I'm shit. Who am I kidding? I knew you were never really good. I was just pretending, and now the world is starting to figure this out.' And yet, you're sophisticated enough to know it's not your fault, but it's a tender sore spot. Is that your ego at work? Absolutely. But don't follow the trap of beating yourself up because it's your ego at work."

This was just as dangerous for entrepreneurs during the highs as it was during the lows. A few days before speaking with Colonna, I had interviewed a software entrepreneur in Colorado named Bart Lorang, who was the CEO of a company called Full Contact and a venture capitalist. Lorang was eager to talk about the daily toll entrepreneurship took on him. "When you work for yourself there's nowhere to pass the buck," he said. "Every single problem or screwup in the organization is ultimately traceable back to you. You have to look at the mirror every single day and look at your failings. Every mistake is actually yours to own. At a larger corporation you can often play the victim and pass the blame."

When I asked Lorang about the roller-coaster ride of entrepreneurship, he confessed that his personal low point was "literally right now." Lorang was trying to quadruple Full Contact's revenue, and this aggressive push had sapped morale, with a number of employees quitting. "I'm waking up every day for the past six months saying, 'Do I want to go into the office and shovel shit in my mouth all day?' My wife's never seen me this stressed out. I came down with shingles two weeks ago. My body is failing. That's what I'm going through right now. I've learned to enjoy and embrace these times but it's hard. I've been depressed, suicidal, and I ask myself, 'Is this something I want to do?' A lot of entrepreneurs go through that. They feel trapped by the thing that they've created. It goes in waves." When I asked Lorang how he planned to break out of this cycle, which was brought on by success, not failure, he said that he just needed to get the company to a $1 billion valuation, to that mythical unicorn status. And then what? He would have a good exit, he said, and "live the life I want to lead." I knew this was a bullshit answer. A roller coaster is nauseating and terrifying, but when people get off them, they catch their breath and jump right back in line.

Colonna told me that the startup myth's online echo chamber made the roller coaster's whipsaw even worse. "The amplitude and frequency of the ride is more intense . . . and that has to do with the way we lionize certain archetypes around entrepreneurship. That drives the highs and lows and makes them more nauseating," Colonna said. "I, as a budding entrepreneur, am not measuring myself by taking pride in craftsman-ship, being kind, making more money today than yesterday, and pro-viding a way for other employees to pay their bills . . . all worthy, noble things," he said. "Instead of taking pride in that, we are constantly mea-suring ourselves into some sort of idealized ideal, and failing."

Money just amplified these emotions, but it was a numerical ba-rometer more often than the cause. One day in California, I received a text message from my brother. "Here's a quote for your book," it read. "The best part of entrepreneurship is the paralyzing dread of looking at your fleeting capital as you look at your bank account." Around the same time, Lauren got a shock when she realized there was just a $1,000 left in her bank account, which had held over $100,000 two years be-fore, when she was employed full-time. "That was horrifying," she said, months later, and it threw her down a dizzying hole of self-doubt. Her business had grown organically the first year, but now it had plateaued. Clients liked her coaching, but she would need many more clients, or a new way to reach a bigger audience, if it was going to make financial sense for us. She wasn't sure what she should do next.

"I have no idea if this is going to work," she told me when I got home from California. "Honestly. It's grueling to not know if you're doing the right thing. It sucks. Is it because I'm not selling it right or people don't want it or it's bullshit? I have no fucking clue. That's the worst part. Just not knowing if it's going to work."

The research linking entrepreneurship with mental health is evolving. Some studies have shown positive correlations between self-employment and overall health, while others have identified the preva-lence of obsession with entrepreneurs. One recent study, conducted by psychiatry professor Michael Freeman, who also coaches entrepreneurs, observed elevated rates of various mental health problems among entre-preneurs (when compared to the general population), including nearly double the rate of depression, six times the rate of ADHD, and three times the rate of addiction. While many have tried to find possible correlations between these conditions and entrepreneurial success (i.e., are those with ADHD natural entrepreneurs?), the negative implications for entrepreneurs are real.

Stress is something most of us experience in some way with work, but for entrepreneurs, it is exacerbated by their financial and mental ownership over that work. Stress is not necessarily bad. My father has always believed that stress is necessary for an entrepreneur, because it keeps them honest, gets them out of bed, and stops them from being complacent. Ute Stephan, a professor who studies entrepreneurship at London's King's College, said the key was the kind of stress entrepreneurs faced. "Challenge stresses" were associated with the highs entrepreneurs talk about, because they came with the opportunity to grow. "That kind of stress over shorter periods of time is quite motivating, especially when you're in control." I saw this in my brother, who was working late into the night but also happier than I had ever seen him, because he was finally doing what he wanted, and with Lauren, who became overtaken with excitement over each new idea and opportunity.

But stress has a dark side, which Stephan characterized as "hindrance stresses." These were stresses out of the entrepreneur's control: economic downturns, conflicts with employees, customers, or partners, and regulatory changes. "There's no upside to it," she said. "They are just stressful." For all that my father valued stress, he had a fraught relationship with it. He slept terribly, waking in the middle of the night with worries about business and money, and had issues with blood pressure, which was particularly worrisome because of his family history. His father, "Poppa" Sam Sax, was also an entrepreneur but a perpetually unsuccessful one, losing a series of businesses in Montreal's garment industry over his lifetime. Though I opened my first book with a story about the smoked meat sandwich that ultimately killed him, the far less heroic truth is that his fatal heart attack was the end result of a career of accumulated hinderance stresses, left unchecked. For an entrepreneur, failure can exact the ultimate price.

DRIVE SOUTH FROM THE NITSCHKES' home in Turlock, through a hundred miles of almonds and raisins and other cash crops, and you get to Holland's Dairy, the De Hoop family farm outside the town of Hanford. The De Hoops are Dutch dairy farmers, and their heritage is obvious the second you walk into their beautiful ranch home. There are racks of wooden clogs, framed prayers in Dutch, art around the home featuring scenes from the Dutch countryside, and windmills on everything from the china to the bath linens. I was greeted in their fragrant kitchen by Ellie (who was busy preparing half a dozen dishes for dinner), her husband, Art, their son Arie, twenty-one, and his sister Catharina, twenty-five (their three other children lived out of state).

Both sides of the family had been "dairymen" back in the Netherlands, and fifty relatives worked on dairies in various states since the family immigrated to America in the 1950s. Art and Ellie had been running Holland's Dairy since 1990, when Ellie's father gave them the business as a wedding gift. Driving through the feedlot with Arie and Art, passing a thousand feet of mooing cows, it was clear just how different an operation Holland's Dairy was from the pasture ranching Nitschke practiced. The dairy was a midsized feedlot operation, with thirty-six hundred cows. It ran twenty hours a day, seven days a week, with the herd being milked twice a day. The cows lived under several long, shaded pens, with concrete pads underneath. They fed by placing their heads through metal gates, in order to reach the troughs where their feed was dished out. Their diet was a mix of different substances, including corn, alfalfa and sorghum, rice and almond hulls, and even dried chicken poop, which were all piled in huge mounds and moved around by tractors. The tractors also spent a lot of time managing the endless manure that accumulated on the feedlot, which had to be moved, dried, and carted off. Beyond the feedlot there were fields for growing feed, a small solar energy farm, and twenty-four thousand almond trees, which the De Hoop family planted five years before as a way of diversifying their income. Their farm's second almond harvest had just begun, and Art got out of the truck to inspect a row of trees.

"Look at that!" he said, picking up a handful of almonds from the ground with a resentful laugh. "A tree full of nuts! It drives me nuts . . . seriously!" The company he'd hired to harvest the trees had done a second-rate job, leaving as many as 10 percent more nuts on the trees than they should have, the difference between a profit and a loss. "Look at the nuts on that tree, man! Drive faster so I don't have to see it," he told Arie as we got back into the pickup. "A tree unshook is like a man standing around collecting a paycheck. Look at this! There's gotta be thousands of dollars of almonds lying around on the ground."

Art De Hoop's frustration was driven by more than just wasted almonds. The dairy business was in crisis, and the prospect of losing the farm was increasingly real. Milk is a commodity, and Holland's Dairy sold it to customers (mostly cheesemakers) at the market price, which had been declining for years. From a high of around $17 for 100 lbs. of milk in 2009, the price was now hovering around $14 for 100 lbs. when I visited in the fall of 2018 (their cost just to break even was around $15.50 for 100 lbs.). American dairy farmers were now so good at breeding and milking their cows that they'd exceeded demand and now lost money on every single gallon they sold. This affected not just dairy farmers in California but all over the United States, with some estimating as many as half the country's dairies had closed up during the past decade.

"We're so efficient in what we do, but we kill ourselves by doing it," Art said. Over the past three years, the farm was operating at maximum productivity, yet lost an estimated $2 million during that time. Exacerbating this were other factors out of their control, including a pending increase in California's minimum wage, attacks on the almond trees from nematodes, new environmental regulations that prevented them from cultivating certain fields because they had microscopic "fairy shrimp" in the soil, and the massive issue of water access, which was exacerbated by California's growing droughts, as well as incoming laws that could divert up to three-quarters of the San Joaquin Valley's irrigation to the ocean.

After cooling off with a limeade made with leftover whey that Ellie was experimenting with as a potential product ("Tell us how it goes," she said. "We'll try anything."), we sat down at the table for dinner. It was piled high with beautiful food they had grown and made, including peppery meatballs from a cow they'd slaughtered, buttery green beans, fresh baked breads, and roast potatoes. Everyone joined hands as Art said grace.

"Thank you, Lord, for the work of each day to make the food we eat, and for the work you allow us to do." Amen.

The De Hoops were at a crossroads. They all believed that the future of dairy farms in California was numbered, but they could not see an easy way out. The more they milked, the more they lost, and diversifying to other products, like nuts, required major investments and five to ten years to turn a profit. They could sell the farm, but then what? "I'm a fourth-generation dairy farmer," Art said. "I've never done anything else but milking cows. So what are we going to do?"

"There's this hope that it's cyclical," said Catharina, "but the belief is that it won't get better."

Her father nodded. "It's not easy to accept that we can't make a living as dairy farmers in California."

"Everyone's in this situation," Ellie said. "Last week we had a friend who said, 'I'm out! I want to sell my cows,' but the government wanted 30 percent of his proceeds from the sale, so you also have no choice but to stay and fight on."

Ellie invited everyone into the backyard for dessert, and we sat under string lights, next to a small chicken coop, as an orange harvest moon hung overhead. The milking barn was just a few hundred feet away, and the contrast of eating Ellie's milk pudding with fresh berries out of Dutch china, while the cowhands hollered and whistled and sung to the animals in Spanish, against a drone of hissing hydraulic milking machines and the ever-present smell of cow poo, made for a heck of a scene.

The cost of toughing things out was more than financial for the De Hoops. Art's last brush with financial failure had nearly killed him. In 2010, as milk prices began falling and the recession spread, their bank called in Holland's Dairy's operating loan. The farm was put into "special assets," a sort of red flagged category that precedes bankruptcy.

"My body went wild for a year," Art said, describing an onslaught of physical reactions to the stress, including sleep loss and blood pressure so high he frequently passed out.

"He was a dead man walking," Catharina said. "The doctor said he could have a heart attack at any time."

Then the bank tripled their loan's interest while downgrading the value of their assets. "You're already down and then they kick you," Ellie said. The family put the farm up for sale, but Ellie's brothers began working with the bankers, floating them for thirty days as they helped renegotiate the loan. It took three years to pay the bank back, three more years to recover the losses to the business, and another three years to get right back into that hole. In 2016, Art contracted Valley Fever, a fungal lung infection that has been growing in the San Joaquin Valley, especially among farmers. He lost all his energy. For two months he slept for twenty hours a day. His doctor said his choice was simple: leave the Central Valley or die. "I considered myself the most unstoppable SOB, but that stopped me cold," Art said. "Whether it is rock bottom or not, you have to hit that point where you realize 'I can't do this anymore,'" he said.

I thought of something I had seen earlier that day, walking through the feedlot with Arie. A cow was lying on the ground, panting and covered with flies, unable to move. She had been sick for a few days, and when I asked Arie what he planned to do if she didn't get better, he gestured at the rifle lying in the pickup truck. With thousands of cows to care for, a bullet was cheaper than a vet and more humane to the suffering animal, he said. Sometimes you just had to recognize a lost cause.

The De Hoops were far from the only farmers facing failure. Climate change, commodity price slumps, Trump's trade wars, consolidation of small- and medium-sized family farms . . . all of these factors had led to the worst financial crisis for American farming in a generation. "It's devastating," said Joaquin Contente, a sixty-nine-year-old dairy farmer in Hanford, who was president of the California Farmers Union. "Within a five-mile radius of my dairy, there's at least twenty-five dairies that have gone since 2009 and will never come back. Some got out gracefully, had equity, and sold it. But others didn't. Some got foreclosed on."

We were having breakfast at a diner in Hanford packed with farmers doing what many here called "coffee shop," chatting about farming over coffee. "Every week, whenever I come across a farmer, the question is always 'What are we gonna do?'" Contente said, stirring four half-and-halfs into his cup. Because most American farmers are male, proud, and socially conservative, they tend to close off their emotions. "Farmers are the most independent of the people you'd call entrepreneurs," he said. "That makes it tougher for them to console with other people when they hit the pits. There's an inherent loneliness to it."

The consequences of that loneliness, coupled with the growing farm crisis, were apparent in farming communities around America: increased substance abuse, marital troubles, domestic violence, health problems, and a troubling rise in farmer suicides. Though official statistics in recent years have been debated, it does appear that farmers in America (and other countries including Canada, Australia, and even India) have some of the highest suicide rates among any profession. Other factors may exacerbate this grim truth. Farmers are exposed to pesticides and other chemicals that have been shown to make certain mental health issues worse and also have easier access to deadly tools (poisons, guns, ropes) than people living in urban areas. Contente, the De Hoops, and others all told me stories of dairymen they knew who had taken their lives in recent years.

Michael Rosmann, a psychologist and farmer in Iowa, who has become a national resource for helping farmers deal with suicidal thoughts, says that more than other entrepreneurs, the farmer buckles down when times are tough, taking on more risk, while isolating themselves. "Those are traits associated with success in farming, but they're also associated with problems coping with stress," Rosmann said. Deepening this was an emotional bond to the business that few other entrepreneurs experienced. The farmer lives on their land and loves their animals. Their business is their home, and its natural cycles dictate everything in their lives, from when they wake and sleep, to what they eat, when they work, and how they relate to the world. So much is out of their control—weather, water, pests, diseases, trade pacts and regulations drawn up in faraway capitals—but the land remains the same, and their bond with it deepens over generations. Rosmann said that many farmers equate the loss of their land with the death of a child or spouse.

"The chances are that when a farm fails, they failed their parents, grandparents and great-grandparents," said Ted Matthews, director of Minnesota's Rural Health Agency, which has been on the frontlines of the farm suicide crisis in recent years. "Emotionally, it doesn't matter if prices were this, or that happened. What matters is they lost the farm, they lost the five-generation farm, and it's all on them. They believe they're a total failure and it doesn't matter why."

The fear of farm loss is existential more than financial. "The farmer's personal identity is so tied to the land that it's like an amputation. You don't see this in other bankruptcies," said Riley Walter, a bankruptcy attorney in Fresno, who worked with farmers around the San Joaquin Valley and had helped to set up suicide hotlines in recent years. "The dairyman is so tied to being a dairyman that his whole identity is tied up in the herd." Even when they move on to work for another dairy, Riley said they are so emotionally destroyed that you can see it on their faces.

In a situation where no good outcome seems possible, death can become a fantasy. When we were eating lunch that first day, Nitschke joked that his biggest missed opportunity was not dying the year before, when he was thrown off Bubbles, his horse. "It was the best business decision I didn't make," he said. "I'd have died with a full beard and wiped out all my debt." It was typical of Nitschke's gallows humor, but it exposed something very real in his soul.

Failure is a remarkably common truth for entrepreneurs. According to US government statistics, only two-thirds of businesses survive their first two years, and half survive to five years. The businesses that last decades or longer are the outliers, not the norm, and the odds are the same regardless of the industry, whether the entrepreneur has a one-man shop or leads a company employing hundreds. But failure is something that has been particularly romanticized by the startup myth of Silicon Valley, where embracing failure is projected as a badge of honor, a right of passage, and a prerequisite to eventual success. Venture capitalists and revered startup figures confidently tell those hoping to learn from them not to fear failure, to actively and openly and enthusiastically embrace it. To fail fast. To fail forward. To fail upward. To fail until success rises from the ashes.

But out in the real world, failure for an entrepreneur is a horrible, life-altering experience, bereft of glory. An entrepreneur risks their money and their home, their health and their family, their pride and identity, and ultimately, their lives when they venture into business. When that business fails, all of that can be impacted. "It really does seem to be a life-changing event for a lot of entrepreneurs," said Ute Stephan, the professor who studied failure's effects on the health of entrepreneurs. "People who say failure is good make the implicit assumption that you can learn from failure and improve the next time. But what if there's a tsunami and your business is swept away? What can you learn from that?"

Failed entrepreneurs in Silicon Valley can go start another company, and many do this, receiving new funding just as easily a second or third time. "In Silicon Valley it's OPM bankruptcies," said Riley Walter, the bankruptcy attorney. "Other People's Money. It is failure at a company level, but not on a personal level, and that failure is more accepted." But farmers and most every other entrepreneur beyond that small, rarefied world don't have the same options. The banks will no longer lend to them. Their reputations are sullied. As entrepreneurs, they often have one chance to succeed. "Farmers don't tend to bounce back," Walter said, "because the startup costs are too high."

Even within the technology industry, glamorizing failure has taken a toll. "I think the mythology around failure is completely unhelpful in this stage," said Brad Feld, a well-known venture capitalist who has written extensively about mental health issues that entrepreneurs deal with over the years, including his own. "Failure is a significant component of entrepreneurship. Failure sucks. It's hard to fail. But acknowledging that it's part of entrepreneurship is key. Romanticizing that it's good to fail isn't helpful."

Jerry Colonna told me that the emotional toll of failure is something all entrepreneurs underappreciate. To protect against the inevitable emotional challenges of their careers, including failure, an entrepreneur needs to cultivate a healthy relationship with their business *and* their life. Entrepreneurs need sleep, exercise, good diets, and other healthy habits, but more than anything, they need community. Entrepreneurship is a lonely endeavor. It isolates the mind and often the soul, in ways that can be liberating, but also dangerous. Entrepreneurs need to know they are not alone. They need a community to share their fears and experiences and problems with. For some, like the De Hoop family, that community came from their church, which was also made up of other Dutch dairymen. For entrepreneurs in the technology business, the community was the "ecosystem" of other entrepreneurs, advisors, and mentors and, if they were lucky, investors who actually cared about the people behind their investments.

But for most entrepreneurs, their community was family and friends, and opening up to them about the challenges of running a business and working for themselves was not easy, especially when the culture stigmatized that vulnerability as a weakness. In a 2017 interview, Gary Vaynerchuk advised his fans to drop a "losing" friend (someone who complains about how difficult things are) and pick up a "winning" one instead. This tip was meant to further the entrepreneur's chance of crushing it like Gary Vee, but I fear that it risked crushing the very lives of entrepreneurs when they needed help the most.

One night, sitting in my hotel in Turlock, I called my brother Daniel and asked how he was doing. I knew he was having a hard time. The ups and downs he was experiencing as he worked to get his business off the ground were taking a toll. He had been up late again the night before, working until 2 a.m., eating takeout food, hunched over his laptop. He wasn't exercising or even leaving the house except for meetings, and I told Daniel that I was worried about him. What followed over the next hour was the kind of frank, open, and loving conversation that I had wanted to have with him for months but was too afraid, or preoccupied, to initiate.

He explained how this business was his dream, and though stressed, he was happier than he had ever been, because he was finally working to create something that he truly believed in. He knew the costs and was willing to endure them for another year or two, until he was in a position to back off. He did not want to ride the roller coaster forever. He wanted a life and a family and the ability to step away from work. But he was glad I had asked him about this. So was I, even if all I did was let my brother know that I cared about him.

"WAKE UP, HENRY," SETH NITSCHKE said, opening the door of his pickup truck, where his son was sleeping with the crumpled remains of a McDonald's breakfast in his lap. "Time to gather some cattle."

It was the Saturday morning after dinner at their house, and we were back in the foothills of Mariposa County an hour after sunrise. The air was cool. A bald eagle flew over us, while a pair of deer looked on from nearby. Seth attached spurs to his cowboy boots and mounted Bubbles, his horse, while Henry got onto an ATV and I sat precariously on the back. We began riding over rolls, looking for the cattle herd. Ten minutes in, we came upon a dozen cows, chewing dried grass. Seth told Henry that he would ride into the gulley to get the rest of the herd, while Henry and I would push this group down to a fence.

"Let's kick 'em down over that hill!" Seth said, as he took off at a gallop and out of sight. Henry turned the crank and the ATV shot forward, while I held on for dear life. Cows darted left and right, and when they did, Henry would turn to outflank them, but the herd kept splitting in two. "It's real hard to gather cattle with just one man," Henry said, and after a few minutes of sudden (and terrifying) zigzagging back and forth, he stopped, scanned the horizon, and waited for his father. A few minutes later Seth rode up over the hill with just four cows in front of him.

"Where are they?" he asked Henry, of the rest of the herd.

"I think they were by the creek," Henry said.

"Well shit, they didn't just disappear," Seth said, resting his hands on the saddle for a second as he looked at the ground. "Summer's been hard on them. That heifer I pulled out there the other day . . . she's gone. Coyotes picked her bones over good."

He rode off again, and we waited atop a hill until he returned. I asked Henry if he liked working with his father. "Yeah," he said, kicking a dried cow patty as far as he could. "It's just fun what my dad does. I like that. But a big part is sitting around and doing nothing." Suddenly we heard a commotion of whoops and hoofbeats and looked over to see the whole herd marching toward us in a line, with Nitschke and his dogs bringing up the rear. Riding high in his saddle with the sun shining on him, Seth Nitschke looked just like a cowboy was supposed to. Henry and I got back onto the ATV and helped rustle the cattle into the corral.

"Good work, Henry," Seth said, giving his son a high five. "Let's let 'em rest and get some tacos."

When we came back from the Oasis, Mica and the girls were there. Charlotte was wearing a pair of cowboy boots over her unicorn pajamas, and Elle was eager to help her dad. "Okay, then," Seth said to her, "let's get to work." He brought her into the corral and gave her a large metal paddle, telling her to stand near the gate that separated one pen from another. "Go slow, always go slow," he said, as dozens of cattle thundered around the enclosed space. "Stand up, don't slouch, and raise your head, okay?" he told her. "C'mon Elle, you look like a damn beat puppy."

Seth got back on his horse and began separating individual cows out of the herd, pushing each one toward Elle, whom he gave a signal to indicate whether she should close the gate and let it pass or direct it to the smaller pen, where it would be loaded onto the trailer, to move to another pasture. Aside from his signal of "yes" or "no," it was quiet, tense work, as the small girl, who weighed less than a hundred pounds, faced down animals that weighed a ton. Mica and Henry looked on from the fence, while Charlotte whined that she needed help putting her boots back on. Between the rising heat, Charlotte's pleading, Seth's concentration, and the lingering atmosphere from the previous night's conversation, the situation was tense, but when the last of the cattle were separated, a huge grin spread across Elle's freckled face. Seth pulled her up onto the saddle with him and they rode around the paddock together.

"You wanna be in charge, honey?" he asked her, beaming with pride. "I'm gonna head to the Oasis and grab some beers, if you wanna load up these cattle."

Later, after Mica took the children home, Nitschke and I drove fifteen minutes to another ranch he leases, with two dozen cattle riding in the trailer. It had been a long day already, and it was far from over. By the time Nitschke wrapped up hauling cattle, storing his trailer, and cleaning up, he would have worked more than fourteen hours straight. But it was a good day, especially with the family there.

"I work by myself, almost all the time, and sometimes it seems like you're the only person who gives a shit about it," Nitschke said. "Isolation is the day-to-day default function, which is not as bad as being lonely. But if you have a bad day, or you're working through personal problems or ones in the business, you do think, 'I wish somebody would help me make this decision.'"

As an entrepreneur, Seth Nitschke was neither a clear success nor a failure. Like most people who start their own business, he was doing work that he truly loved and making a living at it, but he also felt stuck, with no clear path on how to move things forward. "I don't know. I just don't, and it's kinda frustrating," he said. "The handwriting's on the wall, and maybe we have to read it. We need to figure out a way to grow it, or find an exit strategy. That doesn't mean we leave ranching, but maybe we stop selling meat and just raise it and fatten it for someone else." Either way, it was time to make a choice . . . take on more risk, and more debt, or fold up shop. It was the same thing I heard down in Hanford from the De Hoop family, who agreed that a major decision had to be made by the end of the year. Would they stay or go? Fight on or sell the farm?

All economic logic said that both Nitschke and the De Hoops should have thrown in the towel. Their costs were only increasing, while the price of beef and milk declined. Consolidation of their industries was certain to continue, regulations and environmental conditions would only get more challenging, and the risks they bore—to their finances, families, and lives—were sure to grow. And yet it didn't surprise me that both ultimately decided to stay the course. "Our family is basically hunkering down and enduring the storm," Catharina De Hoop wrote me, in an email, five months later. "Dairying is in our blood, it's part of our identity, so it won't be something that is let go easily."

Nitschke was no different. "I love what I'm doing," he told me, as he unlatched the trailer's door and let the cattle into a small holding pen. "I love caring for the animals and the earth, riding my horse, and being outside all day. I love talking to customers who trust us to feed their family." More than anything, it was a fear of going back to a life before entrepreneurship that kept him moving forward. Nitschke had described his part-time feed sales job as the "most boring death you can imagine." More than bankruptcy, his nightmare was being forced to sell life insurance in Orange County, a yuppie suburban wasteland, wearing a polo shirt and khakis. "Here's the thing," he said. "I hated being bored. I can't handle it, roller coaster or not. I don't want to go back to working for someone else."

Nitschke mounted Bubbles. I asked him whether he would do it all over again, knowing how everything had worked out for his business, his family, and his life. He scratched his beard before answering. "I would have made different choices, but I'm happy and recognize I have been very lucky." Who else could become a real-life cowboy in the twenty-first century and make a living from it? "This is dumb! I mean look at me . . . it's patently fucking absurd . . . I'm a hillbilly! Yeah, I'd do it again," he said, asking me, "Would you?"

"Of course," I said, without a second's hesitation. Working for myself was more difficult than I realized. It was painfully lonely, and the mental strain of a career writing books that were more likely to fail than succeed never got easier. There were days when I fantasized about a different life, with the certainty of a salary and the clear tasks of a job. To show up, do my work, and feel secure as long as that job existed. Of course that was a romantic myth of employment, completely divorced from the reality of the working world, with its own stresses and pitfalls. But from time to time, that fantasy crossed my mind.

And then I would look up and realize what I had. I had the freedom to do what I wanted, when I wanted. To pursue *my* ideas, and go where *I* pleased, and have experiences that I would remember forever. To work how I loved. What could be more patently absurd than a guy with no qualifications except his chutzpah spending a year hanging out in hair salons in New Orleans, surfing and eating croissants in New York, touring wineries in Argentina, and helping a cowboy round up cattle in California? We often defined success and failure in entrepreneurship along the economic standards of other business—as profits and losses—but entrepreneurship was richer than that. It was a way of life we had all chosen, and the reward had as much to do with living that life on our own terms as it did with the dollars we won from it. It meant being in the saddle and controlling your own destiny, hoping for a better tomorrow and everything that came with that. That wasn't necessarily logical, but it somehow made perfect sense.

"If I'm going down the road and get a stupid idea, brother, we go forward with it," Nitschke told me earlier that afternoon. Now, sitting atop his horse, as the sun began its descent beyond Silicon Valley, Nitschke got philosophical. "Our ability to accept unproven truths is the key to human existence," he said. "If I stop believing in my story, the business stops tomorrow. If we can't believe in something, in ourselves, in faith, then what will we believe in?"

And with that, Seth Nitschke hollered to the herd, kicked his spurs, and rode off into the sunset.

PART IV

THE SOUL OF AN ENTREPRENEUR

CHAPTER 8

Too Many Ideas

IT WAS A hot and humid afternoon when I picked up my rental car in Boston and began the two-hour trip north to Jefferson, New Hampshire. As I drove through a section of pine forest, a sudden fog set in. Black clouds filled the sky, and a biblical rain began pounding the car, giving way to fat pings of hail, piling up on the road like winter snow. Everyone on the highway pulled over, warning lights flashing, waiting for the storm to stop as the temperature on the car's dashboard rapidly plunged from 92 to 62 degrees in three minutes. In an instant, summer had given way to fall. When I told a gas station attendant about the wild weather, he shrugged. "I guess that's climate change," he said, handing me my receipt.

An hour later I drove down the gravel road to Windhover, John Henry Clippinger's farm to the north of Mt. Washington. Clippinger was sitting on a wicker chair on his wraparound porch with his friend Peter Hirshberg, looking out to the west at a pond, a few wandering chickens, a horse, and the fields, farms, and mountains beyond that made up this little corner of America. Hirshberg had on jeans, sneakers, and a zip-up fleece, while Clippinger was wearing the only thing I have ever seen him wear: hiking pants, a weathered button-down shirt, a worn blazer, and slip-on shoes without socks. Clippinger is solidly built, with thick hands, a booming voice, and a wide face topped by wisps of hair. The two men were furiously typing away on laptops, and the only sound you heard against the backdrop of wind chimes and songbirds was fingers hitting keys. Every minute or so Hirshberg would say something like "Oh, this is interesting" or "Oh, shit!" in his nasal voice, and Clippinger would let out a sort of curious grunt. Hirshberg would summarize an email he'd just received, Clippinger would hum an acknowledgment ("mmmhhhm-mmnnn"), and they'd resume typing.

The two were juggling a flurry of last-minute activity around the Initial Coin Offering (ICO) for Swytch, the company Clippinger had co-founded, which Hirshberg was helping him build. Swytch was a block-chain-powered platform to effectively measure, verify, and allow for the easy trading of renewable energy all over the world. The idea and its underlying technology was incredibly complicated and evolved constantly, but if it worked as Clippinger envisioned, Swytch would accelerate the transition away from an economy based on fossil fuels.

The ICO was the company's first release of its cryptocurrency tokens to public investors, and once this monthlong sale closed tonight at 11 p.m., Clippinger, Hirshberg, and others in the company would know how much money Swytch had in the bank to actually build their technology.

"Now we're literally on the goal line," Clippinger said, as Hirshberg went inside to try to convince a big cryptocurrency investor in Puerto Rico to transfer several million dollars he had vaguely promised them before the deadline. "But we are at the historical point of a reset, so how do you do a reset? If you're sufficiently arrogant to believe you have the solution, then how can you sit on it? There's a moral imperative to act."

While Clippinger was sufficiently convinced of his ability to actually change the world with his latest technology company, he was far from a pie-eyed whiz kid pitching his startup around Stanford. Swytch was Clippinger's sixth venture he had begun as an entrepreneur (or fifth, he had lost count), and with his seventy-fifth birthday coming up later that fall, it was the culmination of his life's work: technologically, intellectually, and philosophically. This is what drew me to his farm, in the opposite corner of the country from Silicon Valley. Entrepreneurship is often misconstrued as a young person's game. To truly understand it, I needed to see what an entrepreneur looked like as he entered his last big project and reflected on what it meant to be an entrepreneur.

"YOUNG PEOPLE ARE JUST SMARTER," Mark Zuckerberg famously said in 2007, when he was just twenty-three years old and already on his way to becoming a billionaire. Bill Gates, Steve Jobs, Elon Musk, Sergey Brin, Larry Page, and of course Zuck himself . . . the most famous entrepreneurs in Silicon Valley's startup myth all created their companies in their twenties, either fresh out of college or right before dropping out. This has led Silicon Valley to value fresh faces over experienced ones. Accusations of ageism in the tech industry are rampant, Silicon Valley's cult of youth is as strong as it is in Hollywood, and venture capitalists have statistically favored investments in companies with young founders over older ones. Y Combinator founder Paul Graham feels that entrepreneurs have a cutoff at thirty-two, because that's the age when they start to get too skeptical. Venture capitalist Vinod Khosla believes, "People under thirty-five are the people who make change happen," while those over forty-five "basically die in terms of new ideas." Startup incubators and accelerators, like Peter Thiel's fellowship, reinforce this youthful bias, as does the growing crop of entrepreneurship programs at universities and colleges worldwide.

But in early 2018, a paper was published by the National Bureau of Economic Research called "Age and High-Growth Entrepreneurship" that revealed a surprising truth. Despite the widely held belief that younger entrepreneurs create better, more successful companies, the opposite was true. "We find that age indeed predicts success, and sharply, but in the opposite way that many observers and investors propose. The highest success rates in entrepreneurship come from founders in middle age and beyond," the authors wrote, noting that the average entrepreneur behind the fastest-growing new companies (especially in the technology sector) was forty-five years old, smack dab in middle age. "We continue to see little evidence, even looking at the very youngest founder, that highly-successful firms are populated by especially young founders. Popular perceptions that celebrate youth as a key characteristic for creating high-growth firms appear largely misplaced."

Eight months after that study came out, I met Clippinger. We were both speaking at a conference about technology in Seoul, South Korea, and one morning, we struck up a conversation over breakfast. I was immediately fascinated by Clippinger and the company he was working to launch, which promised nothing less than the solution to the intractable global problem of climate change. He had the qualities that I had always been drawn to in entrepreneurs: a relentless enthusiasm and optimism coupled with a lack of pretension and an insatiable curiosity about the world. But there was something else . . . his age. It was frankly surprising to meet an entrepreneur starting a business in their seventies, let alone one as ambitious as Swytch. If the recent research showed that the myth of the young founder was largely false, here was the embodiment of that broader reality, someone whose whole life had been defined by entrepreneurship.

John Henry Clippinger grew up in a wealthy Cincinnati family. Though his father was a prosecutor, Clippinger had a rebellious streak, and at twelve he started a car theft ring with other boys. "We hot-wired them, and I had cops chasing me. It was the most exciting thing I've ever done in my life," he said with a smile, as we sat on the porch drinking whiskey, while Hirshberg worked his phone inside. "The frontal lobe was not well developed."

Clippinger eventually went to Yale, graduating in 1966. Initially drawn to the arts ("I wanted to be a painter and philosopher"), he ended up majoring in structural anthropology, studying how language worked, and quickly became passionate about computers and how they could organize information. Clippinger also became heavily involved in social justice. In 1964, he founded Americans for Reappraisal of Far Eastern Policy, one of the first student groups to oppose the Vietnam War, traveled to Selma, Alabama, in 1965, to march with Dr. Martin Luther King Jr. for civil rights, and spent years counseling inner city street gang members away from violence.

Clippinger continued his studies at the University of Pennsylvania, earning a master's and PhD in cybernetics. He focused on the adaptations of new, digital organisms and worked in the emerging field of computer systems design. Clippinger's research focused on making computers comprehend, organize, and use natural language . . . a precursor of the artificial intelligence and machine learning you hear so much about today. (One of his experiments involved having a computer mimic the answers that a psychoanalyst would give to a patient.) What fascinated Clippinger was the notion that a cooperative system (a computer network, a group of people, or something more complicated) could organize and run itself, so long as the proper structures were put in place. "I was interested in how people model different belief systems into technology," he said, "and how technology shapes that belief."

Increasingly inspired by E. F. Schumacher's book *Small Is Beautiful* and the back-to-the-land movement of the counterculture, Clippinger purchased Windhover in 1974, which he named after a local falcon and poem. He built the barn, wired the electricity, and set up the plumbing himself ("very poorly"), got chickens and horses, tried and failed to raise a rare breed of cattle, and grew hay, which he continues to cultivate today on its 283 acres.

Clippinger split his time between New Hampshire and Cambridge, Massachusetts, where he began applying his ideas to business. He created his first company in 1982, called Brattle Street Research, which used machine learning to generate searchable databases from words and phrases plucked from *Wall Street Journal* stories. He funded the startup with a $150,000 mortgage against his home (a massive gamble at the time) and still revels in the war stories from those days, like when he had to convince Wall Street stockbrokers with nicknames like "Hank the Crank" that his system really could help them call the market, even while they called him "an egghead full of shit" to his face.

"For me, being an entrepreneur has a particular meaning," Clippinger said, when I asked him his thoughts on the word. He rejected the steady, comfortable lives his privileged neighbors and classmates from Cincinnati and Yale chose, with their jobs in banking and law, because it was "boring as hell." But Clippinger also remembered how the first time someone called him an entrepreneur, he took it as a slight. "I was always interested to build and fund certain kinds of things. An entrepreneur is someone willing to take on personal risk to execute ideas with the potential opportunity that the public doesn't have, and a product or market that no one else is seeing. You invent a future by creating alternative futures, via technology." Fundamentally, he told me, entrepreneurship was about being your own boss. "For good or bad. I think that's the core of it."

Brattle Street Research was a success, and Clippinger sold it after four years. He took a job as the lead of advanced technology consulting with the blue-chip accounting firm Coopers & Lybrand (now PricewaterhouseCoopers), because he had a baby at home and wanted to learn from an organization. After a few years of well-paid, innovative corporate work, he was itching to pursue his own ideas again ("I don't like to work for other people," he admitted). In 1995, he launched Context Media, an algorithmic publishing platform, which automatically built websites around designated topics.

"I look at John's entrepreneurial behavior as an outcome of the desire to change the world, to really have an impact," said Henrik Sandell, who met Clippinger at Coopers & Lybrand and was his cofounder in Context Media, which ultimately failed after a few years. "He believes that if you're not trying to build something, you're not trying to change things. The challenge is it's hard to stop thinking forward. With building a business, you have to stop moving forward and build on things."

Next up was Lexim, another language-based search company, which quickly raised $30 million during the dot-com boom of the late 1990s and just as quickly lost it all when the NASDAQ bubble popped. "When that hit, you turned gold to lead," Clippinger said, with a laugh. All this time, he maintained teaching and research positions, and he began applying his entrepreneurial ideas to academia. He helped create the Law Lab at Harvard's Berkman Klein Center for Internet and Society, and later, at MIT, he cofounded a think tank called the Institute for Innovation & Data Driven Design (ID3). Both examined the intersection of law, governance, and technology, and allowed Clippinger to pursue his ideas with relative autonomy. He also regularly worked with institutions, including the World Bank, the Aspen Institute, and the Santa Fe Institute, all while advising various companies.

Each entrepreneurial venture—whether it made or lost money, whether it was a for-profit company or a not-for-profit research institution—built upon the experiences, knowledge, and philosophy that Clippinger accumulated in the previous ventures. And all of it was centered around that goal of designing systems that can organize themselves. "We have these cumbersome, unpredictable, politically vulnerable systems," he said, explaining the central question that has driven his career. "So how do you create accountable, decentralized institutions that can withstand that?" How could you embed high-minded goals into technology and make lasting, real change?

"The scope and scale of experiments in digital institution building can go beyond anything practical in the physical world and the results can be easily measured, compiled, and interpreted," Clippinger wrote in his 2007 book *A Crowd of One: The Future of Individual Identity*. "That's the promise of the technology; it can help us learn about ourselves anew." In *From Bitcoin to Burning Man and Beyond*, a book of essays on the future of technology and society that Clippinger edited in 2017, he expanded on this. "A constant theme throughout human history is a deep-seated yearning for a just, perfectible, and virtuous society," he wrote. "How might we design more effective, transparent, accountable, and self-healing institutions?"

Clippinger's daughter Emma told me that her father's belief in this philosophy bordered on an obsession. "And with him, it's totalizing,"

Emma said, of her father's entrepreneurial ambitions. "It's not a way to get coffee in the morning. This is going to be everything. . . . It's all part of a larger belief system, and he's always incorporating new technology, new narratives, new current events to what will be the next thing, but he is able to give the through line and the latest manifestation of his great passion." That all-encompassing approach to entrepreneurship, and life, was frequently overwhelming for Clippinger's family and friends to hear about and endure, time and time again. Emma said that she often cannot talk with her father about her own venture (a nutritional nonprofit in Rwanda called Gardens for Health) because he immediately ties it into his own thoughts, philosophies, and solutions.

Emma personally experienced each boom and bust of her father's entrepreneurship: the thrill of starting up, the stresses of money coming in and going out, and the repeat of that roller-coaster ride over and over. *"We're so close, we're so close . . . oh all is lost . . . the terrible employees! The terrible investors! I hate the whole thing,"* she said, summing up the conversations she overheard growing up. "I rode the wave each time. And it took me a while to recognize that pattern. These are all life-or-death things that people put their life and time into." John partly blames his divorce from Emma's mother on those ups and downs.

Clippinger's entrepreneurship was not focused on winning or losing or getting rich quickly. "I've never been a financially successful entrepreneur," he confessed the next morning, as we walked around the farm's dewy grass. "Never had a big exit in my life . . . 'Oh, here comes John's Learjet!'" he joked. "Some companies made money, and some lost money. . . . Sometimes you do something that has no impact but makes money, and sometimes you make a tremendous impact but no money." Clippinger despised the fetishization of the entrepreneur: the startup's lone hero myth, the veneration of venture capital, and the Big Man's messianic role in laissez-faire capitalism ("Ayn Rand nonsense"). He compared what he saw in Silicon Valley (a place where he witnessed "unparalleled deception and avarice") with the immoral decadence of Weimar Berlin, as young founders awash in riches fiddled with silly apps while the world burned. Entrepreneurship was about one's place in that world and how you deployed your talents in a self-driven way to improve it. "There's no exit here," he said, sweeping his arm around the view of the fields and the mountains beyond. "We can't exit the planet!"

At a time of his life when his peers were mostly focused on golf and grandkids, John Henry Clippinger had arrived at the peak of his purpose as an entrepreneur. He directed it toward the intractable problem of climate change, which he regarded as the most pressing issue in his lifetime. In recent years, Clippinger has witnessed winds coming off Mt. Washington that were so strong they ripped the open doors off of cars like pages torn from a book. The once-abundant moose were dying because of the spread of ticks and Lyme disease (he told me this as we stood in knee-high grass, and I immediately tucked my pants into my socks). The birds' migration patterns were shifting. There were sudden hailstorms, like the one I'd driven through the day before, and record-breaking heat waves (one over the border in Quebec had killed a dozen people the week prior). The earth was changing in dangerous ways. Man was responsible for those changes, as surely as he was responsible for the oil pipeline that ran under Windhover's property. Something needed to be done.

"Humanity has been propelled into a role of ecological responsibility for which it is ill prepared," Clippinger wrote in *A Crowd of One*. He felt an obligation to take everything he had been working on over the past half century as an entrepreneur and do something about it. "How could I sit on the sidelines?" he asked. "I want to see things get made."

THOUGH THE IDEA OF A technology company led by a septuagenarian seems at odds with the youthful image of startup culture, Clippinger is hardly unique in being a senior entrepreneur. Some of the most famous entrepreneurs in American business began those ventures after middle age, from Sam Walton with Walmart to Robert Noyce and Intel. McDonald's, E-Trade, HuffPost, Coca-Cola . . . all of their founding entrepreneurs were in their forties or older when they ran with their ideas about hamburgers and blog posts. As demographics in the developed world skew increasingly older, more individuals in the later half of their lives are going to start more businesses and go to work for themselves.

Cal Halvorsen, who teaches at Boston College's school of social work, has chronicled this shift toward entrepreneurship in later life. In 2017, he noted that while around 7 percent of Americans aged 16 to 49 were self-employed, those numbers grew dramatically as individuals aged, up to 16 percent between ages 60 to 64, and 30 percent between ages 75 to 79. "Almost a third of those who are working over seventy-five are self-employed," Halvorsen said. "That's big." The data were similar for other developed nations. The rate of seniors who are self-employed had also increased over the years and become more diverse, in terms of economic background, race, and gender, owing in part to economic circumstances, like the decline in retirement investments during the Great Recession, which forced many seniors to create a new source of wealth for themselves. "A lot become entrepreneurs because they have no other options," said Halvorsen.

Most senior entrepreneurs are not looking for a big exit or to take on enormous risks, like Clippinger. They want a mix of supplemental income, flexibility in their time, and more than anything, a sense of purpose at a time in their lives when one's identity as a contributing member of society is directly challenged. For entrepreneurs, work represents identity, stimulation, and a reason to wake up in the morning. As my father tells anyone who asks him when he plans to retire, "The day you stop working is the day you start dying." Halvorsen cited the example of his own grandfather, a professor of dentistry in Iowa, who took up the tuba when he retired and saw that one of the reasons the tuba was not as popular as he believed it should be was because it was impossible for small children to hold. So he invented a new tuba stand called the Tubasist, which he sold online. "He didn't make money. He probably lost it. But he patented it and had so much fun," Halvorsen said. "It's not just about making money. It's about making a difference, having a sense of purpose in life, and gaining control. Maybe those don't add up to a bigger paycheck, but they add up on other things."

Older entrepreneurs bring a lifetime of accumulated capital to their ventures; human capital, social capital, and even financial capital. That gives them and the businesses they are pursuing a distinct advantage over those founded by younger entrepreneurs. Senior entrepreneurs see the world through a lifetime of experiences. They view trends and market shifts through the lens of similar ones they have lived through. They see different opportunities than their younger peers do, such as the need for services and products catering to their own demographic, and bring a different set of skills to solve them. Their sum of entrepreneurial knowledge is iterative, acquired one company, one deal, one day at a time. As Clippinger told me, his best defense against fatal mistakes is the instinctual sting of past failures. *"Don't go there!"* he said, mimicking his brain's warning signals. "That feeling is burned into your cortex."

"I think it's important to realize that at every stage of your life you can have dreams and opportunities," said Marci Alboher, the VP of Communications for Encore, an organization that promotes opportunities for work in the latter half of life. "I think there's a real sense that time is running out and that these are either people who feel like there is nothing to lose in digging into something that's nagging them. . . . There's a sense that it's riskier to not do something than do something. They've learned a lot and feel less trepidations to chase that dream."

After our walk, Clippinger and I returned to the house to make more coffee, which he drinks black, as his breakfast, in staggering amounts (his spartan fridge is a tableau of bachelorhood). Hirshberg was up by now, back on the porch with his laptop, typing away. Though he is about a decade younger than Clippinger, Hirshberg has been friends with him for many years and brings his own experiences to Swytch as an entrepreneur and veteran of the technology industry, including nearly a decade working under Steve Jobs during Apple's first years.

Swytch was undoubtedly the most complicated and risky business either man had been a part of. By bringing together the global market for renewable energy with the underlying architecture of blockchain, the company was attempting to marry one uncertain technological solution with another. Somehow they had to convince the world that their idea was both technologically feasible and investment grade.

"I've seen enough patterns that some things become second nature," Hirshberg said, looking at his screen and typing away, as his coffee grew cold. How to grow a market, how to pitch investors, why a lot of young companies pivot too many times, and so on. What emerged, after decades of experiencing these events firsthand, was a second sense for patterns and how to respond to them. Last night's ICO for the Swytch token had closed with less money than forecast (they'd hoped to raise $30 million and got around $11 million), but Hirshberg wasn't worried. You got what you got, he told me, and built your company with that. Patience was the key. "Swytch is a very big idea. It can be all over the place," he said, with the Manhattan accent that forty years of living in San Francisco had done little to dull. "How do you take a very big idea and make it seem like we have a lot of supporters all over the world?"

I asked them what it felt like to be senior entrepreneurs, and they both looked visibly annoyed with the question. "I don't think of myself as 'I'm in my sixties and I'm an entrepreneur!'" Hirshberg said.

"The age thing is really a mentality thing," Clippinger said, his big hands moving excitedly in front of him as he spoke. "A lot of young people are so conservative, and it's really about an openness of mind!"

Did they feel that entrepreneurship kept them young?

"Oh god yes!" Hirshberg said.

"You're open to ideas," Clippinger cut in. "Always open to new ideas. It's a lifestyle thing, a values thing, and you're receptive to that." Physically it was challenging, for sure. Clippinger got inflammation when he flew, especially in his feet, which swelled noticeably, and he was on a plane nearly every week, traveling so frequently between Boston, California, Germany, South Korea, Spain, New York, Puerto Rico, and other global destinations that it took me eight months to find two free days to visit him at Windhover. All-nighters and six cups of coffee for breakfast are a cool rite of passage when you are in your twenties, but the accumulated effects of that, plus the stress, becomes a genuine health concern when you are approaching the average life expectancy for your demographic.

"Yeah, it's exhausting," Clippinger conceded, as a trio of chickens walked by on the lawn below. "But I am genuinely curious about things. I have an idea of how things should be in the world. All the shit we're going through! I see a way we can deal with climate change."

Swytch began in 2017, after Clippinger had a conversation about the emerging world of blockchain technology with John Redpath, an energy commodities trader in Texas who is married to Clippinger's niece. Redpath introduced him to Evan Caron, an employee of his in his mid-thirties, who "has a total hard-on" (Clippinger's words) for both blockchain and renewable energy. The three formed Swytch as a solution to the stagnant market for green power.

What green energy lacked was a transparent, liquid market for renewables, like wind or solar power. As long as fossil fuels are cheaper and more easily traded, they will continue to pollute the world at a rate that makes averting climate disaster impossible. Tracking and measuring renewable energy output was difficult and had no accepted global standard, and the various carbon credits that governments, associations, and even industries had implemented over the previous decades were a mess of conflicting rules and incentives. This had stymied financing for new renewable projects and technologies, to the point where global investments in renewables fell by 7 percent in 2018, the first decline in many years, reversing a shift in momentum that was previously thought permanent.

Swytch proposed a sort of cryptocurrency carbon credit. In the simplest example, you could install a solar panel on your roof, connect it to a smart meter, and connect that to the Swytch app. For every kilowatt of solar energy you generated, Swytch's algorithm (developed by Clippinger) would deposit a certain number of Swytch tokens into your account. These tokens could then be saved, like an investment, or traded on the various global markets where people swap other cryptocurrencies. The value of the Swytch token would automatically shift based on a

variety of factors, from local demand for renewable energy to the particular impact of an offset in reducing greenhouse gas emissions.

The hope was to spark a virtuous cycle of investment. In theory,
the more renewable energy that was generated, the more Swytch tokens were worth, which meant you needed to generate ever-increasing
amounts of renewable energy to receive new tokens, incentivizing businesses to invest in more renewable energy infrastructure. The entire
system would be liquid, decentralized, and supranational, so when a
country pulled out of a climate treaty (as America had with the Paris
Agreement that year), the market was unaffected.

"To accelerate the innovation cycle, you need to reduce cost," Clippinger said. "The goal is to attract capital to go into the biggest re-
gions to disperse high-carbon production in the most frictionless way
possible."

After breakfast the three of us got into Clippinger's pickup truck
and drove half an hour to the famous Bretton Woods Hotel, at the foot
of Mt. Washington. Bretton Woods had been the site of the 1944 conference that established the current global financial system, but Clippinger
and Hirshberg were here to check out Global Economic Visioning, a
two-day summit that aimed to see how blockchain technology could
play a part in creating that system's successor.

Over the course of the next two days, I hung around various events
at the hotel with Clippinger. We listened to talks about climate change
and human termination dynamics, the history of the original Bretton
Woods conference (which established the IMF, World Bank, and the US
dollar as the globe's reserve currency), and a rousing performance by the
jazz pianist ELEW. Clippinger explained Swytch to dozens of people with
the same unbridled enthusiasm I'd first encountered in Seoul the previous year. He told potential investors about the pilot projects that were
already under way with a German utility, an NGO in Puerto Rico (where
much of the power grid was still offline, following hurricane Maria),
the city of Barcelona, and several regional governments in South Korea.

After lunch on the first day, Clippinger, Hirshberg, and Caron (who
had flown up from Austin) sat on the shaded balcony of the hotel and

rapidly talked strategy for Swytch, in a jargon-heavy soup of technical terms and indecipherable acronyms that made my head spin. "Basically, we have evolved Swytch as a verification protocol for attribution-based assets," Caron said, in an attempt to explain their conversation to me, with no real success. What I did understand, the second they began talking, was how alike Caron and Clippinger were, despite the forty-year age gap between them. Clippinger may have advanced degrees, old-money lineage, and an exclusive outfit of L.L.Bean castoffs, but next to Caron, who wore a backward baseball hat and dressed like the owner of a skateboard shop, they were equals. Technically Caron was Swytch's CEO, while Clippinger was its Chief Token Officer, but they were both cofounders, along with Redpath. The way they spoke and finished their sentences, their worldview, their sense of skepticism . . . all of it was the same. Caron had even bought a farm outside Austin to live on after starting Swytch, where his wife raised rescue animals and they grew their own food, after being inspired by Windhover.

"There's people who go through life in a routine and don't have the time to think about the bigger things, like earth, morals, space, and time," Caron said of Clippinger's influence on him as an entrepreneur. "You can check out of the world or check in. I'm more checked-in since I met John."

Both of them felt that their team of intergenerational entrepreneurs was to Swytch's advantage. Caron, Redpath, Hirshberg, and Clippinger all brought their own ideas, energy, skills, and lived experiences to the team, and that shaped their perspective into something far broader than most of the emerging technology companies in the spotlight, which were mostly run by brash young men. There was a maturity in the company's worldview, and that tone was set by Clippinger.

Clippinger's authority and legitimacy were derived from a lifetime of research, knowledge, and firsthand experience on this subject. He brought a perspective that was more patient and long-term than many of the young blockchain entrepreneurs at the conference, who were eager to hack a solution right away, to move fast and break things, regardless of whether their actions had dire consequences for the world beyond. Earlier, Clippinger acknowledged this instinct as a fatal flaw of Silicon Valley's heroic startup myth, whose individualized, selfish drive to action bordered on being "sociopathic," because it ignored the cooperation necessary for lasting, sustainable change.

"Just because you started a company that made money, that doesn't give you authority," he said to me, after a particularly tense session where several Bitcoin advocates were openly calling for the collapse of the global financial system. So much of the cryptocurrency world was tainted by easy money, ego, and overnight expertise, but what changed the world in the long run were always long-term efforts by groups of people, working together with consensus building. Teamwork is what built cities and societies, science and technology, the computer, the internet, and the world wide web . . . not individuals.

"At a certain stage in your life, you have to accept who you are. It's part of the package," Clippinger said the next morning, when I asked him what it meant to live life as an entrepreneur. He was on the porch, drinking his fourth cup of coffee, looking out at the view. Before I drove back to Boston, I wanted to know what kept him going as an entrepreneur, despite the risks, the strain on his health and finances, and the uncertainty. "I'm a person who loves ideas," he said. "I live on ideas. I get high on ideas! They give me dopamine. I love putting things together to solve problems . . . the whole conversation around systems, designing community, the *Small Is Beautiful* philosophy . . . I mean, that's why I moved up here and studied what I did. You're just seeing these ideas flower now. I see solutions, I see my ideas unfolding, and things are finally happening! It's exciting."

Four decades ago, when Clippinger was starting his first company, his drive to be an entrepreneur was primarily financial. He imagined a pot of gold at the end of each idea, but that played with his ego and his sense of self-worth, disrupted his family, and caused him to lose sight of the intellectual curiosity that led him to do his own thing in the first place. Now, after a lifetime pursuing ideas, Clippinger regarded entrepreneurship with a greater sense of purpose. "I feel it's a responsibility," he said, of Swytch. "You have an idea. It has a one-in-a-thousand chance. So what do you do?"

He had the privilege and the education and the skills and connections to make a difference on the one issue that mattered the most to the world right now, and as an entrepreneur, he felt a duty to act, just as he had when he marched for civil rights or protested the Vietnam War. "What could I have done here?" he said. "Could I have done something different? I feel an obligation . . . an ethical obligation. That's my whole reason for being here." Clippinger paused, sipped his coffee, and looked up as the chickadees and finches and hummingbirds zipped around the birdfeeders, chirping up a racket. "I love little birds and swallows. There used to be more here. I love living things!"

Despite her hope that her father would settle down, get a dog, pick up painting, and retire on the farm, Emma Clippinger knew that he would never stop moving from one idea to the next, inventing and theorizing and selling his vision to the world, with the deep belief and conviction that this is what he was born to do. John Henry Clippinger was an entrepreneur, and just like my father, he would be one until the very end. "What makes you think one day that you can just get up and not go to work like everyone else and make up your own thing, and that it's good enough to not only do but get paid for?" she asked. "He showed me that's realistic and possible and viable. This is what makes him happy. This is who he is. He has to experience that for himself."

Speaking to those who knew Clippinger, whether they were longtime friends or those who had just met him at the conference, I saw that it was not going to be an easy road ahead. While people respected his experience, many younger entrepreneurs I met in the blockchain world dismissed Swytch as too complicated, underfunded, and optimistic to work. Others felt Clippinger was too principled and idealistic to succeed in this cutthroat market, that he was tilting at wind farms, a digital Don Quixote wedded to his messianic belief in creating perfect systems to govern the world. But all of them acknowledged that John Henry Clippinger would never stop, never sit down, and never let his ideas remain in his head. He was, as Galia Benartzi, the Israeli blockchain entrepreneur who put on the conference, so eloquently put it to me, "a freedom fighter," one who fought relentlessly for his ideas.

"Ideas," Clippinger said, when I asked what he worried about the most. "I have many more ideas than I have time. I'd like to get something done, so I can do other shit. I'd love to go back and be an artist. To write a novel. There's way more things stuck in my head than I clearly have time for." Entrepreneurship was just a series of ideas that took a lifetime to realize, and like life itself, it rejected any attempt at standardization. Entrepreneurship was the soul of his life, and John Henry Clippinger was going to keep on working at it, right up until the end.

"Success for me is creating the financial instrument to facilitate the flip from fossil fuels to green energy," Clippinger said. "If I have a role in creating that . . . well . . . thank you very much, I'll go to my Maker."

WHAT IS AN ENTREPRENEUR?

That is the question I asked myself when I began working on this book. It is what I asked the hundreds of people I interviewed over the past few years and a question that received an entirely different answer every single time.

Who gets to be an entrepreneur and who does not? What links entrepreneurs together, and why does any of this matter?

If we buy into the myth that has grown out of Silicon Valley, an entrepreneur is a very rare, very specific individual, who engages in the process of innovation and creative destruction, in the model of Joseph Schumpeter's famous theory. This is the entrepreneur you find on the covers of magazines and bestselling biographies. The bold dreamer and inventor of entirely new technologies and industries, who guides us into the future with his endless appetite for risk. He is young and fearless, highly intelligent, and almost always male. A hero who tells their loyal followers to hustle harder, never give up, and embrace failure.

These entrepreneurs call themselves founders, and the businesses they create are called startups. Startups often begin in incubators and accelerators specifically designed to foster their creation and in growing entrepreneurship programs at universities and business schools, who teach entrepreneurship in increasingly narrow terms. The startup founder follows a well-tread path: from the crafting of their initial idea into a pitch deck, through successive rounds of fundraising with investors, into a rapid growth fueled by venture capital, and on to a defined finish; a successful exit or a quick failure. Then they repeat the process again, becoming serial entrepreneurs.

The startup myth is a story of entrepreneurship that holds true for those who take part in it, but it only captures a tiny group of entrepreneurs working in one sector, while excluding the vast majority of the entrepreneurs who build and run the businesses that make up the world's economy.

"The image of the entrepreneur as the great inventor, the great promoter, or the great and daring risk-taker simply doesn't square with the facts," wrote the authors of *The Enterprising Man*. "The reality is far less spectacular than this." The pioneering American study, published in 1964, sought to define how entrepreneurs were different from everyone else. They defined an entrepreneur as someone who took the ingredients of their circumstances, married them with some dose of creativity, and found a way to make a business out of that recipe.

This definition of an entrepreneur was similar to the economist Richard Cantillon's, who first popularized the term in the early eighteenth century. Whether they were a farmer, artisan, or shopkeeper, Cantillon's entrepreneur was defined by two things: they worked for themselves, and they accepted the financial uncertainty that came with self-employment. As Cantillon wrote nearly three hundred years ago, society was broken into two classes: "entrepreneurs and hired workers." The hired worker draws a regular salary, reports to a boss, and works under clearly defined rules. "All the others are entrepreneurs, whether they are set up with capital to conduct their enterprise, or are entrepreneurs of their own labor without capital, and they may be regarded as living under uncertainty; even the beggars and robbers are entrepreneurs of this class."

Now, several years after I began searching for what it meant to be an entrepreneur, I came to realize how little had changed in the centuries since those words were first written. An entrepreneur is not determined by the size of their business, their industry, or any other economic factors, as some academics and experts argue. She is both the founder of a software startup and the refugee baklava baker, the struggling dairy farmer and the millionaire manufacturer, the neighborhood hairdresser and the fourth-generation winery owner. He owns the small business, the medium-sized business, and the giant corporation. An entrepreneur works alone or with partners, their immediate family, or a team of thousands. They go into an office in a suit and tie or sit at home in their sweatpants. They are your brother and father, your wife and friend, the people in your community, and those running the businesses you interact with every single day. Entrepreneurs are both rich and poor, black and white, young and old, highly educated and completely illiterate. They start their businesses because of the pull of opportunity or the push of necessity or both, fund them with savings or debt or outside investments, set them up for the short or long term, and fail more often than they succeed. What unites them are the same two things Cantillon identified: entrepreneurs work for themselves and assume the uncertainty necessary to do so.

The entrepreneur is not someone who is paid a regular salary, regardless of what it says on their business card. They are not the innovator in chief or the intrapreneur within an organization, because these people bear none of the risks or freedom essential to entrepreneurship. Their skin is not in the game. It is just another job. The entrepreneur is also not the on-demand worker, such as the Uber driver or an Amazon warehouse fulfillment contractor, who remains an employee in all but name, with clear rules and rewards dictated to them but no agency to alter that. In order to be an entrepreneur, a person needs to fully own their work and have complete independence over its direction.

I don't have a job or a salary or a boss. I work for myself. I alone decide what to do each day, what to work on, how to do that work, when to work on it, and when to shut off the computer and go paddleboarding. I judge how much risk (financial, emotional, personal) I want to assume in the hope of some future reward. I have complete freedom with my work, with all the joy and terror that brings, and I accept the insecurity that is the price of that freedom. I own my work, and because of this, I feel every dizzying high and nauseating low associated with it. I take everything that happens personally. I always have. I always will.

I am an entrepreneur.

If you do, too, then you are an entrepreneur. Realize that. Say it out loud. Take pride in it. Because if you don't, and if we allow the myths around entrepreneurship to perpetuate and continue to cede its definition and soul to Silicon Valley, then we will see a widening inequality in entrepreneurship, between the narrow few who fit into that image and benefit from its myth and the rest of us who do not.

"I'm glad entrepreneurship is cool, but I think it needs to be something everyday people can see themselves as," said Wendy Guillies, who runs the Ewing Marion Kauffman Foundation, the organization that has done more to promote entrepreneurship in America and around the world than any other. "That's the reality. Everyday people are doing amazing things out in communities. They are just not getting their stories in the newspaper." What the Kauffman Foundation was fighting for, Guillies told me, was nothing less than the core of the American Dream.

Entrepreneurship happens in every single corner of the world, and whether you run a business in China or Ecuador the essence of its soul is universal, but there is something about the way we value entrepreneurs that says something fundamental about the society we live in. A big part of America's founding story was the idea that it was a place where people could come with nothing but ambition, hang up a shingle, and make a go of it:

"In recent years, there has been continuing concern that the social and economic climate of the nation is so changing that both new business enterprise and the entrepreneur will become phenomena of the past," wrote the authors of *The Enterprising Man*, more than five decades ago, citing the fear that "the passing of the entrepreneur and the entrepreneurial tradition means in a real sense, the passing away of a system of values that have always been central to the American way."

What is at stake here is the very heart of capitalism itself. I realize that's a scary word to many people, with good reason. Capitalism has come to represent the unchecked powers of corporations over societies and the legacy of rampant greed, leading to problems as acute as climate change. But at its core capitalism is the economic framework of the open market, and the hope baked into it, that lets anyone take a risk to face the world alone and start a business. To stop asking permission and become an entrepreneur.

That hope is the essential ingredient that links all entrepreneurs together, wherever they are. The hope that your idea has worth. The hope that it will sell. The hope that you have the ability to change your fortune . . . for yourself, your family, the community around you, and maybe even the world. That hope is the persistent faith we gather up in ourselves every single day, as we go out and try to make our ideas work. It underpins the personal risk that all entrepreneurs must accept and allows them to manage it, even when that risk threatens to overwhelm them.

When people talk about the American Dream, they are talking about the entrepreneur's essential hope. But it is this hope that we are putting at risk. When we narrow the meaning of entrepreneurship to an increasingly small elite, who are mostly wealthy, young, white men from Ivy League schools following a standardized, prescriptive model of entrepreneurship, we are cutting off that hope for entrepreneurs of all sizes and ambitions everywhere. We are telling them that their experiences, ideas, business, and dreams are unworthy, because they do not fit into the startup myth's narrow model. That they are not true entrepreneurs. When we write people out of the story of entrepreneurship, we deprive everyone of what is possible.

It is time to reclaim the soul of the entrepreneur. To realize that entrepreneurship is not some magical, rarefied thing that only a select few get to participate in, but something that is open to everyone, everywhere, if they are willing to bear the risk and give it a try. To return the word to its original meaning and the larger group of entrepreneurs that it applies to.

To help them do this, the institutions that have been promoting just one model of entrepreneurship (high-growth and high-tech) need to realize the limits of that and broaden their own definition. Universities, colleges, and even high schools need to study the world of entrepreneurship beyond Silicon Valley's unicorns and its homogenous model of success and teach students that there are actually innumerable paths to pursuing a business that defy standardization.

"It's the everyday entrepreneurs, the people who would turn down that moniker outright as not fitting them at all, they're the ones we should actually be studying, mostly, and whose practices we need to figure out, model and teach," said Sarah Dodd, a British academic who has been at the forefront of calling for this reset among universities, by moving the study of entrepreneurship beyond economics departments and business schools (who tend to regard it as purely a series of inputs that creates jobs and capital), into areas like philosophy, sociology, and anthropology, which can look at the broader role entrepreneurs play in society. "We are responsible for shaping the entrepreneurs of the future: it behooves us to consider who those people might be. And the best way to figure that out is by looking at the folk who are out there now, running small businesses in their millions, without VC funding, or massive media exposure, or appearing on [Shark Tank]. The everyday entrepreneurship of the 99 percent is a deeper, richer, more purposive vehicle for changing lives, individually and collectively."

The organizations that work with entrepreneurs—from nonprofits like the Kauffman Foundation to banks, government programs, and business incubators—need to focus less on creating the next Facebook, or the simple metric of job creation, and develop more tools to support entrepreneurs at every stage of their journey. This includes promoting funding models that are more equitable for startups than venture capital, as well as offering the kinds of business coaching and education that can increase an entrepreneur's odds of success. More attention needs to be paid to the entrepreneurs who have typically been ignored, such as women, minorities, seniors, and those in rural communities, because they start businesses in increasingly greater numbers, and yet they still face obstacles that stifle their enormous potential.

Most important, entrepreneurs require community. They need to know they are not alone. They need people to speak with when the risk and uncertainty seems too much to bear, especially from other entrepreneurs who can empathize with their experiences. This involves breaking down barriers around taboo subjects, like mental health, the fear of failure, and financial troubles, and creating the opportunities for all entrepreneurs to talk openly about what they need, as they bear the uncertainty and isolation of their work.

What is an entrepreneur?

Maybe the more important question to ask about an entrepreneur is not *what* but *why*. Why be an entrepreneur? Why choose to work for yourself, and why continue to do that throughout your life?

For the thrill of starting up, taking a raw idea and bringing it to the world, or because an entrepreneur can start over, in business and in life, even after being uprooted. She can shape a business around the lifestyle she wants to live or build up her community through that business. Entrepreneurs are driven by realizing their personal values or by shaping a family legacy. He will continue to fight through the ups and downs, because all entrepreneurship is fundamentally an act of hope, which builds over a lifetime into a sense of purpose and identity that cannot be uncoupled from who we are.

For me, being an entrepreneur is all of it. It is a set of behaviors and values I inherited from my family, the way I define myself in the world, and the source of both my greatest joys and biggest pains.

Being an entrepreneur means more than just a way to make money. It is an identity intertwined with complicated emotions, swinging between pride and loathing, joy and fear, and the other twists of the roller coaster we strap ourselves into every single day we go to work for ourselves. We cannot separate that from who we are. Like the late Mr. Freeman, whose family immortalized this choice on his tombstone, being an entrepreneur is woven into the essence of our souls. That soul is frequently restless, often innovative, and fiercely independent. It transcends class, race, geography, industry, and generations and resists any form of standardization.

Entrepreneurship is what happens when ordinary people take their ideas about the world and build a business around them. Sometimes these ideas are as vast and complicated as a technological solution to save the world from ecological catastrophe. But more often they are small and simple, like the Waterwheel restaurant up the road from John Henry Clippinger's farm, which served the fluffiest, most delicious blueberry pancakes I have ever encountered.

The Waterwheel was everything I hoped for in a New England pancake house: hand-drawn signs, heavy ceramic coffee mugs, whipped butter, and pitchers of maple syrup made by farmers nearby. The menu featured ads for local businesses; the HVAC repairman, tractor dealer, and other entrepreneurs that made up this community, and as I sat there, drowning those pancakes in that glorious syrup, I realized that the world needed them both—ambitious solutions to climate change *and* blueberry pancakes—and the entrepreneurs who brought them to us. If we can start to shift the conversation back to the businesses that actually touch us every day, perhaps we can reclaim the soul of the entrepreneur.

Acknowledgments

WHILE I'VE MADE A BIG deal about working alone, the truth is that none of this book would have been possible without the support of a tremendous community of people, whom I owe a great deal of thanks to.

Early on, when I was thinking about the nature of self-employment, I tapped the brilliant mind of my friend and noted economist Greg Kaplan, whose probing questions led me to realize this was going to be a book about entrepreneurs.

My friend Coralie D'Souza was kind enough to introduce me to her colleagues at the Brookfield Center for Entrepreneurship and Innovation here in Toronto, including the always-up-for-tasty-lunch duo of Andrew Do and Matthew Lo, who shed some crucial initial light onto the world of entrepreneurship research and its endless paths.

Tea Hadziristic worked incredibly hard sourcing mountains of articles, sources, and leads as a research assistant and is well on her way to becoming a successful and brilliant lawyer.

I owe a remarkable debt to the entrepreneurs who opened their homes, businesses, and hearts to me and endured endless questions about every aspect of their lives: Nikhil Aggarwal and Andrew Chizewer, who fended off an overly aggressive Stanford communications department (and let me buy them an underage beer); the Alsoufi and Alsalha families, who shared their stories and their delicious food (always with extra portions); Tracy Obolsky, who lent me her husband's surfboard and didn't laugh at my poor paddling; Jesseca Dupart, who introduced me as "a nice, white journalist" to her hairstylist; Kevin Mauger, who was endlessly patient, even when explaining conveyor systems for the fourth time; Iduna Weinert, for not holding back and showing me and the family true Mendozan hospitality; Seth Nitschke, for sharing his tacos and philosophy and letting me play cowboy for a few days; and John Henry Clippinger, for hosting me at Windhover, pointing the way to the pancakes, and opening my eyes to an entrepreneur's lifelong passion.

The following people were incredibly helpful with introductions, advice, or just a place to crash through the long years of research. Many of these individuals took an hour or more to chat with me for the book, but they were ultimately not quoted (though their ideas are woven throughout): Roy Bahat, Jon Steinberg (and his dojo), Mara Zepeda, Brian O'Kelley, Derek Lidow, Sigalit Perelson, Jason Meil, Prof. Debra Satz, Todd Krieger, Howie Diamond, Andrew Blum, Sabina Neagu, Devin Cintron, Jim Scheinman, Kent Lindstrom, Rebecca Bortman, Daniel Jacker, Vivek Wadhwa, Adam Gross, Dan Lyons, Drake Huongo, Jackson Eilers, Marina Gorbis, David Paskowitz, Douglas Rushkoff, Eric Paley, Nathan Schneider, Matt Ruby, Michael Mullany, Jonathan Abrams, Craig Kanarick, Prof. Nicholas Bloom, AJ Solimine, Sarah Saska, Mike Murchison, Kamal Hassan, Devi Arasanayagam, Vanessa Ling Yu, Prof. Dan Bender, Prof. Jayeeta Sharma, Prof. Jeffrey Pilcher, Len Senater and Cara Benjamin-Pace, Shuguang Wang, Krishendu Ray, Tommy Le, Johanna Mendelson Forman, Natalie White, Rahaf Alakbani, Sam Sifton, Chris Aylett, Marian Yusuf, Sureya Ibrahim and the women of the Regent Park Catering Collective, Steve Stathis, Rachel Van Tosh, Jessica Feingold, Prof. Zoltan Acs, Jon Shell, Patrick Clark, Jarrett Woods, Cristina Flores, Jason Berry, A'Lelia Bundles, Brandon Andrews, Alicia Robb, Shaynah Solochek, Hermione Malone, LaShauna Lewis, Alex Moss, Ginny Vanderslice, Sara Lawrence Minard, Kara Peck and Cecily Mauran, Jenn Rezeli, Jaime and Isaac Salm, Robert Brown, James Steiker, Daniel Goldstein, Raj Sisodia, Nickolas Sypniewski, Gregory Fresh, David Diehl, Corey Rosen, Richard Panico, Amber Pietrobono, Carmen Rojas, Derek Razo,

Nathan Schneider, Bradford and Bryan Manning, Kris Maynard, Kathy Steele, Phillip Kim, Jason Fried, Hamsa Daher, Bruce Hendrick, Stewart Thornhill, Jean Pitzo, Michael Burdick, Thea Polanic, Rob Hopkins, Ari Weinzweig, Adres Rosberg, Alejandro Leirado, Antoinette Schoar, Judy Green, Ute Stephan, Liya Schwartzman and Gary Peterson, Brandon Souza, Dr. Milena Nikolova, Jolanda Hessels, Rev. Charles Smith, Tom Orvis and Wayne Zipser, Lynne McBride, Anthony Chang, Gary Soiseth, Ron Manderscheid, Jennifer Fahy, Sej Pandya, Galia Benartzi, Marc Freedman, Charlie Firestone, Sarah Dodd, Samee Desai, Barbara Pruitt, Larry Jacob, Richard and Ronald Smith, Steven Kaplan, Sara Bourdeau, Howard Tam, Josh Lerner, Howard Stevenson, Debi Kleiman, Donald Kuratko, Candida Brush, Vanessa Roanhorse, Richard Florida, Louis Galambos, Josh Dale and Ilana Miller, Asher Lack, Steve Hipple. I'm sure there are others that I've forgotten, and if so, I apologize.

One of the best parts of writing a book is getting to speak about it to people who genuinely care, and I owe so much to the wonderful folks at the Lavin Agency for the work they do to make that happen: David Lavin, Charles Yao, Erin Vanderkruk, Tom Gagnon, Gord Mazur, Cathy Hirst, Ken Calway, Sal Itterly, Holly Caracappa, Ruwimbo Makoni, Lucas MacKenzie, Lana Leprich, Abhi Prasad, Stacey Wickens, Linda Cook, and the rest of the team.

James Levine, of Levine, Greenberg, and Rostan, is a true entrepreneur, who transformed himself from a pioneering intellectual in the education world into one of the best literary agents in New York and continues to pave his own path every day (while vacationing without apology). Thank you for your direction and advice at every stage of this book and for the way you painlessly pull clear ideas from my tangled, half-baked notions.

This is my third book with PublicAffairs, so I think it's safe to call them my publishing family. It is a continual pleasure to work with these talented and caring individuals again and again: Jaime Leifer, Lindsay Fradkoff, Clive Priddle, Susan Weinberg, Melissa Raymond, Miguel Cervantes, Melissa Veronesi, Ian Gibbs, and the always impeccably dressed

Peter Osnos, an entrepreneur who stays true to his values and sense of decency.

That decency is something I constantly feel when working with Benjamin Adams, my editor at PublicAffairs, who fled the grind of Manhattan for the genteel breezes of New Hampshire halfway through this book and never missed a literary beat. Ben, it remains a pleasure to continue working together, bearing the risks and hoping for the rewards, while enjoying everything that comes in the middle (usually mediocre lunches).

Finally, I owe a profound debt to my family, who not only supported me with their usual steadfast love and encouragement, but who shaped the way I viewed entrepreneurship. Mom and Dad, thank you for setting the entrepreneurial standard in my life and for cementing that as a value that you passed along to me, regardless of the direction it took. Daniel, thank you for being open about your own experiences and for enduring my pleas to paddleboard while you worked your ass off. Lauren, thank you for shouldering the burden with me: of the home, the children, and the mental weight of going out on our own in this world. I am immensely proud of everything you have accomplished and continue to accomplish every day. I love you all and am proud as hell to be part of this family of unemployables.

Selected Bibliography

General

Bronson, Po. *What Should I Do with My Life?: The True Story of People Who Answered the Ultimate Question.* New York: Ballantine Books, 2005.

Collins, Orvis F., David G. Moore, and Darab B. Unwalla. *The Enterprising Man.* East Lansing, MI: Michigan State University, 1964.

Florida, Richard. *The Rise of the Creative Class.* New York: Basic Books, 2019.

Lerner, Josh. *Boulevard of Broken Dreams: Why Public Efforts to Boost Entrepreneurship and Venture Capital Have Failed—and What to Do about It.* Princeton, NJ: Princeton University Press, 2012.

Shane, Scott. *The Illusions of Entrepreneurship: The Costly Myths That Entrepreneurs, Investors, and Policy Makers Live By.* New Haven, CT: Yale University Press, 2008.

Shane, Scott. *Is Entrepreneurship Dead?: The Truth about Startups in America.* New Haven, CT: Yale University Press, 2018.

Terkel, Studs. *Working: People Talk about What They Do All Day and How They Feel about What They Do.* New York: The New Press, 2011.

Introduction

Aarons-Mele, Morra. "The Dangerous Rise of 'Entrepreneurship Porn.'" *Harvard Business Review*, January 6, 2014.

Additional statistics courtesy of the US Bureau of Labor Statistics (BLS), the Ewing Marion Kauffman Foundation, and the Global Entrepreneurship Monitor (GEM).

Agrawal, Miki. *Do Cool Sh*t: Quit Your Day Job, Start Your Own Business, and Live Happily Ever After.* New York: Harper Business, 2013.

Casselman, Ben. "A Start-up Slump Is a Drag on the Economy. Big Business May Be to Blame." *New York Times*, September 20, 2017.

Dinlersoz, Emin. "Business Formation Statistics: A New Census Bureau Product That Takes the Pulse of Early-Stage U.S. Business Activity." United States Census Bureau Center for Economic Studies. February 8, 2018.

Guillebeau, Chris. *Side Hustle: Build a Side Business and Make Extra Money—Without Quitting Your Day Job*. London: Pan Macmillan, 2017.

Hipple, Steven F., and Laurel A. Hammond. "Self-employment in the United States." US Bureau of Labor Statistics. March 2016.

Hoffman, Reid, and Ben Casnocha. *The Start-up of You: Adapt to the Future, Invest in Yourself, and Transform Your Career*. New York: Crown Publishing Group, 2012.

Kochhar, Rakesh. "National Trends in Self-Employment and Job Creation." Pew Research Center. October 22, 2015.

Lettieri, John W. "America without Entrepreneurs: The Consequences of Dwindling Startup Activity." Testimony before the Committee on Small Business and Entrepreneurship, United States Senate. June 29, 2016.

Porter, Eduardo. "Where Are the Start-ups? Loss of Dynamism Is Impeding Growth." *New York Times*, February 6, 2018.

Samuelson, Robert J. "The U.S. Has Lost Its Entrepreneurial Advantage." *Wall Street Journal*, October 24, 2018.

Vaynerchuk, Gary. *Crush It!: Why NOW Is the Time to Cash in on Your Passion*. New York: HarperCollins, 2009.

Vaynerchuk, Gary. *Crushing It!: How Great Entrepreneurs Build Their Business and Influence—and How You Can, Too*. New York: HarperCollins, 2018.

Wilmoth, Daniel. "The Missing Millennial Entrepreneurs." *Trends in Entrepreneurship*. US Small Business Administration Office of Advocacy. February 4, 2016.

Chapter 1: Starting Up

Aldrich, Howard E., and Martin Ruef. "Unicorns, Gazelles, and Other Distractions on the Way to Understanding Real Entrepreneurship in the United States." *Academy of Management Perspectives* 32, no. 4 (2017): 458–472.

Alger, Horatio. *Ragged Dick: Street Life in New York with the Boot-Blacks*. Auckland, New Zealand: The Floating Press, 2009.

Auletta, Ken. "Get Rich U." *New Yorker*, April 30, 2012.

Cantillon, Richard. *An Essay on Economic Theory*. Translated by Chantal Saucier. Auburn, AL: Mises Institute, 2010.

Carreyou, John. *Bad Blood: Secrets and Lies in a Silicon Valley Startup*. New York: Random House, 2018.

Clark, Patrick. "Entrepreneurship Education Is Hot. Too Many Get It Wrong." *Bloomberg Businessweek*, August 8, 2013.

Fan, Maureen. "Animating against the Grain." Transcript: Stanford eCorner, October 10, 2018, https://stvp-static-prod.s3.amazonaws.com/uploads/sites/2/2018/10/animating-against-the-grain-transcript.pdf.

Griffith, Erin. "More Start-ups Have an Unfamiliar Message for Venture Capitalists: Get Lost." *New York Times*, January 11, 2019.

"Horatio Alger Association Honors Two California Entrepreneurs and Philanthropists, Elizabeth Holmes and Gilbert Edward LeVasseur Jr., along with Seven National Scholarship Recipients from the State." Horatio Alger Association of Distinguished Americans, Inc. via PR Newswire, March 9, 2015.

Isaacson, Walter. *Steve Jobs*. New York: Simon & Schuster, 2011.

Johnson, Stefanie K., Markus A. Fitza, Daniel A. Lerner, Dana M. Calhoun, Marissa A. Beldon, Elsa T. Chan, and Pieter T. J. Johnson. "Risky Business: Linking *Toxoplasma gondii* Infection and Entrepreneurship Behaviours across Individuals and Countries." *Proceedings of the Royal Society B: Biological Sciences*, July 25, 2018.

Kerby, Richard. "Where Did You Go to School?" *Medium*, July 30, 2018, https://blog.usejournal.com/where-did-you-go-to-school-bde54d846188.

Kidder, Tracy. *A Truck Full of Money*. New York: Random House, 2016.

Landes, Davis S., Joel Mokyr, and William J. Baumol. *The Invention of Enterprise: Entrepreneurship from Ancient Mesopotamia to Modern Times*. Princeton, NJ: Princeton University Press, 2010.

Lidow, Derek. *What Sam Walton, Walt Disney, and Other Great Self-Made Entrepreneurs Can Teach Us about Building Valuable Companies*. New York: Diversion Books, 2018.

Lopez, Matt. "The False Promise of Entrepreneurship." *Stanford Daily*, February 26, 2014.

Lynley, Matthew. "Sense Sleep Tracker Maker Hello Is Shutting Down." *TechCrunch*, June 12, 2017.

Mallery, Alexander. "Searching for Steve Jobs: Theranos, Elizabeth Holmes, and the Dangers of the Origin Story." *Intersect* 10, no. 3 (2017).

Marwick, Alice. "Silicon Valley Isn't a Meritocracy. And It's Dangerous to Hero-worship Entrepreneurs." wired.com. November 23, 2013.

O'Reilly, Tim. "Supermoney." In *WTF: What's the Future and Why It's Up to Us*. New York: Harper Business, 2017.

Ries, Eric. *The Lean Startup: How Today's Entrepreneurs Use Continuous Innovation to Create Radically Successful Businesses*. New York: Crown Business, 2011.

Rushkoff, Douglas. *Throwing Rocks at the Google Bus: How Growth Became the Enemy of Prosperity*. New York: Portfolio/Penguin, 2016.

Schumpeter, Joseph A. *Capitalism, Socialism, and Democracy: Third Edition*. New York: HarperCollins, 2008.

Schumpeter, Joseph A. *The Entrepreneur: Classic Texts by Joseph A. Schumpeter*. Palo Alto, CA: Stanford University Press, 2011.

"Unicorns Going to Market." *Economist*, April 20, 2019.

Vance, Ashlee. *Elon Musk: Tesla, SpaceX, and the Quest for a Fantastic Future*. New York: HarperCollins, 2015.

Wolfe, Alexandra. *Valley of the Gods: A Silicon Valley Story*. New York: Simon & Schuster, 2017.

Chapter 2: Starting Over

Blau, Francine D., and Christopher Mackie, eds. "The Economic and Fiscal Consequences of Immigration." The National Academies of Sciences. September 2016.

Bluestein, Adam. "The Most Entrepreneurial Group in America Wasn't Born in America." *Inc.*, February 2015.

Cillian O'Brien, "Immigrant-Owned Firms Create More Jobs Than Those with
    Canadian-Born Owners: StatCan," CTV News, April 24, 2019, www.ctvnews
    .ca/canada/immigrant-owned-firms-create-more-jobs-than-those-with
    -canadian-born-owners-statcan-1.4393134?fbclid=IwAR2nQdO5vJpbrdo
    BUndcFb-6CybXnbcuDeboH8-eXtbN3qlMy3Sbarj6_Qo.
Fairlie, Robert W. "Immigrant Entrepreneurs and Small Business Owners, and
    Their Access to Financial Capital." US Office of the Small Business Adminis-
    tration. May 2012.
Fairlie, Robert W., and Magnus Lofstrom. "Immigration and Entrepreneurship."
    Institute for the Study of Labor (IZA). October 2013.
Herman, Richard T., and Robert L. Smith. *Immigrant, Inc.: Why Immigrant Entre-
    preneurs Are Driving the New Economy (and How They Will Save the American
    Worker)*. Hoboken, NJ: John Wiley & Sons, 2009.
John F. Kennedy's "A Nation of Immigrants" speech to the Anti-Defamation
    League in 1963 via adl.org, www.youtube.com/watch?v=dBVdpH51NyY.
Kerr, William. "International Migration and U.S. Innovation." *National Academies*,
    2015.
Kerr, William R., and Sari Pekkala Kerr. "Immigrant Entrepreneurship." National
    Bureau of Economic Research. July 2016.
Ostrovsky, Yuri, and Garnett Picot. "The Exit and Survival Patterns of Immigrant
    Entrepreneurs: The Case of Private Incorporated Companies." Statistics Can-
    ada. January 2018.
Roberts, Steven. *From Every End of This Earth: 13 Families and the New Lives They
    Made in America*. New York: HarperCollins, 2009.
Vandor, Peter, and Nikolaus Franke. "Why Are Immigrants More Entrepreneur-
    ial?" *Harvard Business Review*, October 27, 2016.
Wayland, Sarah V. "Immigrant Self-Employment and Entrepreneurship in the
    GTA: Literature, Data, and Program Review." Metcalf Foundation. December
    2011.

Chapter 3: Life's a Beach

Atkinson, Robert D., and Michael Lind. *Big Is Beautiful: Debunking the Myth of Small
    Business*. Cambridge, MA: MIT Press, 2018.
Ferriss, Timothy. *The 4-Hour Work Week: Escape the 9–5, Live Anywhere and Join the
    New Rich*. London: Ebury Publishing, 2011.
Marcketti, Sara B., Linda S. Niehm, and Ruchita Fuloria. "An Exploratory Study of
    Lifestyle Entrepreneurship and Its Relationship to Life Quality." *Family and
    Consumer Sciences Research Journal* 34, no. 3 (March 2006): 241.
Marcketti, Sara B., and Joy M. Kozar. "Leading with Relationships: A Small Firm
    Example." *The Learning Organization* 14, no. 2 (2007): 142–154.
Pahnke, André, and Friederike Welter. "The German Mittelstand: Antithesis to Sil-
    icon Valley Entrepreneurship?" *Small Business Economics: An Entrepreneurship
    Journal* 52, no. 2 (2019): 345.
Schumacher, E. F. *Small Is Beautiful: Economics as if People Mattered*. New York:
    Harper Perennial, 2010.

Welter, Friederike, Ted Baker, David B. Audretsch, and William B. Gartner. "Everyday Entrepreneurship—A Call for Entrepreneurship Research to Embrace Entrepreneurial Diversity." *Entrepreneurship Theory and Practice* 41, no. 3 (2016): 311–321.

William Wetzel's "lifestyle entrepreneur" definition via p. 342, *Business Alchemy: Turning Ideas into Gold*. Cobb, William R., and M. L. Johnson, ed. Bloomington, IN: AuthorHouse, 2012.

Chapter 4: Bring 'em Up

Asiedu, Elizabeth, James A. Freeman, and Akwasi Nti-Addae. "Access to Credit by Small Businesses: How Relevant Are Race, Ethnicity, and Gender?" *American Economic Review: Papers & Proceedings* 102, no. 3 (2012): 102.

Austin, Algernon. "The Color of Entrepreneurship: Why the Racial Gap among Firms Costs the U.S. Billions." Center for Global Policy Solutions. April 2016.

Becker-Medina, Erika M. "Women Are Leading the Rise of Black-Owned Businesses." Census.gov. February 26, 2016.

Fairlie, Rob. "Financing Black-Owned Businesses." Stanford Institute for Economic Policy Research. May 2017.

Gill, Tiffany M. *Beauty Shop Politics: African American Women's Activism in the Beauty Industry*. Champaign, IL: University of Illinois Press, 2010.

Gines, Dell. "Black Women Business Startups." The Federal Reserve Bank of Kansas City. 2018.

Harvey, Adia M. "Becoming Entrepreneurs: Intersections of Race, Class, and Gender at the Black Beauty Salon." *Gender and Society* 19, no. 6 (December 2005): 789–808.

"Kauffman Compilation: Research on Race and Entrepreneurship." Ewing Marion Kauffman Foundation. December 2016.

"Laying the Foundation for National Prosperity: The Imperative of Closing the Racial Wealth Gap." Insight: Center for Community Economic Development. March 2009.

Mills, Quincy T. *Cutting Along the Color Line: Black Barbers and Barber Shops in America*. Philadelphia: University of Pennsylvania Press, 2013.

Opiah, Antonia. "The Changing Business of Black Hair, a Potentially $500b Industry." *HuffPost*, January 24, 2014.

Sibilla, Nick. "Tennessee Has Fined Residents Nearly $100,000, Just for Braiding Hair." Forbes.com. March 13, 2018.

"The Tapestry of Black Business Ownership in America: Untapped Opportunities for Success." Association for Enterprise Opportunity. Aeoworks.org. 2016.

"The 2018 State of Women-Owned Business Report." Commissioned by American Express. 2018. https://about.americanexpress.com/files/doc_library/file/2018 -state-of-women-owned-businesses-report.pdf.

Wingfield, Adia Harvey. *Doing Business with Beauty: Black Women, Hair Salons, and the Racial Enclave Economy*. Lanham, MD: Rowman & Littlefield, 2008.

Chapter 5: Serving and Leading

Bernstein, Jared. "Employee Ownership, ESOPs, Wealth, and Wages." Esca.us. January 2016.

"Blue-collar Capitalists." *Economist*, June 8, 2019.

Chouinard, Yvon. *Let My People Go Surfing: The Education of a Reluctant Businessman*. New York: Penguin, 2016.

Friedman, Milton. "The Social Responsibility of Business Is to Increase Its Profits." *New York Times Magazine*, September 13, 1970.

Greenleaf, Robert K. *The Servant as Leader*. South Orange, NJ: Center for Servant Leadership, 1970.

Hsieh, Tony. *Delivering Happiness: A Path to Profits, Passion, and Purpose*. New York: Grand Central Publishing, 2010.

Kim, Phillip H. "Action and Process, Vision and Values: Entrepreneurship Means Something Different to Everyone." In *The Routledge Companion to Entrepreneurship*, 59–74. Abingdon, UK: Routledge, 2015.

Mycoskie, Blake. *Start Something That Matters*. New York: Random House, 2011.

"The One-for-one Business Model: Avoiding Unintended Consequences." *Knowledge@Wharton*. February 16, 2015.

Overman, Steven. *The Conscience Economy: How a Mass Movement for Good is Great for Business*. Abingdon, UK: Routledge, 2016.

Papi-Thornton, Daniela. "Tackling Heropreneurship." *Stanford Social Innovation Review*, February 23, 2016.

Rosen, Corey, John Case, and Martin Staubus. "Every Employee an Owner. Really." *Harvard Busienss Review*, June 2005.

Spears, Larry C. *Reflections on Leadership: How Robert K. Greenleaf's Theory of Servant-Leadership Influenced Today's Top Management Thinkers*. Hoboken, NJ: John Wiley & Sons, 1995.

Wicks, Judy. *Good Morning Beautiful Business: The Unexpected Journey of an Activist Entrepreneur and Local Economy Pioneer*. White River Junction, VT: Chelsea Green Publishing, 2013.

Wirtz, Ronald A. "Employee Ownership: Economic Miracle or ESOPs Fable?" Federal Reserve Bank of Minneapolis. June 1, 2007.

Yunnus, Muhammad. *Building Social Business: The New Kind of Capitalism That Serves Humanity's Most Pressing Needs*. New York: PublicAffairs, 2010.

Yunnus, Muhammad. *Creating a World without Poverty: Social Business and the Future of Capitalism*. New York: PublicAffairs, 2007.

Chapter 6: Keeping It in the Family

Atkin, Tim. "South America's Top 10 Winemakers." *Decanter*, March 23, 2019.

Bhalla, Vikram. "Family Businesses Are Here to Stay, and Thrive." TED@BCG lecture. September 4, 2015. https://www.youtube.com/watch?v=suL-HkP-2Ts.

Bresciani, Stefano, Elisa Giacosa, Laura Broccardo, and Francesca Culasso. "The Family Variable in the French and Italian Wine Sector." *EuroMed Journal of Business* (May 3, 2016).

Catena, Laura. *Vino Argentino*. San Francisco, CA: Chronicle Books, 2010.

De Massis, Alfredo, Federico Frattini, Antonio Majocchi, and Lucia Piscitello. "Family Firms in the Global Economy: Toward a Deeper Understanding of Internationalization Determinants, Processes, and Outcomes." *Global Strategy Journal*, December 2018.

F. R. Kets de Vries, Manfred. "Saving a Family Business from Emotional Dysfunction." *Harvard Business Review*, February 1, 2017.

Family Firm Institute. Ffi.org.

Jaskiewicz, Peter, James G. Comb, and Sabine B. Rau. "Entrepreneurial Legacy: Toward a Theory of How Some Family Firms Nurture Transgenerational Entrepreneurship." *Journal of Business Venturing* (January 2015).

Lopez Roca, Daniel. "¿QUIÉN ES EL NUEVO SOCIO DE CAVAS DE WEINERT?" argentinewines.com. March 13, 2013.

Molesworth, James. "A Sit Down with Bodega y Cavas de Weinert: An Argentine Winery Sticks to Tradition." *Wine Spectator*, November 12, 2009.

Müller, Claudio. "Sustainability in Family and Nonfamily Businesses in the Wine Industry." *International Journal of Wine Business Research* (January 2017).

"Ownership Transitions in the Wine Industry." Silicon Valley Bank. January 2008.

Soler, Ismael, German Gemar, and Rafael Guerrero-Murillo. "Family and Non-family Business Behaviour in the Wine Sector: A Comparative Study." *European Journal of Family Business* 7, nos. 1–2 (2017): 65–73.

Tapia, Patricio. "Zuccardi: Producer Profile." *Decanter*, March 20, 2014.

"Wine Enthusiast's 19th Annual Wine Star Award Nominees." *Wine Enthusiast*, September 6, 2018.

Woodfield, Paul. "Intergenerational Knowledge Sharing in Family Firms: Case-based Evidence from the New Zealand Wine Industry." *Journal of Family Business Strategy* (January 2017).

Chapter 7: A Burrito, Four Beers, and a Roller Coaster

Bruder, Jessica. "The Psychological Price of Entrepreneurship." *Inc.*, September 2013.

Carroll, Rory. "Silicon Valley's Culture of Failure...and 'the Walking Dead' It Leaves Behind." *Guardian*, June 28, 2014.

"Drop One Losing Friend." Gary Vaynerchuk Fan Channel. April 21, 2017. www.youtube.com/watch?v=mCElaIhgKeY.

F. R. Kets de Vries, Manfred. "The Dark Side of Entrepreneurship." *Harvard Business Review*, November 1985.

Feld, Brad. "Entrepreneurial Life Shouldn't Be This Way—Should It?" *Inc.*, July/August 2013.

Fisher, Rosemary, Alex Maritz, and Antonio Lobo. "Obsession in Entrepreneurs—Towards a Conceptualization." *Entrepreneurship Research Journal* (2013).

Fitchette, Todd. "Farmer Suicide: The Topic Few Will Discuss." *Western Farm Press*, June 7, 2018.

Freeman, Michael A., Paige J. Staudenmaier, Mackenzie R. Zisser, and Lisa Abdilova Andresen. "The Prevalence and Co-occurrence of Psychiatric Conditions among Entrepreneurs and Their Families." *Small Business Economics*, August 2019.

Freeman, Michael A., Sheri Johnson, and Paige Staudenmaier. "Are Entrepreneurs 'Touched with Fire'?" michaelafreemanmd.com. April 17, 2015.

Griffith, Erin. "Why Are Young People Pretending to Love Work?" *New York Times*, January 26, 2019.

Hendrickson, Laura C. "The Mental Health of Minnesota Farmers: Can Communication Help?" University of Minnesota. July 28, 2018.

Lahtia, Tom, Marja-Liisa Halko, Necmi Karagozoglu, and Joakim Wincent. "Why and How Do Founding Entrepreneurs Bond with Their Ventures? Neural Correlates of Entrepreneurial and Parental Bonding." *Journal of Business Venturing* (March 2019).

Lerner, Dan, Ingrid Verheul, and Roy Thurik. "Entrepreneurship & Attention Deficit/Hyperactivity Disorder: A Large-Scale Study Involving the Clinical Condition of ADHD." IZA Institute of Labor Economics. October 2017.

LiKamWa McIntosh, Wendy, Erica Spies, Deborah M. Stone, Colby N. Lokey, Aimée-Rika T. Trudeau, and Brad Bartholow. "Suicide Rates by Occupational Group—17 States, 2012." Centers for Disease Control and Prevention. July 1, 2016.

Stephan, Ute, Mark Hart, and Cord-Christian Drews. "Understanding Motivations for Entrepreneurship: A Review of Recent Research Evidence." Enterprise Research Centre. February 2015.

Weingarten, Debbie. "Why Are America's Farmers Killing Themselves?" *Guardian*, December 11, 2018.

Chapter 8: Too Many Ideas

Azoulay, Pierre, Benjamin F. Jones, J. Daniel Kim, and Javier Miranda. "Age and High-Growth Entrepreneurship." National Bureau of Economic Research. April 2018.

Burton, M. Diane, Jesper B. Sørensen, and Stanislav D. Dobrev. "A Careers Perspective on Entrepreneurship." *Entrepreneurship Theory and Practice* (2016).

"Civic Ventures: Entrepreneurship Survey" and "Encore Entrepreneurs: Creating Jobs, Solving Problems." Penn, Schoen & Berland Associates. November 8, 2011.

Clippinger, John H. *A Crowd of One: The Future of Individual Identity*. New York: PublicAffairs, 2007.

Clippinger, John, and David Bollier. *From Bitcoin to Burning Man and Beyond: The Quest for Identity and Autonomy in a Digital Society*. Amherst, MA: ID3 and Off the Common Books, 2014.

Halvorsen, Cal, and Yu-Chih Chen. "The Diversity of Interest in Later-Life Entrepreneurship: Results from a Nationally Representative Survey of Americans Aged 50 to 70." *PLoS ONE* (June 5, 2019).

Halvorsen, Cal, and Nancy Morrow-Howell. "A Conceptual Framework on Self-Employment in Later Life: Toward a Research Agenda." *Work, Aging, and Retirement* 3, no. 4 (October 2017): 313–324.

Schøtt, Thomas, Edward Rogoff, Mike Herrington, and Penny Kew. "Senior Entre-
	preneurship 2016–2017." *Global Entrepreneurship Monitor* (2017).
"Starting Later: Realizing the Promise of Older Entrepreneurs in New York City."
	Center for an Urban Future. September 2018.
Yssaad, Lahouaria, and Vincent Ferrao. "Self-employed Canadians: Who and
	Why?" Statistics Canada. May 28, 2019.

Index

Credit: Christopher Farber

David Sax is a writer, journalist, and speaker who specializes in business and culture. His previous book, *The Revenge of Analog,* became a #1 *Washington Post* bestseller, was selected as one of Michiko Kakutani's Top Ten books of 2016 for the *New York Times,* and has been translated into six languages. He is the author of *Save the Deli,* which won a James Beard Award for Writing and Literature, and *The Tastemakers.* He lives in Toronto.

For speaking inquiries, contact the Lavin Agency: www.thelavinagency.com

PublicAffairs is a publishing house founded in 1997. It is a tribute to the standards, values, and flair of three persons who have served as mentors to countless reporters, writers, editors, and book people of all kinds, including me.

I. F. STONE, proprietor of *I. F. Stone's Weekly*, combined a commitment to the First Amendment with entrepreneurial zeal and reporting skill and became one of the great independent journalists in American history. At the age of eighty, Izzy published *The Trial of Socrates*, which was a national bestseller. He wrote the book after he taught himself ancient Greek.

BENJAMIN C. BRADLEE was for nearly thirty years the charismatic editorial leader of *The Washington Post*. It was Ben who gave the *Post* the range and courage to pursue such historic issues as Watergate. He supported his reporters with a tenacity that made them fearless and it is no accident that so many became authors of influential, best-selling books.

ROBERT L. BERNSTEIN, the chief executive of Random House for more than a quarter century, guided one of the nation's premier publishing houses. Bob was personally responsible for many books of political dissent and argument that challenged tyranny around the globe. He is also the founder and longtime chair of Human Rights Watch, one of the most respected human rights organizations in the world.

•   •   •

For fifty years, the banner of Public Affairs Press was carried by its owner Morris B. Schnapper, who published Gandhi, Nasser, Toynbee, Truman, and about 1,500 other authors. In 1983, Schnapper was described by *The Washington Post* as "a redoubtable gadfly." His legacy will endure in the books to come.

Peter Osnos, *Founder*